YOUR TOWN
Your Real Estate
Profits!

DEAN GRAZIOSI

DEAN ENTERPRISES, LLC.

Your Town Your Profits!
Recession Breaking Secrets To Thrive In Your Backyard.

Published by: Dean Enterprises, LLC
Copyright © 2009 by Dean Graziosi

This and other Dean Graziosi books are available at
www.deangraziosi.com

For information on discounted bulk purchases email us at
specials@deangraziosi.com.

Printed in the United States of America
First Printing December 2009

DISCLAIMER:
To the best of my opinion, all techniques in this book abide by local and state laws. But, as with anything in life you do to make money, please verify that the strategy you use is legal in your area. Also, you are responsible for taxes on all your profits you make. So make sure you keep excellent records of all expenses - for tax reasons and to avoid paying higher than expected city, state and federal taxes.

Cover Design: Freddy Solis
Cover Photography: Chip Brown
Interior Design: Tressa Foster

Dedication

I dedicate this book to all of you who face hardship, negativity, obstacles, naysayers and adversity caused by today's economy. Yet in spite of that, you never give up, never stop seeking new wisdom and are determined to create a better future for you and your family.

This country's greatness was built on the backs of people like you who continue to pursue the American Dream! I applaud you and I appreciate you. You are truly the inspiration that drives me to work harder and be the best I can be.

Table of Contents

Introduction

What do you get when you share the best of the best techniques learned through 20 years of real estate investing and combine it with the secrets of 14 students from all over America who went from worrying about their financial present and future to true wealth and happiness through real estate investing? This book!

Hello, I'm Dean Graziosi and first of all thanks for having enough faith in me to pick up this book. I promise to do my best and to over-deliver on your expectations. What you hold in your hands can be just a good read to kill time or it can be a roadmap to true lifelong financial security for you and your family. The choice is really yours.

If you are one of my current students or have read one or more of my books in the past, I want to welcome you back and say hello, you are going to love this one.

And if you are a current investor who is looking for out-of the-box techniques to make money in today's market, then get ready for some killer strategies to take what you are doing to a whole new level.

Now if you are like the majority of people who have never done a real estate deal, you have little or no money to invest, or you simply don't want to risk your money, we have the program just for you! You might even have decent to really bad credit wondering what the heck you are even thinking about trying to invest in real estate; then let me assure you that you my friend, you have definitely come to the right place. I specialize in YOU!

I ask that you go in to this book with an open mind, leaving your past doubts and skepticism checked at the door for a while. Long enough so I can let you see that this is real. Real for me, real for the student's stories you will read about in this book and countless others across America. I don't care where you live, what you do for a living, how much money you do or don't have; I don't care what your credit score is or if you have a job or not. Your education level does not matter, if you are a man or woman, black or white. If you can have an open mind, follow what you are going to learn, not be afraid to take action and get out there and try it, you can do this. Yes, YOU!

In this book I am going to help you broaden the limits of your thinking and let you see that real estate is not for other people, it's for you. You are going to learn exact techniques from people just like you. They were disturbed with their current life for one reason or another. They didn't want to be left behind, worry about bills, worry about their family and their future anymore. They got my books, learned what they needed to learn, got clarity on real estate investing, took action and simply changed their lives forever. Oh yeah, they made boatloads of money in the process. And they made the money they did, not in spite of today's economy and real estate market but BECAUSE of it.

The students profiled in this book didn't just give their cheerleader story of "rah-rah," they made money. They were gracious enough to share the exact techniques they learned through trial and error so you can replicate what they did. Listen, many were broke with no or bad credit. Many were scared, stressed, depressed and down right worried what their future had in store for them. Others were doing ok in life, they just wanted more. Some were sick of working 7 days a week or 70 hours a week. Some are young couples that want to enjoy life and make their family proud. One thing they all have in common is they didn't let their past or present dictate their future, they took action and changed their lives forever. Now, they have been so extremely gracious to share all they know with you in this book so you can get what they have and more. In the acknowledgements I give them the thanks they so rightfully deserve, so make sure to check that out when you are done reading this book.

If you will take the time to read, fully absorb and reread this book again if you have to, here is what you will get: step by step techniques that have worked for me, the students in this book and countless Dean students all across America. We left nothing out. You will learn techniques that will work in your town, right now with no money and do it faster then you can imagine. You will be amazed how nothing is held back and how if you can leave the "I can't do this" part of your brain on hold; you could be out there making money in as little as 30 days from this very moment.

Before we get started, let me ask you to do a quick assignment that will not feel like work at all and it is free to you now and forever. Go to our social network at ***www.deangraziosi.com*** and spend ten minutes or so and see the wisdom available to you. If you are away from your computer or maybe don't have one then make sure you go there soon. This site is filled with current students of mine from all over the country sharing, caring and helping others become successful all over America. We have truly created a wave of people helping people with real life inspiration and strategies. This will be a place of support whenever you doubt your-self or real estate.

Ok, hope you were able to go there and see just one piece of the support we have for you. I also do live monthly training conference calls that are free and are free to you forever. Make sure to look out in your email box for notifications of time and dates of these calls and other important updates. I do a weekly video blog at *www.**deangraziosi.com*** as well. It comes out on Mondays and yup, it's free as well. These are wonderful, informing and inspiration to get you the results you desire. All I know is that our most successful students are the ones who participate in what we share, heck basically they are participating in their own success.

Remember I can't do it for you. I can supply the wisdom in the pages to come and surely the support and inspire you to the best of my ability, but only you can overcome your fears, step out of what is ordinary and take action. So can you commit to that right now? Go ahead make that commitment!

Also, at any time you would like to talk with one of our professionally trained start up specialists about joining my Real Estate Success Academy feel free to call them toll free at **877-219-1473**. It is unlike anything on the planet and can help you achieve the success you desire like it has for so many before you.

In just a few short pages, you will start getting proven real estate wisdom and knowledge to make money in your town right now! But I'm asking you to trust me on how I deliver that information to you and the few exercises we do first to get you ready to make this a reality for you. All I know is this, if I don't get you to take action with what you are about to learn than this book will be just a good read and I'm not satisfied with that at all.

Let me share with some final thoughts before you start. First, I have countless students tell me that they purchased real estate courses, or at-tended seminars or read other books before mine, but never got results until my book or training. After getting to meet so many students face to face and being at our online social community almost every day and seeing the hundreds of daily posts from evolving and successful students, I think I know why. You see, there are a lot of books and information programs that give you a great overview and give you the "What" of real estate. They bombard you with technical terms and overwhelm you with the "What".

In this book and past books of mine, you get some of the "What." I'll also make sure you know the "Why" you are doing this, but most of all, you will get the exact "How."

Think of it this way. If we related this on how to cook, other books may teach you how to be a chef, share what being a chef is all about. My books and especially this one are more like a cookbook with proven recipes that gets you results. In fact, in this book I will reference recipe style format a lot. Even if you never cooked before in your life and a master chef gives you a recipe for Crème Brule (which is an extremely hard desert to make) and you follow it word for word, ingredient by ingredient, step by step, you can make Crème Brule as good as his. You surely don't need to know what it is like or how to be a chef or go to culinary school for 4 years to learn how to do it.

This book is full of proven recipes from myself and students of mine from all over the country. From big cities to tiny little towns. When you are done reading and if you take action with these recipes, you will be able to cook up successful real estate deals and show the world that you can do it.

I want to share a few quotes. A good friend gave me a copy of Napoleon Hill's first draft of the "Law Of Success." I have not read it yet, but I flipped through it and a few quotes that were highlighted jumped out at me and I knew they were meant to be shared with you.

"A good encyclopedia contains most of the known facts of the world, but they are useless as sand dunes until organized – and expressed in terms of action."

"If you have tried and met with defeat; if you have planned and watched your plans crushed before your eyes; just remember that the greatest men in history were the products of courage, and courage as you know, is BORN in the cradle of adversity."

"There are no lazy men. What may appear as a lazy man is only an unfortunate person who has not found the work for which he is best suited."

"There is a sure way to avoid criticism: be nothing and do nothing. Get a job as a street sweeper and kill off ambition. The remedy never fails."
"Your only limitation, within reason, is the one which you set in your own mind"

"Do not TELL the world what you can do – SHOW it."

If you are unfamiliar with Napoleon Hill, he is a man that spent an entire lifetime interviewing and studying the richest and most successful people of his time. He put in 25 years of active labor to find out what makes a successful person. These quotes come from the people who struggled, faced massive adversity and ended up creating greatness. I though it was an appropriate kickoff to what could be an entirely new life and new way to make money for you and your family.

Now let's get to you, to real estate and to building a solid future for you and your family.

CHAPTER 1
Yes, it works.
Yes, in your own town!

I absolutely don't want to start off on a negative note with you. As you will see, that isn't my style. But I have met many students, before and after they became successful, who have shown me that lingering negative beliefs can exist within us all. So we have to flush out such negative beliefs so that new, positive ones can replace them. So let me take just a moment to address some of those toxic beliefs. For those of you whom this does not affect then congrats, and read on anyway. It's a few paragraphs you can use to help others.

I can't tell you how many times I've heard some variation of *"That won't work."* The negative belief I've heard most in the last 6 months is *"That won't work in my town."* (Hence the name of the book you are reading.) Perhaps you or someone you know has said this? But let's look at this in a different way. I'm sure you've heard about a wildly successful real estate investor who made pots of money with a simple, straightforward strategy. Whether or not you believed that story of lucky success, in so many instances, we have a default mechanism telling us we cannot achieve that type of glory. Instead, we think, "Well, it worked for him, but . . ."

That sentence can be completed by a variety of thoughts; they were in a big city, and you're stuck in a small town. Or, they're booming a small town and you're drowning in the big city. You may default to focusing on negative factors in your area and how it could never work. But those "negative" factors may be the exact reason your area is an unbeatably amazing place to make money.

Whatever your negative beliefs are, they don't make you a terrible person or a doomed investor. It isn't your fault, it's just years of faulty programming from outside influences and life beating you up a bit. Too often in life we focus on the negatives rather than the positives. Rather than say, "that won't work", ask yourself, "how can I make that work for me?"

Let's look at another variation of this quit-before-you-start mindset: *"that won't work in my situation."* You're thinking to yourself, "Sure, she did it, but she had excellent credit and some cash to invest." Then there's the ever-popular *"that won't work in today's markets."* Maybe you have loads of reasons to doubt that you can make lucrative real estate investments. The days of rising home prices are over. How can anyone make money in real estate when home prices are stagnant or falling? There's nothing but unpleasant economic news, mortgages are much harder to get, and negative news about housing is all over the television and the print media. All three of these "that won't work" statements are variations on the belief that you can't make it happen in your town with your abilities and using your resources. Well, I can tell you this: you <u>can</u> make it work "in your town," with your knowledge and financial ability, right now. No matter what!

All you have to do to prove your "that won't work" statements true is to keep saying and believing them. As long as you believe it, it's true for you. But, all you have to do to prove these statements wrong is to read this book and take to heart what myself and real people from all around the country are telling you.

You'll hear from individuals living in sprawling California metropolises and from people sequestered in tiny Mississippi towns. They live east, west and everywhere in-between. Some have money, some didn't have a dime. A few had great credit and the ability to get a mortgage with ease. Most people didn't have it so easy; they had low credit scores and previous financial problems. A few had even experienced bankruptcies. You'll hear from a remarkable woman in the Northeast who fell into a financial mess; as a result, she couldn't sleep and, due to depression, was in poor physical health. She lost her car and was forced to ride a bicycle to work. But she'll tell you, without a doubt, that *"this will work for you, where you are, and in today's markets."* This amazing woman will share all the glorious details with you, including exactly which documents and techniques she used so you can use them as well!

You'll hear from a truly remarkable man in a tiny town in Mississippi who says *"my credit was in the crapper."* And it was! He'll show you how, using not a penny of his own money (he didn't have any) and without any credit, he managed to put tens of thousands of dollars in his pocket and build a massive monthly cash flow. He did all of this while working 10 or more hours a day in construction. This man was so limited on time during waking hours that he had to study and read in the middle of the night or early morning hours before going to work. Finding even one hour per day to study and learn was not easy, but he did it, and now he no longer works 70 hours a week. Wait until you hear how he did it and how you can do it, too!

If, for some reason, Greg's techniques don't seem to work in your area, it's not a problem. There are many incredible techniques in this book shared by wonderful students who are living it everyday. These generous individual will share all their secrets with you; actual strategies, bona fide deal details, and even copies of their transaction documents. Remember, what works for one person in one area may not be right for you. However, mixing and matching the deal recipes I give will create the winning combination for you in your town, with your ingredients.

Though you'll be powerfully affected by these stories, the goal of this book is not just to inspire or to motivate you. It's a factual, detailed textbook of authentic real estate investment deals, in towns all around the country, made by people just like you. These deals are recipes for success, and that's how we'll share them with you. You'll get the ingredients with step-by-step instructions to end up with a deliciously successful deal. Like most recipes, there isn't only one way to make it happen. Variations in ingredients and preparation can produce an equally scrumptious dish, just as it can produce every bit as profitable of a deal.

You'll also learn how to make your town any town you want it to be. I don't mean moving. It's about investing where you can find the best opportunities. Once these students show you how they use today's technology, you can pick a town with the greatest profits in real estate, do your research, and make it "your town" for real estate investing. We'll demonstrate exactly how to move from the "big picture" of the national real estate markets and drill down to your area of choice. I'll show you how to conduct market research and assemble a team that will bring success after success after success, even if you're in Florida and buying rental properties in Iowa. That's exactly what Angie Novigrod has done, and she's never even visited Iowa! You'll read Angie's deal recipes later in the book.

I will also be giving you a comprehensive database with resources for financing, banking, locating properties, evaluating suitability, determining true value and walk-away prices, and more. You can find this in the resources section at the end of the book. We will refer you to it frequently to support the decisions and methods our students used in their deal recipes.

The resources section will also bring greater clarity to the stories about my students, giving you my perspective and providing alternative routes to same successful endings. For example, you'll learn how to approach a bank about REO properties. What should you say in a letter, email or phone conversation? How do you deal with a listing real estate agent who is reluctant to present your low offer on a property? How to get a bank to say "yes" when most banks say "no." How to turn a lease option into a no-money-down machine. It's all in here, with everything you need to cook up your own lucrative deal recipes.

These real world deals will do two things:
1. Convince you that there are many ways to make money in today's real estate economy right in your local area.
2. Arm you with the receipes you need to model the wild success of these deal makers.

Bad news is not only irrelevant; in many cases, it can also mean there's an opportunity for you to use my strategies and put money in your pocket. Always remember: in most cases, you are not taking advantage of someone's misfortune. In fact, you may be helping provide a solution to their problem. If misfortune is involved, you didn't cause it, and someone is going to buy or make a deal anyway, so why not you? In many cases, the techniques I teach actually help a desperate seller out of an ugly situation. Let's take a look at the economy and current state of the national real estate market. Here are just a few of the amazing profit opportunities:

Bad News: "Prices are deflated due to competition from foreclosures."
The Opportunity: Who can argue with the opportunity to profit from buying properties at prices well below their actual market value? Prices haven't been this good for decades. Plus, lowered values cause banks to make insane deals to incentivize people to buy the bank-owned properties (REO's) on their books. If the banks don't sell, they could go out of business.

Bad News: "People are losing their homes all around the country."
The Opportunity: Most of these situations are not caused by lost jobs or income, but by poor mortgage choices and practices. The people who have to move from a foreclosure still need a place to live and can afford rents that make your deals profitable.

Bad News: "People don't have down payments and can't qualify for mortgages under newer, more stringent guidelines."
The Opportunity: Here's that "need to rent" opportunity again. Most people still have their jobs and want to remain in the same area, but need to rent while they rebuild their lives and financial status. In his deal reci-

pes, Greg Murphy will show you how to work with these people, how to make money when they move in, while they rent and how to cash out big when you sell to them a few years down the road. With this no-money-down technique, you can help people own their own home when others simply tell them "no."

These are just a few examples of how, when taken appropriately, seemingly bad news is really great news for you!

It's all about recognizing opportunity in every situation. In order to survive, the media need headlines that sell newspapers. They have no interest in the effect their headline has in your life; nor do they care what you do for a living. Don't take my word for it; keep reading. You'll recognize yourself in many of these people. And you'll see how your local real estate market is similar to one or more of these markets. Once you see how other people with problems like yours make it happen, there will be no stopping you.

Many of my students' stories mention my Web site and being motivated by discussions with other investors. They tell you that they learned not only about successful deals, but also about mistakes and failures. They came to the site with questions, fear and doubts that may sound familiar to you:

• What if I don't have money?
• Can I have bad credit?
• Can I really do this?
• What do I need to get started?
• How do I know what to do from day one?

- How do I find deals?
- What if I have additional questions after reading the book?
- What if I fail?
- Do your family and friends tell you that you are crazy for trying real estate?

FREE BONUS

If you have not already spent 10 minutes at my Web site (which is 100% free), please take a few minutes and check it out at *www.deangraziosi.com*. It's more than motivation!

You may have more questions, and that's OK. We learn best when given more than just instructions. We need real-life examples, and that's what you get in these stories and deal recipes. It would be like giving you a recipe for a dessert dish and keeping one or more of the most important ingredients a secret. This book is your real estate investing success cookbook, and there's nothing left out.

To get the most out of this book, you just need to see pieces of yourself in one or more of these amazing people. Once you see that they're not better at business than you, go out and put what you learn into practice. Combine their stories, the deal recipes and my guidance, and there's absolutely no reason you can't be your own success story in a reasonable amount of time.

I've already said this, but it's really important: the people in this book are ordinary people just like you! One day, they woke up and decided they'd had enough and that today was the day to do something different! They decided to take action, just like you did when you purchased this book. You're different from most others that want something more; you decided to take action and that's the first step toward your next success! Each day you do something to get closer to your goal, you should be commended. How often do people start off strong with a New Year's resolution, but by January 10th it may already be a forgotten thought. But I am confident this will not happen to you. You are determined and you will achieve success!

Your Town Tips:
- Practice the P's to success: Passion, Persistent, Patient, Press while being Polite and Professional!
- Never give up or give in. You will do it!

As you read through this book, you'll find numerous tips, techniques, strategies and action steps. The more you put into action, the more you will get out of your effort. Remember, you are no different than the people featured in this book. Most of them started in the same situation you're in. Most overcame challenges greater than having no money or bad credit. They made it happen; so can you! And yes, you can make it happen in your town!

Your Town Action Item:
Life is good!
List 3 times in which you had a perfect day and why it was perfect.

_____

_____

_____

CHAPTER 2
Why are You Doing This!?

When I was young and played baseball on the playground, whenever one of us would hit the ball into a neighbor's yard, we'd yell, *"DO OVER!"* It gave us a second chance to hit a homerun. How often in life have you wished you could get a "do over?" Sometimes, we wonder if we missed the opportunity of a lifetime and wish we could have a second chance. This could be your second chance!

You have passion and a desire to succeed with real estate investing, but may not know the best action to take after reading this book. The best advice I can give you is to be dedicated to your education and to take action with what you learn, no matter what. Each day, learn something new; whether from my books, from ***www.deangraziosi.com***, from our success academy or from technqiues designed to further your goals. You took action and started reading this book because you want something better, you want something more! Continue this action by finishing this book, don't let anything or anyone stop you. When you're done reading, go out and apply what you've learned. There is no other way to success. But I promise the end result can be life-altering. You don't have to miss this second chance at the life you deserve. If you need to reread a section, then read it over and over until you understand the concepts and how to use them. How do great athletes and performers make it look so easy? Practice and preparation!

How often do we buy something that comes with instructions? It's easier to follow the instructions, but most of us chose the "faster, easier way" and ignore them. After I assemble a new toy for my children, invariably, there are leftover parts. That's when I realized I needed to look at the instructions for those "extra parts".

Your real estate investing should be the same approach. Study each and every part so when you are ready to take action at the end, there is nothing left over.

You Need A WHY!

Do you know why you ordered my book? You may know the reason, but in most cases, there is a deeper answer motivating your actions. What makes you happy? What do you want out of life? What do you _really_ want? Sometimes, as you decide what to do, you need to sit down and figure out why you want to succeed in real estate. Once you figure out your "why," nothing else will matter.

In an activity as simple as a trip to the grocery store, humans never start to do something without some idea of why. The grocery store is easy, you need a loaf of bread. It's not complicated, but there's a definite reason for our trip. When you bought this book, you had a reason, even if you didn't sit down and consider precisely what it was before the purchase. The complexity of human behavior also can mean that the reason at the top of our minds isn't the real reason or motivator for what we're doing.

In some of my seminars and classes, I use an exercise called "The Seven Levels." I've experienced the power of this exercise in drilling down to the core reason that I write books and teaching others. It has changed my life. Take just a few minutes to complete this exercise; I think you'll find it will give you a laser-like focus in reading the rest of this book and fulfilling your desires.

Seven Levels Deep

I don't attend many seminars; there just aren't enough hours in the day. A few years ago, I paid $25,000 to join a group of some of the deepest thinkers I've ever met. This is an amazing bunch of guys, each makes money by helping others advance to the next level in their lives. Run by my good friend Joe Polish, the 25K Group gets together three times a year to brainstorm on how to take what we do to the next level. On a side note: I've found that paying $25k makes me pay a lot more attention!

Early in my in my life and business ventures, I didn't benefit from this type of networking because I didn't know they existed. I followed the hard road, learning by doing, failing, and succeeding when I'd learned enough from my failures and mistakes. So it was a big deal for me to join the 25K Group, as it was one of the first times I decided to let others help me by sharing their knowledge. Let me tell you; it's much easier to learn from _other_ people's mistakes and failures. It's similar to taking the express lane on a crowded highway. And it's what you are doing by reading this book.

So back to my 25K Group story. Before we started brainstorming at these gatherings, we'd do thinking exercises designed to open our minds to new ideas. I need to help you do that in this book as well. Jumping directly into details and strategies isn't the way you'll learn or adopt these tools for success. I need to help you open your mind to the possibilities, as well as the fact that, yes, you can do this, and you can do it where you live.

You're reading this book to improve your life by creating a more secure financial future. It really doesn't matter if you're moving away from or toward something. If you've made financial mistakes, lost your job, or just haven't managed to save anything toward retirement, you want to move away from these failures. If you're reasonably secure and not burdened with debt or financial problems, you're reading this to move toward something better. Either way, you are in the right place at the right time.

Know that the path I am taking you down is specificaly designed to get you the results you want. I'm not here to get you "pumped up" and then let you drift back into a life you are not 100% happy with. I have been self-employed for over 20 years, and I have been blessed to make lots of money, experiencing lots of failures and accomplishments along the way. I've had the chance to meet and learn from great people: Joel Osteen, Michael Jordan, Hugh Downs, Richard Branson, and many more prolific entreprenuers who started with nothing and went on to greatness.

So I took all I learned about setting a path for success and set a course of action for you within these pages. In preparation for this book, I flew in the deepest thinkers I know, and together, we brainstormed how I can do a better job of helping you, my reader, learn real estate investing and get the most out of my materials and instruction. It's important to me that this book does more than just teach you. I also want to motivate you and lead you step-by-step through the process of fulfilling your dreams and goals for financial success.

Experience has taught me that I can provide excellent material and tools, and still have people not put them into play, or fail in their use, simply because I failed in giving them what they needed to make it happen in their lives. Something was lacking, something allowed my students to be knocked off track, never getting out there and putting our great tools into practice. Even when our comfort zone isn't comfortable at all, it's all too easy to go from an early failure right back into our old ways, never venturing out to try again. So I brought this group together for the sole purpose of helping me give more to my students and to those who buy this book.

I sat down with Joe Stumpf, an amazing thinker and someone who has helped me immensely. The first thing he said to me was that NOTHING can get you off track if you are crystal clear on what you really want and why you're doing what you're doing. Things like a failed deal, problem Realtors, difficult financing, or any of the other things we run into every day in doing what we do, can get you off track if you do not absolutely KNOW why you're doing it.

We sat down to do the "Seven Levels Deep" exercise together. Now, if you received my e-mail on this exercise and watched the video documenting this technique at my live "Gain the EDGE 2009" event, awesome. If you didn't, then at the end of this section, I'll give you the URL so you can see it. It's great stuff!

Joe started the exercise by asking me why I was doing this. I told him that it was *to get better results for my students.*

Level 1: He asked why that was important to me, and my response was that I *wanted to help more people succeed*. Joe just kept questioning with "Dean, it's great that you want to help more people succeed. But why is it important to YOU to help more people to succeed?"

Level 2: I thought a minute, and I told him that it was important to me to have a *reputation as someone who provided true and effective capabilities* that work and are not just hype. Still, Joe just kept on questioning why it was important to me to have that reputation.

Level 3: Each question took a little more thought and time to answer. I didn't want to say only what Joe wanted to hear, but really give my true feelings. I told him: *"It's important to me to have this reputation because I want my business to grow based on solid values."* What do you think was next? Yes, Joe wanted to know why it was important to me to have my business grow based on solid values.

Level 4: *"Because I want longevity and security in my life"* was my answer after a moment or two of thought. Here I am, four questions into the exercise, and it's getting more intense, as I dig into my true self and feelings. Of course, Joe wasn't finished, asking next; "Why is longevity and security in your life important to you?"

Level 5: The answer came to me pretty easily this time, with ***"I never want to go backwards in my life."*** I didn't like where I came from, and I never want to go back there. I was thinking we'd finally drilled down into my psyche as far as necessary, but then he hit me again with, "Dean, I understand and appreciate what you said, but why is it important to you to never go backwards?"

Level 6: I really had to dig deep this time. I thought a bit, and I found that the answer was that ***"I never want to be unable to support my family."*** No matter how well I'm doing, or how much money I have, this answer showed that I still worry about being in a place where I can't support my family. Well, just when I thought we had it, Joe says, "Dean, I appreciate that feeling and your ability to voice it, but one more question: Why is it important to you that you are never in a position where you can't support your family?"

Level 7: It took a moment or two of thought to get this one out. ***"Because I want to be in control of my life so that I can help everyone I love around me to evolve to the next level."***

If someone asks you why you're reading this book today, you may jump to answer, "financial security" or something similar. But I bet it goes a lot deeper than that. There are motivators in our lives that we keep buried deep inside ourselves. When asked a question, such as why we bought this book or why we want to learn real estate investing, our first answer is usually a shallow one. You've just walked with me through my Seven Levels Deep exercise, so you know why I wrote this book: so I can have control of my life, help you to evolve to the next level, always support my family, never go backwards in my life and well, you know the rest.

There's plenty of amazing material in this book, with inspirational stories from people just like you who have made real estate investing their path to security and financial freedom. I guarantee you'll be far more likely to join them if you do this exercise right now. Once you're crystal clear on WHY you're doing this, nothing will stand in your way. When the Realtor tells you that your strategy "won't work in this market," or a family member reminds you of a past investing mistake, you'll let it roll right off, simply because you're absolutely clear about why you're reading this book and taking these tools out into your market to build your real estate investing business.

Your Seven Levels Deep Exercise

What is important about this book to me? I don't want to suggest answers to you, because your answers are unique to you. This is the question that gets you started on your seven levels deep analysis. It's not one of the seven levels, as your first answer is. But, to help you to get started, here are a couple of answers others have given:

I want to learn what I need to know to apply it to successful real estate investing, OR
I want financial security, and I think I can learn how to do it with real estate by reading this book, OR...

Don't just grab one of these answers if it's not your true feelings. This first one is pretty easy, as it's the most surface-focused. You'll really begin to dig in as you move through the seven levels. Your answer to this first question becomes Level 1.

Now, ask yourself the WHY of your first answer. As an example, if you answered "to gain financial security in real estate investing with the material in the book," then ask yourself WHY that's important to you. The answer to that question is your Level 2. Just keep moving on, asking the WHY of each of your answers, digging deeper each time to try and dig down to your root emotion and motivation.

FREE BONUS
Go to *www.deangraziosi.com/yourtown/7levels* and I have a video clip of this exact exercise being shared at my live event. Plus I've prepared for you a blank 7 levels deep template to print out and use. It's the exact form I used when I did this life changing exercise.

Once you've reached the Seventh Level, are you surprised by your core WHY for reading this book? It is normal, as most of us don't spend a lot of time deeply examining of our motives. If you blew it off thinking, "Hey, this is great Dean, but I want to get to the real estate stuff," I say, you trusted me enough to buy my book, trust me enough to do this exercise. Listen, I'll admit that I'm guilty of moving way too fast in life, and in the past, I might have blown right past an exercise like this. But I would have been foolish and missed important steps that I don't want you to miss. So take a few minutes and do this, not for me, but for you and your family.

After Joe and I did this exercise together, if I wasn't convinced of its power, I surely was after Joe told me how he used this questioning technique on his daughter. When she asked for a new "flip" cell phone, he told her that she couldn't have the phone unless she went through the Seven Levels Deep exercise with him. We'll look at only the first and last level answers:

Level 1: Because everybody thinks flip phones are cool.
Level 7: Because I'm usually sitting alone at school for lunch. I think that if I had a flip phone out, others might want to sit with me because it's cool and they want to see it.
Being the father of a little girl who will grow up sooner than I want, that almost brings tears to my eyes. If Joe hadn't taken the time to go through that with his daughter, he never would have known her true motives or be able to help her.

Now, Joe could have just given her a "yes" or "no" answer to the "can I have it" question. But, by going through the exercise, deeper reasons come out than "I just want to look cool." Think about doing this every time you are considering a major purchase. You just might find that it isn't as important as you thought, or maybe its even more important!

Once you complete the Seven Levels Deep exercise, keep a copy of your answers in your wallet or purse. You might even want to write them down from number 7 at the top working down to number 1. This puts them in order of importance. If you're feeling down, perhaps because of a refused offer on a property, take out your list and remember WHY you're doing this. It's how you'll realize your goals and dreams.

Okay, now that you know your "WHY," you want to make sure you stay on track and always keep that burning desire of the "WHY" you want to do this no matter what challenge you may face. Each day you face a new challenge, but know that you will achieve your goals if you have a plan, stay on track and do the right things. The DG Web site (***www. deangraziosi.com***) provides information, support and inspiration as you face these daily challenges. Many of my students have described how the

"DG Web site family" (as they call it) has become integral to their invest-ing lives. Whether my students had to deal with naysayers or just wanted to be around like-minded people to learn, the DG Web site is the place to go. It's helped and supported many of my most successful students, and this Web site family waiting to help you!

Your Town Action Step:

Print and complete the "My Why Commitment" form (see below):

Go to **www.deangraziosi.com/yourtown/7levels** for the "My Why Commitment" form, print it out, and hang it on your refrigerator, bathroom mirror, or computer screen.

The My Why Commitment form distills all you learned in this section onto one page and makes it easy to remind yourself of the commitment you made to succeed and why.

My Why Commitment

Your Name _____
Your Town _____
Your Why (list top 3 answers) _____
_____
_____

My Why Pledge!
Today is the day that I have committed to change my life! I will do whatever it takes to make a change in my life. I will take immediate action by getting started today and always staying the course. I may encounter brief moments of frustration, fear, or insecurity, but I know that is normal and I will never quit! I know my "WHY" and I am confident and committed to make this happen. There may be some additional challenges along the way. With wanting more out of life, I am sure to face naysayers that tell me I can't do this. However, I will come back to the "My Why Commitment" and remember my WHY! I commit to persevere and push through adversity to reach my goals, my dreams and my plateaus of success! Today is the first day of the rest of my life.

Sign: _____ Date: _____

Attach photos of the people, places or things that will remind you of your WHY!

Congratulations for completing the "My Why" Commitment form. You just reached another level of your plateau for success. This exercise really makes you dig deep and really explore "WHY" this is so important to you! This is a good time to take a brief recap of where we are at. We know your "WHY" which is very important, we also know the who is you, the what is real estate, the where is your town, the when is right now and the how is my books and programs.

CHAPTER 3

The Clarity Begins

"It's a small world after all"!
— *Disney Company*

If you've used Google Earth (earth.google.com), you've probably been pretty impressed. From an image of the globe, you can zoom in on a country, state, zip code, all the way to a specific street address. It's like you're in a space ship, approaching the earth with a pre-programmed course to a pinpoint destination. I can play with this free service forever, checking out my home, the nearby shopping centers, streets, parks and major sites around the area.

FREE BONUS
In fact, we liked that concept so well we used it to create a killer analytical tool. Take a few minutes right now and go to *www.totalviewrealestate.com*. This is a remarkable tool that took many months and several thousands of dollars to create. Wait until you see the potential in this Web site! Just imagine how valuable it will be for you to have so much information about one piece of property all in one place and right at your fingertips. Yes, it really works and it's free to you in order to help you succeed.

If real estate is fairly new to you, it can feel overwhelming, almost an entirely new world. At times, it can be difficult to try new things that are out of your comfort zone. We fall into routines and become comfortable with our habits. I remind you of this because I want you to be aware that change is scary. Don't let that fear of something new stop you from moving forward. If you don't change, predicting your future is pretty darn easy. It's just more of what you currently have. And if that frightens you, then let's work together on something new.

By trying new things, you open up your "sphere of influence." You meet new people, you see different things and you open your life up to new opportunities. As you see, change is good.

When it comes to real estate research in your town, it's a bit like Google Earth or the www.totalviewrealestate.com program. I'll show you how to use these tools and strategies in your town; the people in this book are living proof that it can be done. Remember, no one just "lucks" into real estate profits. It requires research, and that includes learning about your town, about how you see your town, and more importantly, how others see your town.

Starting the Analysis

We will start with some basic analysis and getting a pulse for your community. The Internet saves so much time and effort, it is amazing. Get online and view new property listings in your area instantly. These listings contain a variety of information, including photos and facts about the home and surrounding area. Two of the most frequently visited Web sites that you should explore are www.realestateagent.com and www.craigslist.com. If you Google "association of real estate agents" with your city and state name, you'll discover Web sites that have a "public" view section that will give you some, but not all, of the information on properties listed in your area. It's a great resource!

On the www.realestateagent.com Web site, listings are searchable by city and state or by zip code. You can narrow your results by indicating specific search criteria. Each property listing has a number at the top called the Multiple Listing Service number or "MLS" for short. You want to become an expert of your local area of interest; I cannot stress this enough. The real estate agent.com site is one of the best places for you to learn about your market place; you'll find new property listings, changes, price reductions, and much, much more.

You want to become familiar with the following:
• Your local target area of interest
• The price range of the homes that you are considering investing in
• The selling price of the houses on the blocks in your overall area of interest

On the www.craigslist.com Web site you can search property for sale or for rent. You can search by state and drill down by city. You can also search "properties for sale by owner." Craigslist.com is currently a free resource to post classified ads with photos for properties for rent, properties for sale or properties wanted. You can use Craigslist.com to learn about properties currently available in your market. It's also a great way to discover perspectives and opinions about a specific area; you can interact with other users by asking questions about their properties or inquiring about the surrounding area. We will discuss the value of Craigslist for your real estate investing activities later in the book. Many of my students have utilized this Web site to locate deals or even find buyers.

Your Town Tips:

• You want to know what properties are on the market in your local target area, what they sell for and how many days it took each to sell.
• You want to know the prices of properties on the market in your area. When new listings hit the market, you want to know the street, the other properties for sale on the block and even have an educated guess as to the price of the new home listing.

Your Town Action Steps:

• Explore www.realestateagent.com. Become familiar with that site and the information it provides.
• Take look around www.craigslist.com for you area. Get a feel for their ads and how to fine-tune your searching.
• Find a MLS real estate agent site for your area that has a "public" option. You'll find tons of information for studying listings in your area of interest.
• For extra credit - Take a different route each day as you go through your routine and see all that you have not seen in your town.

Getting Familiar with your Area

Everyone likes finding something on sale and in today's market there are many sellers that want to sell even if they are selling their property at a loss. As soon as they sell, there's a sense of relief because it's one less thing to worry about. So if you like shopping and looking for "sales," this is exactly what you get to do in real estate. You want to find motivated sellers eager to put their property on the market. They normally list their property less than the fair market value or will accept less in order to sell the property quickly. The more "on sale" the property is, the better the opportunity is for you the investor! So let's take a look at how we find these properties and what our plan of action involves.

First, get familiar with the neighborhood and your target area of interest. You can gather information on your own, as well as by visiting a few different real estate agents. Sometimes the smaller, independent offices have an agent or broker that's an expert on the market and will spend that extra time with you to answer your questions about the area. These smaller offices, which may have been in the community for years, often strive to provide superior personal service in order to compete against the larger chains in the area. Their knowledge can be priceless, especially if they share insights to the current market. If you have identified a potential area of interest, discuss it with the real estate agent and ask the agent generate comparable sales reports of similar homes that have sold in the area during the past six months to one year.

In later chapters I will go into greater depth about how to find the perfect real estate agent and how to get prices and a feel for the community at warp speed. Plus, I can help you with your investing needs and the techniques you need to build an entire "A" team of professionals to help you reach your goals in real estate investing.

Anytime you start something new, it can feel a little intimidating, especially when you don't know your way around. Compare it to going out of town on vacation; it's your first time in a new place and you don't know your way around. You want to get out of the hotel room and hit the ground running, but part of you thinks you should have a plan. By the time you learn your way around and feel comfortable, it's time to return home.

When it comes to real estate, I think it's okay to explore the first few days to get familiar with your surroundings and with what's available to you. After you visit a few local real estate offices, you may want to start looking through printed sources, such as newspapers or the free real estate booklets found at grocery stores. These sources will also help you become familiar with the layouts and sources of listings.

Are you ready? There's a variety of ways you can gather additional data and save time. On any given weekend, there will be multiple "Open Houses" in your area. An open house allows any and all buyers to view the home without scheduling a prior appointment, so you can usually see several homes in only a few hours. This is a convenient way to meet local real estate agents and become more familiar with the style of homes in your area.

Your Town Action Item:

• This weekend, visit a few open houses in your area. Be sure to get a listing sheet on the home and a business card from the real estate agent hosting the open house.

• If the owner holds the open house, be sure to get a listing sheet and the owner's contact information.

Another way to see a large number of homes in a short period of time to attend an event called a "Parade of Homes." Usually sponsored by a local broker and held on weekends, a parade of homes allows you to tour a series of homes in your area. You may even be able to find an event during the week, so be sure to check with your local real estate agents about any special events coming up.

Your Town Action Item:

• Contact your local brokers and find out when the next Parade of Homes is being held.

Recently, real estate agents are even sponsoring tours of foreclosed properties. Several areas now sponsor bus trips that take you on a tour of that area and show the foreclosed homes. If you have an interest in foreclosed homes, this could be the ideal tour for you.

Your Town Action Item:

• Contact your local brokers and find out if there are any tours of foreclosed properties in your area.

List Price vs. Fair Market Value

This is one of the most critical areas of real estate investing. You need to understand the difference between the list price and the fair market value of a home. We will also cover the after repaired value, too. This information is the foundation for determining whether or not a property is a deal.

The fair market value (FMV) is the perceived price that the market would normally pay for a property. The list price is what the property is listed for and what the buyer is hoping to get. The after repaired value (ARV) is the price you could expect to sell a property for after you make necessary repairs or improvements. Remember, the true price a property is worth is what someone is willing to pay for it. When buyers are emotional about a property, you can expect to get a higher price.

There's one more price I use. My students and I call it the "SFV," sell fast value. If the seller wants to resell or flip the property fast, this is the price it would sell for. Later on, as you learn to calculate your deals, this is a great number to work backwards. For example, if you buy a home that you hope to sell for $100,000, but you know from your research and your real estate agent that you could get the $100,000, but that it will sell fast at $90,000. You can work your profit backwards using the "SFV" value. If you can't profit from the "SFV," then walk away.

Gary and Jill from Florida, who made over $500,000 since reading my book, had a fantastic phrase; "We buy really low and we sell sort of low." They learned that the right house, in the right area, at the right price always sells, even in a down market. The best part is that a good real estate agent will be able to tell you in seconds what people will ask for a home, what a fair price is and what price the home will sell fast in only a matter of days.

Your Town Tip:
• A property is only worth what someone else is willing to pay for it.

Your Town Action Item:
• Do not get emotional about having to buy a property. If you do, you will probably overspend for that property. Get excited over the numbers of the deal, not over the property itself.

Because properties are considered unique, there is no standard blue book to guide you. Most values are based on comparable properties in a comparable area over a specific period of time (usually within one year). Compare it to artwork: the price someone will pay for one painting may be totally different than what someone else would offer. So we see that emotion can get in the way of judgment.

Another good example is a car dealership. A car dealership may sell 25 of the exact same model car in a given month. The 25 buyers that purchased the vehicle probably all paid different prices for the exact same vehicle. The buyers are probably happy, so did anyone really overpay? You want to base your pricing on facts and what others may pay for a property. The greater the potential profit in a property, the more margin for error you have to work with. If you purchase a home for more than 50% off FMV and sell it a year later for 20% over FMV, you still made a solid profit on the transaction.

If you are new to all of this, please do not get overwhelmed. I put this book together so that anyone, form beginner to expert, will walk away with the knowledge and confidence necessary to go out and start making money. But writing a book is not easy, and I may not be perfect in my delivery. So know this: all the information you need to succeed is within these pages. If move too fast with a topic in Chapter 4, odds are that I will sum it up and make you totally understand it in another chapter. So, read the entire book, don't get overwhelmed and trust me. I assure you; it will all come together.

State, County and Town Research

At any given point in time, some states are better than others at attracting business, commerce and industry. There are many reasons for this; for one, states can offer tax incentives to attract large employers. States are also heavily involved in education at all levels. Many people choose one area over other similar places to live because of the quality of education. In this stage of information gathering, you want to follow state news or trends that influence employment, education, moving patterns, and commercial and residential development.

Locate your state's government Web site at http://YourState.gov, as I did with the state of Alabama. I went to their press release section, which contained news about economic initiatives: http://www.alabama.gov/sliverheader/Welcome.do?url=http://ado.alabama.gov/. You can easily find something similar for your state. Don't forget to look for an email newsletter service or the RSS news feed.

Another resource is the state chamber of commerce Web sites. You can find your state at the U.S. Chamber of Commerce Web site: http://www.uschamber.com/chambers/directory/default. I clicked on Colorado on the map, which directed me to the Colorado Chamber of Commerce Web site (http://www.cochamber.com). I also found more than two dozen chamber sites for cities in Colorado.

Find out if there's an economic development committee in your area. This is a group focused on maintaining and expanding business in the area. Look for an "economic development" link on your city or town's Web site, inquire at your town hall or do a quick Google search. If there is, find out what they are up to, what they are pushing or what's on their agenda.

You can find out about a new factory, a major government infrastructure construction project, or a large corporation relocating their headquarters. Positive or negative, it's valuable information. You wouldn't want to purchase a rental home in an area that relies heavily on a single employer if there's news reporting that this company is considering leaving the area. It can happen, and this kind of news reduces prices. With state, county and city research, what looks like a bargain can turn out to be a burden.

MARKET CYCLES – Supply and Demand

To understand pricing and data in a real estate market, it is important you know the types of real estate market cycles. If you understand what type of cycle you are in, you will be better prepared to find and negotiate deals. Real estate market cycles can be rising, declining or flat. The cycle of the real estate market can be driven by various factors. As in any market, supply and demand affect pricing. If there is a low supply, you expect a high demand, causing prices to go up. Inversely, if there is a large supply and a lower demand, you expect prices to drop.

It is important to consider various factors when reviewing markets throughout the country. For example, over 10,000 people a month move to the city of Phoenix, Arizona. On the surface, you may think, wow, this is a great place to invest because the demand must be extremely high. Yes, demand is very high, but what about the supply of various homes? By doing your research, you discover that bad loans caused many foreclosures, which brought prices way down. There is a fortune to be made in Arizona right now, but it may just be a different strategy then what you may think from first glance. So, do not let me confuse you with the back and forth of this explanation about Phoenix. Yes, people are migrating in; but over-speculation by developers and high foreclosure rates has caused more "supply" than "demand" and therefore, the market has dropped significantly. It simply means you have to buy really low and sell sort of low, like Gary and Jill are doing in another hard hit area; Florida.

There could be a tremendous opportunity based on what you discover in your research. If you discover that a new IMB plant is coming to your area and there will be more houses needed than available, you may want to use a different strategy, like Chad from California. You'll hear more about Chad and his unique situation later. I promise you this: there is something for everyone and you can make money in your town no matter what! Be patient, we are getting there.

The key here is to learn your market and then determine the best strategy for the market that you want to invest in. As I write this book, there are numerous properties on the market and most areas of the country are experiencing declining or rock bottom prices.

Remember the earlier point: everyone likes a sale?
• Everyone likes to buy things that are on sale. It's the reason why people purchase summer gear at end of summer sales.
• Think of the "Black Friday" crowds; the people that line up in the middle of the night at stores throughout the country for the day after Thanksgiving sales? This real estate market is 10 times better than any after Thanksgiving sale!
• Buy gas on Monday through Thursday morning because the price of gas is higher from Thursday night through Sunday.

When you go to the super market, you're familiar with most of the prices of the items on the grocery list. Even if you do not know each and every price, you know that a full cart of groceries costs more today than it did a few years ago. If you have a budget of $50 per trip, that $50 does not go as far as it once did. What happened to that $4.99 case of your favorite beverage? Today, that same case is $5.99 to $8.99 and some of the beverage distributors now manufacture 20-pack cases. What happened to the other four cans or bottles?

We love buying things that are on sale; so much so that we often buy more when it is on sale. Today real estate is on sale, a massive sale. You are learning how to find the insane bargains, keep them for rental income, buy clean and flip for a profit, or use no-money-down techniques to pass that killer deal off to someone else and profit in the middle. Today, when I talk about the super market, I am not talking about groceries, I am talking about real estate and it's a "**SUPER MARKET**"!

Your Town Tips:

- Know the cycle your current real estate market is in. Is the market declining, flat or on the rise? The change in pricing of properties should follow the demand of the market.
- Speak to at least 3 real estate professionals and get their opinion on the cycle of the local market.

Your Town Action Items:

- Assess what is happening in your local real estate market area. Are prices declining? Are there many properties on the market? What is happening in your local area?
- Speak to at least 2 other real estate professionals and get their opinion on the pricing in the local market.

When You're Investing Out of Your Area

I have a number of very successful students who chose to invest in areas where they do not live. Some are investing in states more than 1,000 miles from their homes. With today's technology, e-mail and the Internet, you can study an area, build an investment team, and communicate very effectively without having a physical presence.

You may get a deal referred to you by a friend, bank, or other business associate that is out of your area. This can be an amazing opportunity filled with the profit and results you desire. Of course, the deal is in another area, so you'll need to do your homework.

First, do exactly the same research for any area of interest. Go to the state government site, chamber of commerce sites, and local real estate search pages. All you're doing is changing the state, county and town. You can get a very accurate picture of the economy and local real estate market, no matter how far it is from where you live. Sure, you can't drive around, and that's a significant limitation. Therefore, your first important relationship should be with a great real estate agent and possible a property manager. Make your decision about investing in the area based on your research and what you find from a team of professionals in the area.

If your interest is in flipping properties, then finding a real estate agent should definitely be your first step. If you plan on buying and holding for rental income, a property management professional would probably be better. Many of them are agents as well. The point is that these professionals will be in tune with areas and home styles that rent well. Remember: it is not important to have the right real estate agent or broker. It is essential.

Later on, we will discuss in greater detail how to build the professional team that fits your needs and empowers you for massive success and less risk, whether investing locally or across the country. The real estate agents who work with investors tend to specialize in that activity, as it requires a different mindset and approach to the business.

It doesn't hurt to lay the foundation for your team in a remote area before the research. This can help you to do your investigating. No sense in spinning your wheels or doing double the work. You will learn how Angie has her team do everything in Illinois, while she lives in sunny Florida. Angie now has five deals and has never even looked at any of them! She has raised her net worth over $100,000 and has a healthy monthly positive cash flow. She created a killer team, based buying decisions strictly on the numbers, and is doing amazing things. She is on track to retire in five to seven years.

Try using Web site research to locate a Real estate agent or real estate agent. What you're looking for isn't a real estate site with the usual hype about "top producer" or biggest company with the most agents. Try doing searches on the city name and statistics, like "Denver real estate statistics," or "Houston real estate sold properties," or "Miami real estate trends." These searches turn up Web sites of real estate professionals who track and measure such statistics. You may not be able see the most up-to-date numbers, but an e-mail or phone call can get one of these professionals to run a current report for you.

In fact, this number running could be your first contact with a future valuable team member. If the agent is prompt to respond, and can pull MLS reports giving you sold property prices for the area and neighborhoods of interest, he or she may be just the person you want to work with on your deals.

The vast majority of real estate agents work in a "retail" environment. That's why you want to locate those who are experienced in working with investors for your team. It's great when you find one, because he or she can help you identify opportunities in your town. But, you don't want to rely completely on real estate people, as a great many properties will come onto your radar screen from sources not related to listed properties or the MLS. You want the knowledge to quickly evaluate every one for profit potential, and then apply more detailed analysis to those that seem to warrant it.

So, you want a real estate agent on your team as one of your resources. But, you don't want the agent to be your sole conduit for potential deals. You want to become an expert in your real estate market. You can bounce ideas off of your agent, and use him for contracts and deals when appropriate. But, you want to be able to locate your own opportunities, recognize them for what they are, and act on that information with confidence.

FREE BONUS
In my previous book, "Profit from Real Estate Right Now!," on Pages 111-119, you'll find a section that specifically details how to find the right real estate agent. If you do not have my previous book, you can go to *www.deangraziosi.com/yourtown/ findagent* and get that section of the book for free!

Do not let doubt about your abilities creep into this market research process. You don't have to be an accountant, real estate broker, mathematician, or master negotiator in order to become an expert in your town real estate. Everything you need is in this book. You'll learn the details of everything: how deals are located, the negotiation process, and the outcomes with financial specifics. You'll find information specific to different towns, properties, and people who, using my books and seminars, have successfully implemented the strategies they learned.

In the student story and deal recipe chapters, people will share the details of their best deals; how they found them and how they made them happen. After the recipes in every chapter, they talk about the tools and resources they used to prepare their deals. What if you do not have access to one or more of these tools or funding resources? I'll help you with alternatives, other ways you could have made that same deal happen for you in your town. As you know, most cooking recipes provide alternative ingredients or cooking directions; my students' successful deal recipes are no different.

Always strive to continue building your knowledge and education in real estate and soon you will find your own niche. There are many ways you

can broaden your knowledge including:
- Joining a local investment club
- Rereading this book or other real estate books
- Joining the DG family at the ***www.deangraziosi.com*** and being an active member. The Web site is totally free and packed with information and inspiration!
- Look in to my Success Academy; there may be a coaching program that is right for you. **Call anytime at 877-219-1473.**
- Attend real estate training seminars or events such as our annual "Gain the EDGE" event live event. Take a look at the "Gain the EDGE 2009" event at ***www.deangraziosi.com/yourtown/edgeevent***

Summing It Up

As we move to the deal recipes from my students, I hope you're excited about this journey we are about to take. Because of the variety of strategies utilized by my students, each person needed to develop a structured and organized approach to locating the right properties for each strategy. We will also cover specific topics in greater detail. For now, I'll just cover the highlights so you can watch for these vital tools, essential tips and valuable resources as you read.

Market Overview Questions – A set of questions that focus on the characteristics of the real estate market in your town. In the "Knowing the Market in Your Town" chapter in the Resources section, we'll show you how to use them in your town.

Web site Real Estate Listing Search Sites – There are a huge number of Web sites that allow you to search listed properties, but they all aren't the same. We'll show you the differences and how to use them to your advantage.

Print Media for Research – Do you read the local homes magazines? They aren't just pictures and listings. There are articles as well. No information is unimportant.

News That Yields Opportunity – Do you read the real estate section of the local newspaper? If not, you may be missing out on announcements about new parks, commercial building or other things that will influence how you do business in your town.

Real Estate Brokerage Ads Tell Us a Lot – Real estate agents make a living helping sellers to market their homes. Some pay marketing professionals to draft ads for them. Pay attention to their ads for tips on wording and what's hot in your town.

FSBO Ads Can Be a Gold Mine – FSBOs, For Sale By Owner homes, are a very profitable niche, and bring with them special issues of marketing and negotiations. Some of our student deals will show you how they worked with FSBO sellers. This topic gets a whole chapter in the Resources section.

Homes for Rent Ads Bring Sellers – In this section, Greg Murphy shows you how he uses "for rent" ads to locate both buyers and sellers. Greg and I give you even more information in the Resources section; there's an entire chapter on Greg's highly successful lease purchase and lease sale strategy.

Taking the Open House Approach to Learning Your Market – Real estate agents know the value of caravans to view listed properties. You'll find that this first-hand viewing of what's on the market is invaluable. I'll show you how to use open houses to "know your market."

Your Own Caravan Approach – Joe takes a very organized approach to a nice Sunday drive. But, you can still have fun when you're gathering data about your town.

Forms to Help You Gather Information

An organized approach to market study isn't going to be a burden, as you can utilize several forms that take the marketing research and make it easy to note down what information you need to know, and what information you'll want to refer to later. The process will involve taking the "drilling down" approach, from local area information described, right down to data on individual properties.

FREE BONUS

We can't show you all of them here, but they're waiting for you for free at *www.deangraziosi.com/yourtown/forms*. Here's a partial screen shot of one of the "Market Composition Analysis" forms. There is no substitute for market knowledge, and these forms are designed to get that knowledge collected and recorded so that you can use it for profit later. The key is to use whatever process works for you.

Name of Town or city:					
Zip Code:					
Date:					
Zip Code	Number of SFH	Number of Condos	Number of Townhomes	Commercial	Multi-Family
Price Range	Number of SFH	Number of Condos	Number of Townhomes	Commercial	Multi-Family
Under $50,000					
Under $75,000					
Under $100,000					
Under $125,000					
Under $150,000					

Are you getting the idea that this isn't one of those books long on inspiration, but short on "how to?" You're just getting started. The next 9 chapters are student stories and deal recipes. You get everything, including why they started investing in real estate, their financial situations, some inspiring stories, and a lot of deal detail in their recipes. You'll meet different people, in different towns, with different deal strategies. You'll find someone just like you, in a town just like yours, doing deals you'll want to do. Let's get started!

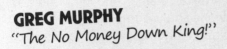

CHAPTER 4

GREG MURPHY
"The No Money Down King!"

Mississippi contractor
Turns His Life Around!

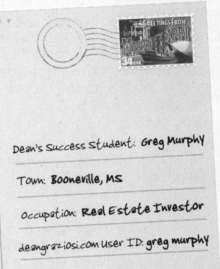

Dean's Success Student: Greg Murphy

Town: Booneville, MS

Occupation: Real Estate Investor

deangraziosi.com User ID: greg murphy

"My credit was in the crapper!"
—Greg Murphy

Maybe your credit situation is the same as Greg's. You want and need to make a change in your life, and are searching for an answer. Real estate investing sounds appealing, but you wonder, "how can I make money in real estate without any of my own money and without any credit?" Well, this is exactly what Greg Murphy has done. To those who question his no-money-down technique, Greg replies, *"If I just had no money that would have been easier. I also had a pile of debt and was working 70 hours a week. But with this technique, I've had success with real estate investing with no money, crappy credit, and no bank loans!"* We will meet Greg and discuss this system that he has been able to perfect. I believe Greg is the "No Money Down King!" How would you like to be like Greg, a real estate investor that uses none of his own money or credit? It sounds too good to be true, doesn't it? Let's take a closer look into Greg's story and the ingredients for his recipe for success.

Before we begin, I want to let you know that we are profiling 14 (some are spouses and partners) students in this book, all with their own great stories and strategies. Some students will give you more wisdom than others; some will give more inspiration and hope. This group of students was specifically chosen to give you the perfect balance and create success in your life! But with that said, I want to stress the importance of this chapter. It is the chapter that anyone can use to profit in their town right now, with no money, no credit and without having to take ownership of single property. It is jam packed with a tremendous amount of information; you'll be given all you need to do what Greg has done so well. Of course, I want you learn from other tremendous people like Joe and Stacey Jurek and their magic email. But if you use only Greg Murphy's lease-option strategy, you could be making money in no time, with no downside and no risk. Okay, let's get started!

Like most hard working Americans, Greg worried about his family's financial future. He was employed in a solid trade and made decent money, but no matter how many hours he worked, he could just not get ahead. Often he would work 60 to 70 hours a week and still struggled to pay his bills.

Then one day, Greg fell off a ladder, and realized that when missed work for several days, his income stopped. What would happen to his family if he was hurt for an extended period of time? If he missed work for two months, he could lose everything he had. Greg said, "when you're young, you feel like you can run through a brick wall, but as you get older, you begin to realize some things and discover you may not be as invincible as you once thought you were." What would happen if you experienced the same accident? Greg decided he needed to find another way. He knew there had to be a better way, and was determined to find it!

Greg was working construction in 2007, with a low credit score and no cash to invest. He had tried one real estate deal on his own without guidance from anyone, buying homes to rehab and sell. It didn't go well; he paid more than he should have, and barely managed to get out of the deal. This was extremely scary because he was already behind on money each month and a bad deal could have crippled him. I'll let Greg tell you:

"My financial situation was horrible. I was working sunrise to sunset and still couldn't make my bills. I was just surviving, and my credit rating was in the toilet. When I had tried real estate investing in the past, I bought three homes at once, paid too much, and bought in the wrong areas. I had no training in real estate investment, did no research, lost a lot of money, and just had a horrible experience."

Greg's brother had ordered some "real estate guru" materials, books, tapes and CDs from someone else and loaned the materials to Greg. Greg spent many late nights reading and listening to sessions, but still nothing worked. He couldn't find the information he needed, but even more so, he lacked encouragement and the knowledge that others were making it happen by using those materials. It just wasn't enough to help him to get past the fear of failure from his previous experience.

"Those materials just didn't make any sense to me. You can't start out talking about capitalization rates when I don't know the first thing about real estate investing. I needed something that could take me from newbie through each step to make it happen."

"I knew there had to be a better way, but I hadn't found it until late one night, I saw one of Dean's infomercials. I didn't watch it just once. The burning I took in my past fling at real estate investing gave me a lot of doubt. I watched several times, and finally decided that it was worth the cost of the book and I gave it a try. I really believed that Dean was sincere and could understand what he was saying. This was so important because when you are talking with someone that has never done real estate before, you do not want to take people too deep into these concepts too quickly because it can just go over their head."

Greg ordered and read all my other books as well. He had to read and study late at night. Or he would get up at 2:00 or 3:00 am to read for an hour before going to work in the morning. When people are determined to succeed, anything is possible. Greg even made the commitment to join my Real Estate Success Academy because he was truly determined to succeed.

"It was more than the classes, training and those things keeping me accountable. These guys were here for me every time I needed them. Heck, I would call them a few times a day sometimes when I was working on a deal and felt bad. They were always there with real advice. You can tell in minutes that these guys know their stuff. If someone is a little nervous like I was, the Success Academy is the way to go."

Greg found the academy invaluable; the coaching staff was always available to assist him with his action plan, provide motivation and answer technical questions. Can the Success Academy help you too? You bet! Give them a call to see if it is a fit at **877-219-1473**.

Greg claims he was a slow starter, taking several months to digest the material and create an action plan before his first deal. But Greg isn't a slow starter; everyone is different, and each of us have lives and situations that determine how quickly we can start something new.

Truth is, nothing will help you or your family have a better future or feel more secure if you don't commit to changing your financial future forever. I know, at times you may feel helpless or even hopeless. But you need to have hope, because there is a way to turn your financial situation around, just as Greg did. I know it stinks that Greg had to get up in the middle of the night to find the time to learn my techniques. But that period time in which he was inconvenienced is a small price to pay for a better quality of life. Would that be worth it? As Greg would say, "Heck yeah!"

As inspiration to keep reading and learn Greg's techniques, know this: now is not a time to do nothing. Now is the time to take action with those things that can propel you to wealth. You're going to be doing it with realistic, applicable skills to profit in a down market, with no money and no credit. Could that be the foundation for a new start on your whole life? You bet!

Greg lives in Booneville, Mississippi, in the eastern part of the state, 110 miles from Memphis, 200 miles from Nashville. It's definitely not a big city; recent census data states the population is around 9,000 people.

Greg needed to limit his early activity to something that was low risk, required little or no cash, and definitely didn't require financing, a good credit rating or a bank loan. So he settled on his own variation of "lease with option to purchase."

Greg's plan was to lease a home with an option to purchase from a homeowner desperate to sell. Then he used creative marketing techniques (which he learned here) to find a "tenant buyer" who would lease option the home. This strategy is often called a "sandwich lease option" because you work in the middle of the buyer and seller. This technique allows you to make money upfront and in the middle, with a bigger payout at the end.

Let me explain this as simply as I can before we get in to all the details:

first, Greg built a buyers' list and separated into two parts; investment buyers and tenant buyers. An investment buyer is someone who has cash and is ready to buy. A tenant buyer is someone who can't qualify for a typical loan, but can afford a slightly higher monthly payment and a fractional down payment. The tenant buyer wants a home, but does not have the tools or time to find the deals you can find. In most cases, you are working with people who are behind in their payments, are about to lose their home, and do not want to face foreclosure. Good news: you can help them. You can negotiate to pay their payments to date, make their payments moving forward (you are going to lease it with an option) and at anytime during the lease, you can buy the home for what is owed on it.

Okay, so now that you have your list of tenant buyers and investors, go out and find homes with desperate sellers. You then lock up those houses on a lease with an option to buy. Then you simply match that house with people on your buyer's list. If there is a lot less owed on the house then it is worth, you could flip the contract to a cash investor putting a profit in the middle for you. On the other hand, if the house is worth about what is owed, you can offer it to a tenant buyer who will put a minimal payment down that covers the back payments of the owner plus some extra for you (profit up front). Rent the home to the tenant for an amount greater than the monthly mortgage payments (profit in the middle with cash flow) then the tenant buyer's purchase price would be set at true value at some future date, locking in a nice profit (the big payoff at the end).

If that was a little confusing, here's an example of a deal Greg is working on right now. I'll use round numbers to make it easy. Through his marketing efforts, Greg found a family three months behind on their $500 per month mortgage. They are stressed. Greg told them that if he can find a buyer, he would make their late payments and pay their mortgage to take the burden off of them (all the paperwork and conversations to have are later on). In order to avoid foreclosure, the family agreed that Greg could buy the house at anytime for what is owed.

Next Greg went to his tenant buyer's list and told them that he has a great little house that they can take a lease option on with $3,000 up front ($1500 goes to catch up payments, $1500 is Greg's profit up front). He set the lease option rent at $650 per month (profit in the middle of $150 a month) and told the tenant buyers that they could purchase the house in the future for the fair market value. Since we are at a bottom market, Greg expects them to close in a year or two and the property to go up between $20K to $40k (the big payoff in the end).

Why would a tenant buyer do this? Because they can't put the 20% down to purchase a house, or their credit is not good enough at this point in time. As a tenant buyer, they can get in a house for a minimal down payment, a little extra each month, and some of their rent goes towards the purchase of the home. That's better than throwing it all away on rent each month. This is a win-win for all parties involved. The desperate seller gets out of payments they can't afford, the tenant buyer gets their family in a home, and Greg makes money for being smart and ambitious enough to put this deal together.

Greg closes deals like this over and over and over in his tiny town. Of course, we will explain all the additional details so that nothing is left out. But I hope you can at least start to see that with this no-money-down technique, you can make money anywhere and never even own the home.

The basics of Greg's plan include the following 5 step system for lease options:

1. Build your Real Estate Professional Team
2. Build your Investor Buyer's list
3. Build your Tenant Buyer's list
4. Find properties that meet your criteria
5. Close the deal and generate cash

Build Your Real Estate Professional Team

A team with the right experts can save you time, work and money. With the right real estate investment team, you have a valuable resource in each professional's area of expertise. Greg's "A-Team" consists of the following:

- Real estate attorney
- Mortgage broker
- Realtor
- Title company
- Accountant
- An established credit repair company
- Escrow company
- Construction contractors
- Contacts at the county courthouse (to assist in gathering and recording information)

You will not need all these people all the time for each deal. But like a tool shed in which you can grab a tool when you need it, it's great to have these team members ready when you need them. In later chapters you will learn how to choose and pick the best people to be on your team and when to call upon them. Remember, these team members are not getting paid unless you are putting a deal together and making money. In fact, a worthwhile real estate agent will work his or her tail off for you in hopes of profits down the road.

Tenant Buyers

Once he had his A-Team in place, Greg built a list of buyers for properties he hadn't even yet identified. As previously mentioned, he was looking to attract the perfect tenant buyer by running ads, placing bandit signs and hanging flyers to interest people who can't buy but want to. (You get the exact ads and how to place them in this chapter, so we make that part easy for you!) Greg is attracting people that need to work on their credit and/or cash for a down payment. He's not advertising specific properties, remember, he doesn't have any. Instead, he tells callers that he's moving properties through all the time, and gets their information, which is crucial. He is not only getting their names but also building a profile on potential buyers; what type of home they want, the amount of money they have to put upfront, what they can afford to pay on a monthly basis, what area would they hope to be in, and their credit score. After Greg finds out what they need and puts it in his list, he is off to the races to find a home for them. But remember, that list grows fast so a home that is not right for one person on your list may be perfect for another. Greg stated that he has something for every buyer in his list, whether that buyer has good credit, bad credit, or no credit.

> **"It's all about your lists, man."**
> **—Greg Murphy**

Investor Buyers

If you think there are no investors out there with cash, you are absolutely wrong. Investors are cashing out of the stock market or are sick of getting 1.5% interest on their money in the bank and looking for a place to invest their cash. Greg uses bandit signs, Craigslist ads and flyers to find these potential buyers and now has something that others don't think exists: a pile of investment buyers with cash.

Build your Investor Buyer's list

"The key closing an assignment deal with an investor buyer is making sure you leave plenty of meat on the bone." – Greg Murphy

Let's take a look at what makes a good candidate for an investor buyer. First, he or she must have cash or access to cash and be able to buy and close a deal within 2 weeks or less. The more profit potential you can pass on to the investor, the better the chance for future deals with that investor.

Greg uses bandit signs, flyers, bulletin boards, business cards and ads in the small local newspaper such as the "penny saver" publications. He posts his flyers in delis, grocery stores, Laundromats, apartment complexes, bookstores, convenience stores and supply houses. He has found that a handwritten flyer works best because it appears less threatening to a motivated seller. A bright yellow or red flyer with black lettering is a reliable way to draw attention to prospective motivated sellers.

Take a look at a few actual bandit signs and flyers Greg uses to attract Investor buyers:

Do you have cash?
I need to sell my home fast!

Steal my home today!
Call 555—1212

HELP Desperate owner!

3/2 house must sell fast!

2 Bedroom/2 Bath Home
in nice area, 50% below
appraised value

Call 555—1212

Greg also calls the "for rent" ads in the classified sections of the news-paper. Building inspectors are a resource as well, they are the ones who know who has what going on all around town. Run some ads on various Internet sites (including Craigslist), and you'll have a steady stream of people to talk to and add to your buyer list as cash investors.

Okay, now I hope your eyes are opening up to first parts of these no-money-down techniques. Of course you need to know how to put that deal together once you line it all up. We'll get to that. Right now, I want you to see and learn exactly what type of ads Greg runs and what they say. He likes cheap or inexpensive ads, keeping the wording short, but the marketing principles are still there to draw the buyer to his advertisement.

Greg gets his supplies from Walmart: a black Sharpie marker and pre-cut 10x14 white poster boards. He then creates "bandit signs" to reel them in. Greg posts his bandit signs on street corners to generate calls. Here are a few examples:

"Desperate owner 3/2 house must sell fast"

"2 Bedroom/2 Bath Home in nice area, 40% below appraised value"

"3/2 Home, FSBO, owner must sell fast!"

You want someone who can pay cash and close in 2 weeks or less. Remember: the investor buyer wants an unbelievably good deal . . . even an insane deal. They don't want a marginal deal; there are already too many marginal deals in the market place. Starting to get the idea? It's taking what you know the active real estate investor is seeking and putting it out there.

When investment buyers call Greg and he does not currently have any homes available, he may tell them that a specific home has sold, but he's working on a similar deal. The investment buyer gives Greg their contact information and criteria they are looking for and Greg goes to work to find a deal that will appeal to them.

Greg completes a portfolio sheet on each investment buyer, including property criteria and location. For example, an investor might be inter-ested in duplexes under $50,000 in a certain zip code or part of town or in single family homes that can be bought for 30% to 40% off of fair market value (FMV). Once Greg finds a deal that matches the investor's criteria, he contacts the investor and tells him or her the details. Greg creates a file for the profile of each of his potential buyers and uses it as an easy reference to match the perfect deal with the perfect investor.

Greg finds the buyer first, simply because he doesn't have the money to buy a property and then resell it to the buyer. He needs a ready buyer before he can find a seller. Thus, Greg is the matchmaker who creates win-win deals for all the parties involved. "If you create win-win situations for these investors, they will be coming out of the woodwork to buy these deals," he says.

Greg can assign his interest in the deal to the investor and makes a quick and tidy profit. The investor buyer is happy to pay Greg the assignment fee and "steps into Greg's shoes" to complete the deal with the motivated seller.

In an assignment deal, you sell the equity or the right to the deal in your contract. That amount can be negotiated to whatever you think is fair. Like Greg says, "leave some meat on the bone and they'll come running back for more deals." Basically, if Greg finds an amazing deal, he marks it up enough to make a nice profit while still keeping the price way below FMV. So many of my students use assignment deals to make a fast profit in the middle. You will learn how Chip and Andrea did it to make $44,000 in less than 2 months with no money of their own. It is a wonderful strategy. Instead of a long chapter on assignment deals, I'm going to give you yet another bonus. I covered assignments in great detail in my past book. So below you can get link that will take you right to that section.

FREE BONUS
You can find detail on how to do an assignment deal, including the forms to use, in my previous book, "Profit from Real Estate Right Now!" Check out pages 151, 153, and 164-170. And if you do not have my previous book you can go to *www.deangraziosi.com/yourtown/assignments* and get that section of the book for free.

Build your Tenant Buyer's list

"All real estate buyers love a good deal, so I give them one!"
— Greg Murphy

Now, let's take a look at some of the characteristics that makes a good candidate for a tenant buyer. Greg doesn't like to use the terms "renter," "lease," or "renting." He is searching for people who want to own a home, but have poor credit, or don't have the down payment, or both. These people are motivated by the desire to be homeowners, not just "renters." So, Greg markets to his potential tenant buyers in just that way. He uses the same marketing, media, and methods, but just changes the wording a bit. Some of his ads may read as follows:

• 3/2 home, great location, owner financing
• 2/2 house, available as a rent-to-own
• Homes available with a buyer assistance program
• Homes available: no credit, low down payment, no problem!
• Buy a home, don't rent, with buyer assistance and poor credit
• Why waste money renting when you can own with our help

3/2 HOME

GREAT LOCATION

OWNER FINANCING

Homes available with
buyer assistance
program.

Call 555—1212

BUY A HOME,
WHY RENT?

Low down payment!

Call 555—1212

Again, Greg uses wording that appeals to his target market. He has found that the people who respond to these ads will be very amenable to buying a lease to own home, working to repair their credit, and paying a higher-than-market rent for a home if they can own it within a reasonable period of time. Greg believes that the ideal number of tenant buyers on your list should be around 10 to 15 buyers with a $2,000 to $5,000 down payment.

Greg does his homework and contacted his mortgage broker for the latest client application requirements. He wants to stay current on the various loan programs and his mortgage broker can provide an updated list of what a prospective tenant buyer needs to qualify for a loan. Greg has his tenant buyers complete an application that authorizes the broker to run the prospective buyers credit. This application asks for the following information:

• Authorization to run credit – Greg knows the minimum that is acceptable
• Monthly income of tenant buyer
• Job history of tenant buyer
• Current and previous addresses
• Social security number
• State and Driver's License Number
• Amount of down payment tenant buyer has available

Greg will usually take 8 to 10 applications to his mortgage broker to run credit checks and determine which buyer could qualify the fastest for a mortgage and at what amount. When a prospective tenant buyer calls Greg, he has them complete this application to determines if this buyer could be ready or may need some additional assistance (such as working with an advisor on credit repair). Greg always strives to assist each prospect, even if the tenant buyer may not be able to qualify for one of his lease option programs. He provides the best advice he can and offers referral advice to the buyer for other programs in the area.

If the buyer does not qualify, Greg informs the buyer that he does not have anything at this time but provides information on other programs or services. Greg may even refer the motivated seller to any number of investor buyers that he has on his list in case they want to talk with the motivated seller and possibly pursue a short sale. Greg wants to ensure that he does not burnout his mortgage broker by sending over everyone that calls. He can pre-qualify the tenant buyer, which saves everyone time, and effort. Remember, he is also looking for people who do not qualify now, but with a little credit repair, could qualify in 6 months or a year.

(There's more in later chapters how to find the perfect mortgage broker, how to pre-qualify applicants, and who to forward to your broker.)

Greg loves the new tighter mortgage requirements, because they yield many more prospects for his tenant buyer programs. He puts people into contact with his credit repair company, gets them started in raising their credit scores, and finds a home that meets their size and location needs. He tells us that getting a couple dozen buyer prospects quickly with these ads is very possible. But he never stops advertising, as prospects move away, get locked into long leases, or become non-prospects in various ways. It's a constant process. He also passes their information to his mortgage broker to find out how close they are to being able to get a mortgage. The ones that have only a little way to go with qualifying go to the top of the list.

Later in the chapter, Greg will share much more of his strategy and methods after I give you his deal recipe. Since all of his deals are very similar, just multiply this one out, as that's what he's doing successfully over and over.

Find Properties that Meet your Criteria

"What if I could just take over these payments for you until we can find a buyer? Would that help you out? We can step in and make the payments until we find a new buyer."
— Greg Murphy

Greg has a nice long list of prospects that include both investor buyers and tenant buyers. He has a profile of each buyer with notes on the size of home they need, bedrooms, baths, location, etc. Now all he has to do is kick in the second half of his successful matchmaking strategy. It's time to find the homes that are right for this "no money out of pocket" strategy. Greg takes a broad-based approach:

• Scours For Sale By Owner ads
• Drives around looking for FSBO signs
• Talks to his professional real estate team for word of mouth referrals
• Goes on the Internet and to Craigslist to scout out motivated sellers
• Uses bandit signs with this revised message

I BUY HOUSES
Any Condition
Any Area
CALL 555—1212

Facing foreclosure?
Behind on Payments
We can help!
Call 555—1212

Need to sell
your home fast?
We have a program
for everyone!
Call 555—1212

His favorite prospect is a very motivated seller, usually 3 to 4 months behind with their payments, and staring foreclosure in the face. They may have been trying to sell their home for several months, and may have had it listed by a real estate agent in the past. They have reached the point in which their credit score is being hurt and they fear losing their home altogether. Some ways to find these motivated sellers include the expired MLS listings that Greg's local real estate agent can share with him or the FSBO ads on Craigslist. Greg will start with the oldest FSBO ads on Craigslist first and then call to inquire about the seller's home. Chances are, if the seller has still not sold their home, they are even more motivated to sell now.

Greg tries to work with sellers to create a win-win deal. Here are his action steps:

• Find a motivated seller that may lead to a lease option deal.
• Call the seller and begin to carefully build a no-pressure relationship.
• Build the relationship by making a few calls, ask some questions without pressure, and finding out their true situation.
• Be a good listener and empathize with the seller's situation.
• Ask the seller if they would be interested in discussing a way Greg could:
  - Provide a program to offer some debt relief
  - He can take over their payments
  - Catch up back payments
  - Make repairs and improve their home for a sale
  - Take care of the payments until Greg can get the home out of their name
• Start the process quickly if they want to move forward. In 9 out of 10 cases, the sellers are ready now.

Don't get too personal on first phone call; just listen to the seller. The seller wants to explain what happened and you want to listen. If the preliminary information sounds like a potential deal, Greg will schedule a time to view the property with the seller. As Greg speaks with the seller, he cultivates a relationship.

• How many months is the seller behind on their payments?
• What is their payment each month?
• What is the total amount they are behind, including penalties and late fees?
• What is included in the mortgage payment (such as principle, interest

insurance and property taxes)
- Whose name(s) are on the current deed? Is the property in one name or, if a couple, in both names?
- What is the total amount of the mortgage owed?
- Does the seller have any other liens or mortgages against the property?
- Are there any minor or major repairs that are needed for the home?
- Greg asks, "What if I could just take over these payments for you until we can find a buyer? We can step in and make the payments until we find a new buyer. Is this something that would interest you?"

As Greg gathers this information, he qualifies the seller and the property for two options. One, to see if the seller would be open to a lease with option to purchase or, second, to see if the seller's property has some instant equity.

Greg will schedule a time to walk through the home to determine if there are any repairs that may need to be completed prior to locating a buyer for the home. He also confirms that the seller is only seeking debt relief and will be happy for Greg to assist with their current situation.

If the meeting goes as planned and both parties are happy, we move on to the next level. To have both parties happy means that the home owner wants to have his or her payments caught up, and their mortgage paid each month until their home sells. They also agree to sell Greg the house for what is owed on it. They're happy because basically, they get to wash their hands of a stressful situation. For Greg, being happy means that the house has appeal, will fit with someone on his buyer's list, that there is not more owed on it the home than it is worth and that he can make money with it. (More on this in a minute.)

At this point, Greg has several forms that will need to be completed with the motivated seller. He schedules an appointment to meet at his attorney's office with the seller. It is important to have an independent third party, such as a real estate attorney, to assist with the completion of the forms. The real estate attorney can notarize the forms upon completion. Greg has the attorney prepare the following documents:

1. Release of Mortgage information from the motivated seller's bank that holds the mortgage
2. Agreement to Lease with Option of Purchase
3. Memorandum of Option

Greg trusts the seller's responses but realizes he must always verify all the information he gathers. Part of Greg's due diligence is to verify the mortgage rates, terms and conditions. To verify the mortgage balance information, Greg would ask the seller to sign the Release of Mortgage information from the bank that holds the mortgage, so that Greg can verify the information provided. Greg will also want to run a preliminary title search as well. In Greg's area, his real estate attorney can assist him. In your area, a real estate attorney or a title company could be of assistance. You want to ensure there are no other attachments on the property such as an IRS lien, contractor's lien or even a second mortgage.

Greg will then review the title search information with his attorney. He will also review the amount and the terms of the mortgage. Greg wants to ensure the mortgage terms are acceptable with what he wants to do with the home. Once he gets this information and the review completed, he can then determine if the home is a good candidate for a tenant buyer or an investment buyer. If the title search and the mortgage confirmation come back without any issues, Greg can move forward and record his Memorandum of Option at the local county court house. The Memorandum of Option provides a notice to others that you have an option on the property; it is kept in the County Recorder's office. This should prevent the original seller from attempting to sell the property if they have already granted you a lease with an option to purchase.

> **"Remember, don't get too personal on the first phone call and just listen to the seller. The seller wants to explain to you what happened and you want to listen to them. Once your listen and they unload their problems, you will become their new best friend."**
> **— Greg Murphy**

Sure, this all sounds straightforward and you're excited about the possibilities, but you're now thinking, "wait a minute Dean, how do I know if I'm getting a good deal on this property?" Well, that should be rather easy to figure out. You want to determine the current fair market value of the property based on comps of similar homes that have recently sold in the local area and then project the value of what the home you now control may be worth in a few years. This way, you can be sure the lease with option to purchase contract that you execute with your tenant buyer with a pre-negotiated price factors in potential appreciation for the property. When he first started, Greg drove his area and looked at various properties for about two weeks. He wanted to know what properties were selling and renting for.

Once Greg determined the fair market value, he would exercise his due diligence in inspecting the property. Greg completes an inspection sheet that he has created and makes any notes as to what the property may need. In Greg's area, there are many prospective tenant buyers that have a minimal down payment but are very willing to earn a little sweat equity by completing some of the needed repairs. Greg always tries to work with each tenant buyer to create a win-win deal. Even if the initial profit is not as great when the tenant buyer moves in, if the home has positive cash flow and a big payday once they close on the home, it is well worth the effort.

Each property represents a new and different opportunity for you. If the current mortgage balance owed is equal or only a little more than the future purchase price, it should be a good deal to move forward. If the future purchase price is tremendously more than what will be owed on the mortgage, this is a slam dunk! Another key to remember here is the purchase price you negotiate with the original seller is always equal to the remaining amount of the mortgage when you finally exercise your option and close with the original seller. This is very important because you will realize the benefit of any mortgage pay down as your tenant buyer makes their monthly mortgage payments to your escrow company.

FREE BONUS
You can go to www.deangraziosi.com/yourtown/gregforms
and get Greg's exact forms and documents that he uses
for the ease with option to purchase deals. Oh yeah,
that's another free bonus just for you!

Closing the Deal and Generating CA$H

**"The only thing that limits you with lease options is
how hard you want to work!"
— Greg Murphy**

When Greg finds a deal, he first tried to do an assignment to an investor buyer to see if he can make a fast $3,000 to $5,000. This is easier if there is a good amount of equity in the property. For example, if the motivated seller owes $100,000 on the property, yet with a tiny bit of clean up, it is worth $150,000 or more. You may be able to assign the deal (as we discussed previously) for a nice little profit in the middle, making it a win-win for all.

Next, if the house has little or no equity, or no investors want the house at that time, Greg offers the property to a tenant buyer. Each deal depends on the buyers you have on your list and what you want to accomplish. You can make fast cash assigning a home to an investor but if you have more time, you can offer a lease option to sell the home to a tenant buyer and potentially make a significant amount of more cash over time.

Remember with the lease option, Greg makes money on the transaction on the front end of the transaction, he makes money on the middle of the transaction, and he makes money at the end of the transaction. How great is that?

Deal Recipe # 1 – A Tired Landlord Wanting Out

The Ingredients
• A motivated landlord wanting to sell the home he was renting out
• A tenant buyer who needs to lease purchase
• Tenant buyer needs time to build credit rating
• A home that meets the tenant buyer needs
• Low mortgage balance in relation to value

Desired Result
Greg builds his tenant buyer list and, on the other side, locates highly motivated homeowners in danger of losing their home or just wanting, but unable, to sell. He negotiates a lease purchase from the current owner, and then places one of his tenant buyers into the home on a lease purchase. The deal needs to be done with little or no cash out of Greg's pocket. Ultimately, Greg will sell the home to the tenant buyer at a nice profit (greater than the loan balance at which he agreed to buy it from the original motivated seller).

Preparation

- Greg has a potential tenant buyer on his list, along with their needs in a home, such as bedrooms, baths and location.
- In this case, he was calling "for rent" ads and found a landlord who really would like to sell, but couldn't in the current market.
- The home is owned free and clear, so the motivation is simply to sell and quit being a landlord.
- The homeowner is highly motivated, accepting a lease purchase deal that allows Greg to take control of the home.
- Greg agrees to a purchase price of $29,500, well below the true value of the home.
- He executes a purchase contract and a deed to allow him to sell the home later to his tenant buyer.

CONTRACT FOR THE SALE AND PURCHASE OF REAL ESTATE

The Seller hereby agrees to sell and the Purchaser agrees to purchase the hereinafter described property on the terms and conditions stipulated as follows:

PROPERTY located at: _10)_ ▓▓▓▓▓▓▓
(house #, street/road)
Booneville, MS, 38829.
(city,state,zip)

Legal description attached: Warranty Deed or Survey

PRICE: Total purchase price of the property agreed upon $ _29,500_

TAXES and INSURANCE: All taxes for the current year will be pro-rated between Seller and Purchaser. Adequate Harzard Insurance shall be provided Purchaser at closing as required by Mortgagee.

TITLE: Mortgagee will require a Certificate of Title from a reputable title

More in this contract in this excerpt:

12. TIME IS OF THE ESSENCE IN ALL MATTERS OF THE AGREEMENT
13. OTHER TERMS:

Failure to pay Deed will go Back to Charles Roberts. Buyer has the Right to assign the Property to another investor at any time during the Length of contract, or the Right to Renew at the end IF he has performed in a timely manner. Deed will go Back to Charles Roberts in the that will Fail to do everything that we say in contract.

The undersigned agree to buy and sell on the above terms, have-read, fully understand and verify the above information is being correct. All parties acknowledge that this is a legally binding contract and are advised to seek the counsel of an

- He gets a deed, giving him the flexibility to go through with the process and sell the home to the tenant buyer.
- Getting the deed in your name is not required, but it adds an extra level of protection for all sides. If you do this, you can add a clause like Greg did above stating that if the buyer's failure to pay occurs, the deed goes back in the seller's name.

WARRANTY DEED

███████ ██ ████████   **GRANTOR**

TO

GREG MURPHY   **GRANTEE**

   FOR AND IN CONSIDERATION of the sum of **TEN DOLLARS** ($10.00) cash in hand paid and other good and valuable considerations, the receipt of all of which is hereby acknowledged, I, ████████████████████ do hereby sell, convey and warrant unto **GREG MURPHY**, the land lying and being situated in Lee County, Mississippi, more particularly described as follows, to-wit:

Part of ████████████████████████, bounded as follows:
Beginning at the ████████████████████████████, more or less, to the
████████████████████████████████████ more or less, to the ████████████████ to the Point of Beginning.

Also: Commencing at the ████████████████████████████
and run thence ████████████████████████████████
████████████ feet to the Point of Beginning.

The warranty in this deed is subject to rights of way and easements for public roads and public utilities.

   WITNESS, my signature this 5th day of February 2008.

He completes the lease purchase contract with the tenant buyer at a positive cash flow rental amount, and with a down payment that covers his up-front costs. Notice the purchase price of $72,000. What a great profit Greg will have down the road!

Greg receives a down payment from the tenant buyer that covers all of his out-of-pocket expenses in the deal; in this case, the down payment was $3,000.

The tenant buyer even volunteered to do some improvements to the property. Often improvements can create more appeal or value to a property and if a tenant buyer is paying for them out of their pocket, encourage them to do as much as they desire!

Greg structured this deal so he did not have to make a payment for the first few months. The payments were eventually around $300 per month and Greg had the home lease optioned to a tenant buyer for around $600 per month. That is a positive cash flow of $300 each and every month!

When Greg closed the deal he made $37,000. Way to go Greg!

CONTRACT FOR THE SALE OF REAL ESTATE

The Seller(s) agrees to sell and the Purchaser(s) agrees to purchase the described property on the terms and conditions listed below:

Property located at: ___*102*_____
(street address)

Booneville MS. 38829
(city, state, zip)

Legal description attached: Warranty Deed or Survey

Price: Purchase price of property------------------------------- $ _*72.000*_____

Earnest Money: The Purchaser(s) deposited (___) Cash (✓) Check in the amount of $ _*3,000.00*_ as earnest money with _*ESTHR*_ .This money will be applied to purchase transaction.

Closing Date: Closing date will be on or before _*FEB. 15 ·08*_
Possession Date: Possession date will be on or before _*FEB. 15 ·08*_

When the tenant buyer is ready to purchase, he sells them the home at the retail price they agreed to in the beginning of the lease purchase.

Garnish and Presentation

This is an amazing process, and Greg gives us this example with the statement that he's doing it over and over again. He uses none of his own money, locking up this property in December of 2007, places a tenant buyer in it right away, and at a nice positive cash flow until they are able to buy the home. Then, he helps his tenant buyer to get to the point where they can purchase, and at a price that's at true market value.

So, he buys it for $29,500, with none of his own money on a lease purchase. He gets paid every month on a second lease purchase until it's ready for sale, then he sells it for $72,000. Out of that money, he's paying the $29,500 purchase price, keeping the $42,000 difference, less closing costs. He helps the original homeowner sell the home and helps a tenant buyer to get the home of their dreams. And all at a nice profit! Could you use an extra $300 per month as Greg earned? Just think what you could do with the $37,000 in profit Greg earned when he closed this deal! Folks, it doesn't get any better than that!

120.	Gross amount due from borrower:			72,376.01
200.	Amounts paid by or in behalf of the borrower:			
201.	Deposit or earnest money			3,000.00
202.	Principal amount of new loan(s)			56,000.00
203.	Existing loan(s) taken subject to			
204.				
205.				
206.				
207.				
208.				
209.				
Adjustments for items unpaid by seller:				
210.	City/town taxes	1/1/2008	to 3/14/2008	20.68
211.	County taxes	1/1/2008	to 3/14/2008	29.20
212.	Assessments			

This is the best of all worlds. Greg's business model makes him money, but it also gives him a sense of fulfillment when he can help people on both ends while he's doing it. Way to go, Greg!

Deal # 2 – Creating a Variation of the Same Recipe

The Ingredients
• A ready-to-rent owner occupied home
• Low loan balance and very low mortgage payment
• Ready tenant buyer willing to pay market rate rent until purchase
• 5 years on the buying side before Greg must pay off the home
• 1 year on the tenant buyer's lease purchase agreement

Desired Result
Just like in his first deal, Greg wants to locate someone wanting out of a home with a low mortgage balance in relation to value. The interest rate and payment he's assuming are also low enough to allow a nice positive cash flow. So, Greg has positive cash flow every month for the entire period he's holding the home.

He does the lease purchase to gain control of the home for a much longer period of time than he's setting up the tenant buyer. This gives him time to complete the deal, but also time to find another tenant buyer if the first one doesn't perform according to their agreement. He makes a nice profit on the resale at the end.

Preparation
• Greg makes his deal with the homeowner for a five-year lease purchase at $33,000, the loan value.
• He will catch up her past due two payments and continue to make them in the future, and it's only $138/month.
• This owner is getting government assistance on her payment, and that will go away, so the payment will increase to $245/month.
• He places his tenant buyer in the home at a lease amount of $475/month, and an agreement to purchase the home in 12 months for $75,000.
• Because taxes and insurance are part of the payment escrow, Greg is making a nice cash deposit into his bank account every month, and stands to make a $40k+ profit in 12 months if the tenant buyer exercises their right to buy.

Agreement to Lease With Option to Purchase

Parties: Buyer _My Mmphy_ of _Market / Homes_
and
Seller, ████████ of _____

In consideration of the payments, covenants, agreements and conditions herein contained the above parties hereby agree to lease

With an option the following property:

Subject Property Address: _1600_ ████████ _____

Legal Description: _See attments_ _____

_____

Personal Property included _O_ _____

Personal property to be transferred at closing by bill of sale free of any encumbrances.

Existing Loans- At time of closing buyer may elect to take title subject to the existing loans to _FHA_ _____

In the amount of $ _33,400_ bearing interest rate of _6_ % payable _FHA_ (P & I)

Or the loan will be paid off by the seller.

Loan Number ████████ Date last payment made _____

Other Liens, back taxes, etc. _in escrow_ _____

Term of lease and option _5 years_ months beginning _6 22-08_

Monthly Payment $ _137.99_ due on the _7_ day of each month beginning _6-7-09_ 20 _09_

Monthly credit toward purchase price when rent paid on time $ _O_ _____

Purchase Price $ _33,000_ + , additional option consideration _O_ to apply towards purchase price.

1. TERMS: Seller agrees that upon the exercise of the option they will assist in financing by taking as part of the purchase price a note in the amount of $ _33,000_ with payments of $ _137.99_ beginning _12-7-09_ .
2. MAINTENANCE: The buyers shall pay for all repairs costing less than $ 100.00 each month. Repairs costing $100 or more will be paid by the owner. Should the owner fail to make repairs to maintain the house in its current condition, the buyer may have said repairs made and receive a credit equal to 200% of the cost of the repair toward the purchase price and a full credit toward the next payment due.
3. SELLER'S AGREEMENT NOT TO FURTHER ENCUMBER: Sellers agree not to refinance the property, nor to modify any existing loans, nor to transfer any interest in the property during the term of this agreement.
4. PAYMENTS ON EXISTING LOANS, TAXES AND INSURANCE: Seller shall be responsible for paying the taxes, loan payments and for keeping the property insured for its full replacement value during the term of this agreement. In the event seller fails to make payments when due of taxes, insurance, or loan payments, buyer may elect to make said pays due payments and receive 200% of their amount credited toward the purchase price and full credit toward the next payment due the seller.
5. PRORATIONS: Taxes and insurance and loan interest shall be prorated as of the date of closing of the purchase.

Agreement to Lease With Option to Purchase

Parties: Buyer ▓▓▓▓▓▓▓▓▓▓▓▓ of ▓▓▓▓▓▓▓▓▓▓
and
Seller, _Greg Murphy_ of _Market / Homes_

In consideration of the payments, covenants, agreements and conditions herein contained the above parties hereby agree to lease

With an option the following property:

Subject: Property Address: _1600_ ▓▓▓▓▓▓▓

Legal Description: _see attach A_

Personal Property included _O_

Personal property to be transferred at closing by bill of sale free of any encumbrances.

Existing Loans- At time of closing buyer may elect to take title subject to the existing loans to _Greg Murphy_

In the amount of $ _75.000_ bearing interest rate of _____ % payable _____ (P & I)

Or the loan will be paid off by the seller.

Loan Number_____ Date last payment made_____

Other Liens, back taxes, etc._____

Term of lease and option _____ months beginning _____

Monthly Payment $ _475.00_ due on the _7_ day of each month beginning _6 ~ 12_ 20 _09_

Monthly credit toward purchase price when rent paid on time $ _475.00 FOR 12 months_

Purchase Price $ _75,000_ , additional option consideration _5,700_ to apply towards purchase price.

1. TERMS: Seller agrees that upon the exercise of the option they will assist in financing by taking as part of the purchase price a note in the amount of $ _75,000_ with payments of $ _475.00_ beginning _6-12-09_ .
2. MAINTENANCE: The buyers shall pay for all repairs costing less than $ 100.00 each month. Repairs costing $100 or more will be paid by the owner. Should the owner fail to make repairs to maintain the house in its current condition, the buyer may have said repairs made and receive a credit equal to 200% of the cost of the repair toward the purchase price and a full credit toward the next payment due.
3. SELLER'S AGREEMENT NOT TO FURTHER ENCUMBER: Sellers agree not to refinance the property, nor to modify any existing loans, nor to transfer any interest in the property during the term of this agreement.
4. PAYMENTS ON EXISTING LOANS, TAXES AND INSURANCE: Seller shall be responsible for paying the taxes, loan payments and for keeping the property insured for its full replacement value during the term of this agreement. In the event seller fails to make payments when due of taxes, insurance, or loan payments, buyer may elect to make said pays due payments and receive 200% of their amount credited toward the purchase price and full credit toward the next payment due the seller.
5. PRORATIONS: Taxes and insurance and loan interest shall be prorated as of the date of closing of the purchase.

The original mortgage payment was for $137 per month under a FHA loan. When Greg took over the mortgage payment, the monthly payment increased to $245 per month because the owner was no longer living in the house. No worries, for Greg was getting $475 per month as positive cash flow on this $230 per month. He had also received a $3,000 down payment for this property and the tenant buyer had agreed to do some additional repairs as well. Greg advises to not get too hung up on making a huge amount at the beginning of each deal, because over time, the money will come as the deal matures.

Garnish and Presentation

There's no arguing with success, and Greg has a thriving system going. He is quick to point out that it's satisfying on several levels. He has a positive cash flow of $230/month until the tenant buyer is ready to close. Then he pockets a profit of around $40,000 when the tenant buys the home. Yes, he does make money, but he's also helping both a seller and a buyer realize their goals. He has little or none of his own money invested, gets a rent check every month for more than the payment he's making on the home, helps the tenant repair their credit and ultimately buy a home, all with a really nice profit in his pocket.

Utensils and Preparation Tips

Matching a Motivated Seller with Greg's Buyers

Greg told us how he builds his buyer list and fills it with people who want to own a home, but can't buy right now due to bad credit and cash problems. He tells them that he'll find them a home and help them to lease it until they have repaired their credit, let them apply some of the rent toward the down payment, and complete the sale when they're able to get the financing.

Now, all he has to do is to keep working the other side of the deal by running ads, and by calling on ads, to find someone who fits his seller profile and has a home that meets his buyer's needs. Once he's located this seller, he goes to work to lock up the property and get his tenant buyer moved in.

How Greg Locks Up the Home for His Buyers

Either Greg is talking to a landlord who's tired of the renting life, and wants to sell the home, or he finds a homeowner in trouble that really needs to sell the home right away to avoid foreclosure and a bad credit hit. The loan balance and payments need to be low, and he then makes an appointment to talk to them.

By showing these owners how he can take their payments off their back, and get their home sold without any more damage to their lives, financial future and credit history, he usually gets them to let him do a lease purchase for the amount of their loan and a monthly lease payment for their current payment amount.

The Tenant Buyer Side of the Deal

Greg knows his costs, and he knows the market rent he can charge his tenant buyer is higher. Before he ever locked up the other side of the deal, he had his tenant buyer on board and wanting the home. So, now he just needs to get their lease purchase signed and get them moved in.

This tenant buyer wants to buy a home, not be a renter. They are doing this as a "lease purchase," and are more than willing to make the down payment to lock in a deal on a home they want. Now Greg moves them into the home with a lease purchase and helps them to reach their goal of buying it in a few months or a year or two if necessary.

Alternative Ingredients or Preparation Tips

- It's hard to suggest different ways to go about such a successful deal recipe. Greg is doing it over and over again with great success in his town. Rather than suggesting any "better" approach, what might your town or your situation require that you do differently to get similar results?
- If you live in a larger city, you may have advertising advantages not available to Greg.
- Maybe your desired tenant buyers would not have the $3,000 that was required for a down payment in the deal Greg shared with us. Far from a deal-killer, you'll just need to look at the many short-term funding options I give you in the "Funding Your Real Estate Deals" chapter in

the Resources section. One that jumps to mind is using a loan from a relative and offering them a nice short-term interest rate. Let's say that your tenant buyer could have come up with $1,000, but not the $3,000 that you need to do this deal with no cash out of pocket. You allow the tenant buyer to pay an extra $200/month the first year, and your friend or relative gets this money, which amounts to a 20% return on their investment. Or, it could be $300/month for 8 months, or $400/month for six months. It's a win for everyone!

Your Town Action Items:
- Go to Craigslist or your local classifieds and see how many for rent ads you could call to see if the landlord is tired and may want to sell.
- Start drafting your classified ads directed to both tenant buyers and investors.
- Run some of them if you're ready, and practice your responses to the different callers you'll get.
- Start your buyer list and your file of potential properties for purchase.
- Put your team together, and consult an attorney about how to do what Greg does in Your Town.
- Read the chapter in Resources "Lease-Purchase & Lease-Sale Strategy."

Putting It All Together

> **"I have something for every buyer and
> every situation in my program."**
> — Greg Murphy

Some investors may not want to learn a new concept because it may seem a little difficult. However, if you learn this lease option concept, it is so powerful because you can make money with no money and no credit.

Greg believes a key is to succeeding with lease options is to not over think the process, but take action and just do it because it works. The best advice is to figure out what you can do in real estate and take action. For Greg, his options were limited because he had no credit and no money so lease options were his choice because he viewed it as something he could do that would be risk free. When you start out, you may not truly understand how real estate transactions work, but doing a few lease options will really teach you about how the process works. Greg said he never wants to use his own money and still looks for no money down lease options deals.

The biggest thing that people do not understand is how you can buy and sell a home if you do not own it! Greg stated it is only paperwork. He takes a simple lease option contract and makes it work for him when he buys and when he sells a property. He added some bells and whistles at times for some of his tenant buyers that may need the assistance of a credit person or a good mortgage broker. The key is you own the contract and control the property. Greg credits his success to the power of a good system. Once you get your system in place, everything else will come together. Greg said the system is so easy that anyone can do it with virtually no risk. If you do not have any money or do not have any credit then this is the perfect system for you! You do not have to deal with any bank loans and the only thing that might hold you back is how hard you want to work on this method.

I am proud of Greg for taking action and making a difference in his life. Greg looks great, has lost weight and he is really enjoying himself. Greg feels so much better about the future and is not worried about living paycheck to paycheck anymore! He now has even more time for his family and is able to do things with his family that he previously could not. It is an inspiration to so many others that may be starting with no money and bad credit. Greg decided to find his niche with the tools and ingredients he could use. He improved not only in his physical health, but also his financial health. You, too, can make a difference and start cooking up some no-money-down deals! Greg has changed his future in his own town and you can do the same! It does not matter where you live, whether it is a small town like Booneville, Mississippi or a metropolis like Chicago, Illinois. The mechanics are the same for any deal whether the homes cost $40,000 or $1,000,000. Greg uses lease options on the way in and on the way out. The key is to have a pool of qualified potential buyers and become a matchmaker for deals.

I know that was a lot to digest. You can always go back and read it many times over. There also are lots of people at the DG Web site using similar techniques and you can ask questions. The whole point is that action and mistakes always outweigh analysis and paralysis.

CHAPTER 5

STACEY & JOE JUREK
"The Amazing Adventure!"

Dean's Success Students:
Stacey & Joe Jurek

State: **Indiana**

Occupation: **Entrepreneur and CPA**

Stacey's deangraziosi.com User ID:
Chasing the Dream
Joe's deangraziosi.com User ID:
Indiana-Joe

Couple Experiences Growth at a Break-neck Pace!

Everyone loves the thrill and excitement of a new adventure! You may not know what to expect or what may be around the next turn, but you are excited to discover and learn. Whenever you begin an adventure, it helps to be prepared and have someone to support you along the way. It is always more fun to share the journey with someone you love. Joe and Stacey have formed an ideal team as they pursue adventure and profit in the world of real estate investing.

Now before I go any further, I want to say that Joe has been amazing in sharing everything he and Stacey have discovered. I ethically stole (because he wanted me to) everything that he is doing to be successful. I appreciate his passion to help others so that now you, too, can use Joe and Stacey's techniques and get the results they are getting.

Joe and Stacey Jurek are like many of the hard-working families in America. Joe is a Certified Public Accountant (CPA), working for a not-for-profit social service organization. Stacey left corporate America to become an entrepreneur, owning and operating an Italian restaurant.

In their words, "We are the typical middle class average family from the Midwest, trying our best each day to enjoy life." Indeed, with very little free cash and lots of debt, many of you will readily identify with their situation. Joe writes: "Each day we were working harder, making less, and not getting ahead. We wanted to secure our future and get out of debt. We did not want to rely on Social Security or a 401k for our retirement. Thus, we saw real estate as a way to secure our future."

Right now, many of you see yourself in the Jurek's situation. It's a tunnel with only a tiny light at the end, you both work at jobs, yet all your effort just seems to maintain the status quo. It's more of the same next week, next month, and next year, with a comfortable retirement just not in the picture. Take heart though, because their success could also be yours, and a lot sooner than you might think.

Your success isn't related to the real estate market conditions!

Please remember that Joe and Stacey experienced their success during what is being called the worst real estate market in history. Is it really the worst? Are you ready to be open-minded, think outside the box and become an investor?

Joe says: "*We saw Dean's program on television. It caught our interest because everything he was talking about we could relate to. Dean appeared to be very honest. We had faith that this was the best route for us to pursue. We had a few other investment properties, but stopped after Stacey opened the restaurant. We did not know how to acquire additional properties with limited resources.*"

First, they read all my books and attended my "Gain the EDGE 2009" event in Phoenix, Arizona. Joe stated *"the "Gain the EDGE 2009" event changed our lives. It reignited that burning desire to succeed at something again. The event provided so much information, tips, techniques and strategies that it felt like we were getting a treasure map with our own personal tour guide as we set out on this new adventure!"*

 Want to see Joe and Stacey in a video and learn more about the "Gain the EDGE 2009" event go to www.deangraziosi.com/yourtown/theedge

Another factor in their success that they didn't hesitate putting my strategies into practice while still studying the materials. Before we go into details of their highly successful transactions, what did Joe and Stacey do to lay the foundation for success besides putting my techniques into play immediately?

Research. They made it a top priority. Research is how you get a handle on your local market and choose the right strategies for your area for current conditions. They made it a daily ritual to learn at least one new fact about their local real estate market. Their research paid off in their first deals.

Their goal was to buy and hold properties for long-term rental income and speculation. So their strategies and property decisions were always pointed in that direction. As I mentioned, they did a huge amount of research, and keeping up with your local market is critical. Things can change quickly, and your strategies for profit in a deal may need to change with them.

Joe and Stacey went through MLS property searches online, searching hundreds of properties in their neighborhoods of interest. They tracked recent sales, days on market, foreclosures, price reductions, and trends for all of these factors. Once they focused in on a property, they examined its value and characteristics, the surrounding area, and market trends they found in their research.

Though long-term rental income was a primary consideration, future appreciation would be a welcome additional benefit. Their secondary plan was to wait for a better real estate climate and leverage their returns by selling some appreciated properties to pay off others and free up capital for more purchases. They believe it is always good to have a "Plan B" or multiple exit strategies.

We're building a picture here of two investors who immediately understood the value of real estate investing, studied my materials, and put them into practice as quickly as possible. They did their homework, researching in depth, and relating each considered property to the market as a whole and local market trends. And, when they found a property they liked, Joe said: *"We would look at properties and if the property 'screamed deal to us,' we were making offers. We would try to make creative counter offers and use additional "gut feelings" when presenting low or creative offers."*

You may identify with Joe and Stacey, their backgrounds, financial situation, and desire to do more to secure their future. If one of the ingredients isn't something you have available, or one of the processes isn't something you can do or want to do, refer to the alternative ingredients and preparation tips at the end of the chapter, and the Resources section at the end of the book. Every deal could have had one or more changes to the ingredients or methods, so don't dismiss any of them until you've checked out other ways to get it done. Let's take a look at these successful real estate deal recipes from Joe and Stacey.

Deal Recipe # 1 - Aggressive Deal-Making - Staying True to the Ingredients

The Ingredients
• Highly motivated seller, probably a foreclosure, pre-foreclosure or short sale
• Major discount (50% or better) to asking price and value
• Location near employment, education centers and recreation
• Features in demand for the area
• Reasonable costs to rehab for a long term rental property
• Cash out of pocket without financing to purchase & rehab
• Positive rental cash flow for the long haul

Desired Result
When Julia Child decided to study cooking at Le Cordon Bleu in France, she entered a world of male chefs-to-be. She didn't let that deter her from her dream to learn French cooking and bring it to the typical American kitchen. When you read how Joe and Stacey set their offer price for this deal and stuck to it, you'll see how being aggressive and sticking to their plan made this a very successful deal recipe.

That's why you want to have multiple projects and potential deals on your radar. You need to be able to walk away in order to make the very best deal. Joe and Stacey took this attitude to the bank with their first deal.

*"When I first learned Dean's concept to not be afraid to make offers for up to 50% or more of the asking price it was a bit unsettling. But the more I read, the more students at **www.deangraziosi.com** that were doing successfully, the more confidence I got to go for it. I was motivated and now agreed with the theory of offering 50% or less for a property because there were so many new properties coming and staying on the market."*

This is the aggressive approach, and you'll see that it worked wonders for Joe and Stacey in this deal.

More from Joe: "*I found the REO that changed our lives thanks to Dean's strategies and techniques. We looked at a rough 3-bedroom property that had great potential. Along with 3 bedrooms, it had an eat-in kitchen and laundry room. It also featured a very large 2 1/2-car garage. I know that people in the Midwest love garages because of the snow in the winter.*" Here's some of that research paying off. Joe knows the buyer's hot buttons. "*The property is on a double lot in a mixed residential and commercial area. Thus, there could be potential for future commercial zoning, which may increase the value of the property.*"

Preparation

- Drove neighborhoods to locate and compare properties
- Targeted bank owned REO properties for the greatest bargains
- Looked first at properties on the market for more than 90 days
- Targeted multiple properties, making offers 50% or less of asking price
- Located homes in good rental communities close to local business, employment, colleges and recreation
- In an area of commercial and residential mix, possibly leading to zoning changes and appreciation
- On a four lane state road with high visibility and traffic count, again possibly indicating future value increase from commercial development

"*The property was listed at $69,900, and we decided to offer low at $20,000. The offer was turned down and not countered by the REO bank asset manager. A few weeks passed, and the property went under contract, so we decide to chalk this one up and started to look for another deal.*" Notice that Joe stuck to his goals and plans, not trying to chase the deal with a higher offer. We'll see that this was a great strategy.

"*Then, I couldn't believe it. The property reappeared on the market online, listed for sale at $49,900. I contacted the listing broker to ask about the current situation. The broker stated that the bank wasn't happy with the deal falling through when the buyer backed out. After much discussion between Stacey and I, we decided to make an offer, this time for $10,000! Thanks to Dean, I had the courage to ask for the low offer and then wait for the broker's response. The listing broker asked 'Did you say $10,000?' I stated that's exactly what I said. The response was a stuttering agreement to present the offer.*"

"*A little later, the listing broker called to let me know that the bank was rejecting the offer. I didn't make another offer, just kept the property on my radar. In a few weeks, I saw that the listing price had dropped*" *below $40,000. I again approached the listing broker with my previous offer of $10,000, but this time it was my best and final offer. He agreed to present it that way, and I waited a tense two days before a response. The listing broker called to say that the unbelievable had happened: they had accepted my offer! It was a voice mail message, so I saved it as proof, and called my wife with the awesome news."*

PURCHASE AGREEMENT
(IMPROVED PROPERTY)

1 Date: February 27, 2009
2
3 **1. BUYER:** _____ Joe Jurek _____ ("Buyer")
4 agrees to buy the following property from the owner ("Seller") for the consideration and subject to the following
5 terms, provisions, and conditions:
6
7 **2. PROPERTY:** The property ("Property") is known as _____ 2323 ▓▓▓▓▓▓▓▓▓
8 in North _____ Township, _____ Lake _____ County, ▓▓▓▓▓▓▓▓▓
9 Indiana, ▓▓▓ (zip code) legally described as: ▓▓▓▓▓▓▓▓▓ Add _____
10 All L 17 & 18
11 together with any existing permanent improvements and fixtures attached (unless leased or excluded), including,
12 but not limited to, electrical and/or gas fixtures, home heating fuel, heating and central air-conditioning equipment
13 and all attachments thereto, built-in kitchen equipment, sump pumps, water softener water purifier, gas grills,
14 fireplace inserts, gas logs and grates, central vacuum equipment, window shades/blinds, curtain rods, drapery poles
15 and fixtures, ceiling fans and light fixtures, towel racks and bars, storm doors, windows, awnings. TV antennas,
16 satellite dishes and controls, storage barns, all landscaping, mailbox, garage door opener with controls AND THE
17 FOLLOWING: _____
18
19 _____
20 _____
21
22 EXCLUDES THE FOLLOWING: _____
23
24 The terms of this Agreement will determine what items are included/excluded. All items sold shall be fully
25 paid for by Seller at time of closing the transaction. Buyer should verify total square footage, land, room
26 dimensions or community amenities if material.
27
28 **3. PRICE:** Buyer will pay the total purchase price of $ 10,000.00 _____ for the Property. If Buyer obtains an
29 appraisal of the Property, this Agreement is contingent upon the Property appraising at no less than the agreed
30 upon purchase price.
31
32 **4. EARNEST MONEY:** Buyer submits $ 1,000.00 _____ as earnest money which shall be applied to the
33 purchase price. The listing broker shall deposit earnest money received into its escrow account within two (2)
34 banking days of acceptance of this Agreement and hold it until time of closing the transaction or termination of this
35 Agreement. If Buyer fails for any reason to submit earnest money, Seller may terminate this Agreement.
36 Earnest money shall be returned promptly in the event this offer is not accepted. If this offer is accepted and Buyer

Being aggressive and sticking to their offer paid off for the Jureks in this deal. By being patient, not chasing the deal, and sticking to their plan, a $70,000 initial price turned into a $10,000 purchase. This sounds like a best case scenario, but Joe has more for us.

"Well, it got better. At closing we received credit for unpaid property taxes that were due toward the end of the year. I had provided an earnest money check of $1,000 with the executed contract, and then based on the credit we received for taxes, we only had to come to closing with less than $7,000. I was in a state of disbelief! It was the answer we were looking for to help us to get out of debt. That answer was real estate investment. We realized that properties such as this could help us to get out of debt and on a path to financial freedom!"

Think about this tax thing for a minute. Notice on the contract, that this deal took place early in the year. The tax credit was like receiving a tax-free loan for nine months. This helped the Jureks get the property with less cash at closing, get it ready and rented, and pay taxes at the end of the year with help from proceeds from rentals.

111.		
112.		
120. GROSS AMOUNT DUE FROM BORROWER		10,249.07
200. AMOUNTS PAID BY OR IN BEHALF OF BORROWER:		
201. Deposit or earnest money		1,000.00
202. Principal Amount of New Loan(s)		
203. Existing loan(s) taken subject to		
204.		
205.		
206.		
207.		
208.		
209.		
Adjustments For Items Unpaid By Seller		
210. City/Town Taxes	to	
211. County Taxes	01/01/08 to 04/02/09	2,531.91
212. Assessments	to	
213.		
214.		
215.		
216.		
217.		
218.		
219.		
220. TOTAL PAID BY/FOR BORROWER		3,531.91
300. CASH AT SETTLEMENT FROM/TO BORROWER:		
301. Gross Amount Due From Borrower (Line 120)		10,249.07
302. Less Amount Paid By/For Borrower (Line 220)		(3,531.91)
303. CASH (X FROM) (TO) BORROWER		6,717.16

The deal closed in April 2009, and Joe had this to say: "*I would never have attempted this if not for Dean and his program. This was my Deal #1, and it was truly a start to an entire new life for me and my family*"

Garnish and Presentation

After the closing, Joe and Stacey followed my suggestion to invite friends over to help with some cosmetic work on the property. They cut back trees, fertilized the lawn, re-coated the driveway, did a little painting, put in new carpet and cabinet handles. When Stacey contacted their insurance agent, the amount of coverage suggested for value of the property was $100,000. That's ten times what they paid for it! It was after this deal that the Jureks attended my "Gain the EDGE 2009" event. Joe says "*this event exceeded all of our expectations and changed our lives forever!*"

But, there's more to this story. The Jureks put about $5,000 into property improvements, making their total investment around $15,000. They currently estimate the value at $120,000. It is rented out at $1,000 per month, for a projected positive cash flow of $8,700 annually. The numbers are impressive: $8700 / $15,000 yields a pre-tax return of 58% on cash invested the first year!

Could this deal be a one-time success story? Not a chance! I'll give you the details on more of the deals Joe and Stacey successfully closed.

Deal Recipe # 2 - Straight to the Source Buy

The Ingredients
- Duplex in a good rental area
- Close to local business, employment, colleges & recreation
- Features in demand
- All brick construction
- 2 car garage
- Offering price below market with positive rental cash flow goal
- Purchase price within cash available for no mortgage
- Bank REO at auction

Desired Result
Joe and Stacey's favorite business strategy is to do a lot of market research. They watch their local market closely, and do a huge amount of online and drive-by searching to locate deal opportunities. They also

target bank-owned properties that have been on the market for a while and have decreased in price.

On this particular deal, the bank put the property up for auction, which is where the Jureks found it. But they didn't want to compete for it at the auction, as this almost always drives up the purchase price. After all, that's what the auctioneer gets paid to do.

Preparation
• Contact the bank directly to short circuit the process before auction
• Make an offer well below its true value
• Do a cash deal for a purchase with no mortgage
• Keep the property for rental with good positive cash flow
• Joe negotiated the deal with the bank in March of 2009, with the ultimate purchase price $22,500 cash. The earnest money deposit was $1,000, and the closing date to be in May 2009.

PURCHASE AGREEMENT
(IMPROVED PROPERTY)

Garnish and Presentation:

What's going to make this a very successful recipe is the true value of the property after rehab work is done, and the rental income it will produce. The Jureks put $17,500 into improvements, making their total investment

$40,000. The estimated value of the property after the improvements is $135,000, increasing their net worth by $95,000.

		41
120. Gross Amount Due From Borrower		
200. Amounts Paid By Or in Behalf Of Borrower	$22,853.00	42
201. Deposit or earnest money		50
202. Principal amount of new loan(s)	$1,000.00	50
203. Existing loan(s) taken subject to		50
204. Commitment fee		50.
205.		50<
206.		50!
207.		506
208.		507
209.		508
Adjustments for items unpaid by seller		509
210. City property taxes		Adj
211. County property taxes 01/01/08 thru 03/31/09		510.
212. Annual assessments	$7,099.03	511.
213. School property taxes		512.
214. Association Dues		513.
215. Maintenance Fees		514.
216.		515.
217.		516.
218.		517.
219.		518.
220. Total Paid By/For Borrower		519.
300. Cash At Settlement From/To Borrower	$8,099.03	520. T
301. Gross Amount due from borrower (line 120)		600. C
302. Less amounts paid by/for borrower (line 220)	$22,853.00	601. G
303. Cash From Borrower	$8,099.03	602. L<
	$14,753.97	603. C:

The HUD-1 image and the check show the cash they brought to closing was reduced by the tax credit, and they closed with a check for $14,753.97. As an investment, their rental positive cash flow of $14,000 for the year is a whopping 35% cash-on-cash invested return.

With an excellent rental market for the area, which is a major reason they were attracted to this property, they were able to rent it out for $1,750 per month. The Jureks project their annual positive cash flow will be about $14,000. They are considering taking a mortgage on this property to provide funding for more projects.

When the Jureks were able to get an accepted contract on this property, they decided to sell one of their vehicles and also liquidate an IRA. Joe stated that he knew they would have to pay a penalty and taxes for an early withdrawal, but decided to do it because of the recent stock market avalanche and his confidence in real estate. He told me in person it was the best move he ever made. This may not be not for everyone, but it worked for the Jureks.

Deal Recipe # 3 – Brick Single Family Home

The Ingredients
• All brick 2 bedroom ranch style home
• Fenced yard, three car garage and central air conditioning
• Community close to shopping, employment, colleges and the Interstate

Desired Result
Joe and Stacey's desired result is to locate a home in an area that can command a substantial rental income, make offers at 50% or below asking price, and go with the deals that accept their deeply discounted offer. It's a plan they execute over and over with great results, so why change it?

Of course, this plan requires that, besides their deep discount purchase, the rental income should produce a nice positive cash flow while they wait for opportunities to refinance or sell at a profit to free up cash for other deals.

Preparation
- Do daily searches of the MLS listings online to locate homes that may fit their plan requirements.
- Found this home and used a real estate agent.
- They negotiated with resolve and got the home under contract at $17,500.
- They received tax credits at closing to offset some of the initial cash investment.

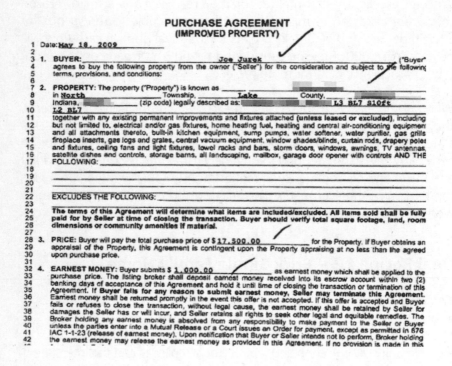

Garnish and Presentation

With only $2,500 needed for repairs on a home in great condition, they have a total of $20,000 invested as a cash deal. The estimated value of the home is $75,000, resulting in immediate equity and an increase in net worth of $55,000.

Here's the breakdown from the HUD statement:

Hammond, IN 46327 Lake County, Indiana	Statewide Title Company, I	
	PLACE OF SETTLEMENT	
	617 ▮▮▮	
	Crown Point, IN 46307	

J. SUMMARY OF BUYER'S TRANSACTION		
100. GROSS AMOUNT DUE FROM BUYER:		
101. Contract Sales Price	17,500.00	
102. Personal Property		
103. Settlement Charges to Buyer (Line 1400)	248.45	
104.		
105.		
Adjustments For Items Paid By Seller in advance		
106. City/Town Taxes	to	
107. County Taxes	to	
108. Assessments	to	
109.		
110.		
111.		
112.		
120. GROSS AMOUNT DUE FROM BUYER	17,748.45	
200. AMOUNTS PAID BY OR IN BEHALF OF BUYER:		
201. Deposit or earnest money	1,000.00	
202. Principal Amount of New Loan(s)		
203. Existing loan(s) taken subject to		
204.		
205.		
206.		
207.		
208.		
209.		
Adjustments For Items Unpaid By Seller		
210. City/Town Taxes	to	
211. County Taxes 01/01/08 to 06/23/09	4,945.35	
212. Assessments	to	
213.–219.		
220. TOTAL PAID BY/FOR BUYER	5,945.35	
300. CASH AT SETTLEMENT FROM/TO BUYER:		
301. Gross Amount Due From Buyer (Line 120)	17,748.45	
302. Less Amount Paid By/For Buyer (Line 220)	(5,945.35)	
303. CASH (X FROM)(TO) BUYER	11,803.10	

The home is owned free and clear and has a tenant in place at $850 per month in rent. This will produce an annual positive cash flow of $5,700 and is expected to appreciate more in the future. Their current goal is to investigate if a mortgage can create funds for other deals. If they can take cash out while maintaining a positive cash flow, they will have intelligently leveraged their ability to increase their investments.

Deal Recipe # 4 - Creating a New Deal Recipe from Scratch

The Ingredients
- Four BR, 2 BA home with attic, basement, garage & fenced yard
- 100% financing from the bank with the REO
- Cash from the seller bank for rehab and repairs
- Financing that would allow for positive cash flow
- Financing with below-market interest rate for at least five years

Preparation
Joe and Stacey are action people, and on their flight home from my Live "Gain the EDGE 2009" event, they began to put together their action list for getting more deals cooking. Joe says, "On our list it included contacting at least 3 local banks to inquire about REOs." That's exactly what he did when he got home.

Joe started calling local community banks in the area to inquire if they had any REOs. He had the goal of contacting 3 banks about REOs and was able to accomplish this feat in less than 2 hours. He was so amazed at how easy it was that he decided to contact more banks just to inquire about their REOs and build a file of future contacts. Joe went on to say, *"I would always get the REO Asset Manager's direct phone number and email address. I wanted to email the contact at least once every few months to stay in contact with them. I was always very surprised that none of the banks were rude when I called and almost all were very friendly in providing the information. I was extremely surprised that if you were friendly, they were eager to provide the information. Another tip was to be polite but confident. These calls went so well, I started to call a few banks in Illinois and Michigan just to see if they had anything that would work for us. I always tried to find out the decision maker for the bank REOs and make sure I had all their contact information."*

We can't list all of Joe and Stacey's deals here, just like we couldn't for any the students I am profiling. But so you know, Joe and Stacey closed two deals between their first deal and this one. Through a tax sale, they were able to purchase a small commercial building in a desirable part of the town's business district and three commercial lots for pennies on the dollar. These commercial parcels were located on a four-lane state route road that is popping with various commercial developments. These four properties purchased at a tax sale have raised their net worth nearly $200,000. Yes, real money and real deals.

Now back to this deal, it's my favorite Joe and Stacey deal. After Joe's calls to the banks, they were ready to tackle REO's, or real estate owned properties that banks had taken back. (You will learn all about REO's in a later chapter) They knew that banks are flooded with them and, for the first time in many years, eager to get those properties off of their books and sold. Which means lots of opportunity. Besides all the other factors in finding the right home at the right price in the right area, Joe wanted to cook up something a little different to make the deal not just good but spectacular. And what do you know, it worked. Now, Joe didn't find this deal recipe anywhere. He dreamed it up, and decided that a really great deal would result if he could put these ingredients together in the right way. So, after contacting several banks and talking to several REO asset managers, he located the house that fit. They also realized that flexibility in negotiations and the right proportions of ingredients would be required. With banks being desperate, the complete opposite of just a few years ago, there were lots of variables, including price, financing with great interest rates, special terms, money back, and more.

1. The bank was asking $120,000 for the home. Joe didn't make a price offer, but a terms offer first. His initial offer didn't mention price, but required 100% financing from the bank, and $10,000 in cash to complete cosmetic repairs.
2. With his offer, he told the bank that he wanted to create a win-win for both parties, and that he could offer a higher purchase price with "great terms," or a lower purchase price with "good terms." He would leave the choice up to the bank. (He did this via email; you'll see the emails below.)
3. It took a few weeks to hear from the bank, but the call came from the bank president. He apologized for the delay in calling. The counter offer he presented was for a purchase price of $115,000. No cash for repairs would be included, and the interest rate on the 100% loan would be 7.25%.
4. Joe says he "*almost fell out of my chair when I realized they would do 100% financing.*" But the other terms weren't to his liking, especially the interest rate, which would put the payments at an amount that would be tough to cash flow. Joe presented a recap of the expenses the bank had in keeping the home on its books, a breakdown of the

sluggish area economy, and that he would be unable to pay their asking price with the high interest rate and no cash for repairs. Joe's emails and counter offer correspondence with the bank are below:

Email # 1 – From Joe to Bank Vice President

Good Afternoon Mr. Banker,

It was a pleasure speaking to you regarding the home located at 789 Washington Street (please note: this home is 1,057 sq ft). As we discussed, the home is in a nice location and does have potential. However, I believe this REO has become a greater liability for your bank over the years considering, utilities, general security and upkeep, insurance and property taxes ($4,134.68 annually). Thus, I would estimate the annual expenses for property taxes, insurance, utilities, exterior maintenance, caretaker and security are probably closer to $7,000 per year.

Similar homes on the market and homes that have recently sold include:

- *1627 Alice Court (1,044 sq ft home) listed at $42,000*
- *3655 Ewing Ave. (1,264 sq ft home) listed at $54,900 (new listing)*
- *180 Wabash (2,064 sq ft home) listed at $58,900 (can't sell; lowers price monthly)*
- *1664 - 175th Street (1,368 sq ft home) listed at $63,000 sold for $54,900*
- *319 Avenue G (1,748 sq ft home) listed at $64,900 sold for $59,000*
- *1060 Addison (1,344 sq ft home) listed at $72,000 sold for $59,250*

The real estate market has become very slow and potential buyers have become limited. I heard several people are now scared to purchase a home because of the current state of the economy and the lack of financing options.

There are several issues that would need to be addressed with the 789 Washington property, that would include, but not be limited to, the carpeting, interior doors on closets, new hot water heater, general finish work, etc. The exterior would require painting, siding, and eventually a new roof. Thus, the home at 789 Washington would probably be listed in today's market at $79,900 or less.

I would be open to negotiate a deal that would work for both of us. I could offer a higher purchase price (near asking price) with great terms or a lower purchase price with workable terms. Please advise your preference as to price or terms. I want to purchase this home if I can work out a deal that makes sense and would cash flow itself.

I look forward to working with you and your bank to create more affordable housing to make a difference in our community. Thank you for your time and consideration. Have a nice day.

– Joe

Banker's phone call voice message to Joe in response to Joe's Email #1

Hello Joe,

Mr. Banker. The bank would like to offer you the home at 789 Washington Street for $115,000 and we could offer 100% financing amortized over 30 years with an adjustable rate of 7.25% for the first 5 years. So, let me know if you have a deal. Thanks.

– Mr. Banker

Email # 2 – From Joe to Bank Vice President after his phone call

Re: follow-up to the Banker's phone call and voicemail message.....

Good Evening Mr. Banker,

Thank you for the call on Friday afternoon regarding the 789 Washington Property. You indicated the bank was looking at selling the property at $115,000 and offering a 30-year mortgage with an adjustable rate of 7.25% for the first 5 years.

I apologize if I was not as clear in my previous email in which I discussed I could offer a higher price with a good interest rate or a high interest rate with a good price. However, I would not be in a position to offer a high asking price with a high interest rate.

The home does require approximately $10,000 in additional finish work. Thus the $115,000 offer price and interest rate would not allow this property to run a break-even cash flow. I am sure you can understand my position. The 7.25% adjustable rate (non-owner occupied interest rate) is also high based on other local banks' current interest rates and www.bankrate.com.

Also, the real estate market is still on the decline. Currently, in the market there are much larger homes on more desirable blocks in the $75k to $99k range. If the home on 789 Washington was listed by a real estate agent, it would be priced at $79,900 or less.

Thus, I would like to propose an offer of $64,900 with the 30-year mortgage with an adjustable rate. The first 5 years would be at the rate of 6.25%.

Or

I could go as high as $89,900 with an interest rate tied to the current prime rate (3.25%) amortized over 30 years with an adjustable interest rate that would be tied to the prime rate for the first 5 years.

Other terms and conditions:
- *No penalty for early mortgage pay-off.*
- *All unpaid property taxes to be pro-rated and credited to me (the buyer) through day of closing*
- *Seller to satisfy all other liens and bills accrued to date against property prior to closing, including but not limited to, the water and other gas and electric utility bills*
- *Buyer to receive title insurance reflecting clear and equitable title for the property.*
- *First mortgage payment to be made 60 days after closing*
- *Property to have interior painting completed*
- *Entire property including, basement, and garage to be left in a clean condition and free of debris.*
- *Plant sod in the front of the property where the grass area is now dirt.*

Please advise if either of these options is acceptable to the bank.

I want to create a win-win transaction for both parties. In the event we do not reach an agreement on this transaction, I would appreciate it if you could contact me in the future if you acquire any other REOs. Thank you for your time and consideration. - Joe

As you can see, Joe's confidence in doing deals has grown. He is asking for it all and then some. I love it. And it gets even better!

Email # 3 Banker's response to Joe after Joe's # 2 Email

Joe,

We would agree to a fixed rate for the 1st five years at 4.50% then adjusted to prime plus 1.25%. The loan would be amortized over thirty years and we will accept an offer of $94,000.00 with all your other terms as satisfactory.

– Mr. Banker

Email # 4 Joe's to Banker after Joe received Email #3

Good Morning Mr. Banker,

Thank you for the email and the follow-up information. If I understand your current offer correctly, it would be summarized as follows:

Purchase Price: *$94,000*
Interest Rate: *first five years at 4.5% and then adjusted each 5 years to 1.25% over the Prime Rate; Amortization of mortgage for 30 years*
Mortgage Amount: *Would consist of the net of the Purchase Price less '"other terms" being paid and satisfied or credited to buyer as discussed in other terms. All other terms note in prior email are to be accepted by the bank.*

I desire to move forward in closing the deal. Please indicate when it may be convenient to complete the written purchase agreement, title work and close on the property. I appreciate your efforts with constructing a deal that can be a win-win for both of us.

Thank you for your time and assistance. Have a nice day.

– Joe

Email # 5 - Banker to Joe with acceptance

Joe,

We accept.

Our attorney can prepare an offer to purchase with all the terms and conditions that we discussed and he will need to know how you want your name on the deed, etc.

You will be sent monthly statements for the payments, therefore, we need a mailing address.

I will be out of the office this afternoon. Thanks

– Mr. Banker

Is that awesome to see that communication in real life, with a real student, with a real bank, making a real deal that is making them money, right now? Let's recap this incredible deal that could only happen because of today's market. It's a great time to be a real estate investor!

- Paid $94,000 purchase price (Current value =$110,000)
- Secured a low interest rate of 4.5% and fixed for the first 5 years.
- Future five-year interest rate adjustments would be tied to an amount equal to the prime rate plus 1.25%
- The first payment would not be due for 60 days after closing to allow time for repairs and location of a renter

At the time of this counter offer, the prime rate was at 3.25%. This meant that Joe was asking for a significant drop in price coupled with a much lower interest rate than the bank put forth in their offer. I'll let Joe tell you the outcome:

"To my disbelief, that is exactly what we received! We got a purchase price of $94,000 (probably more like $88,000 after a property tax credit), and a fixed interest rate of 4.5% for the first five years. The mortgage would be amortized over 30 years, with the first payment due 60 days after closing. I still can't believe it! We are ordinary people achieving extraordinary things thanks to Dean Graziosi. His books, programs and Web site are what provided the knowledge, direction and inspiration we needed to succeed."

Deal Garnish & Presentation

The total investment in this home was $99,000, which included about $5,000 in improvements. However, the Jureks didn't bring a check to closing, they got one! With the tax credits, they ended up walking away from the closing table with a check for $5,765.05

With the current value estimated at $115,000, the Jureks increased their net worth by $16,000 with this deal. And the projected positive annual cash flow from rental is estimated to be $4,200. To learn more about REO's look at Chapter 15 in this book to see extensive information. More from the Jureks:

**"I want everyone to know that they can do this too!
That is why I'm providing this amount of detail to help you
in your local area to do the same type of deal. Dean, thank you
for all your inspirational guidance, and we really appreciate
all the inspiring members on the DG Web site too. Good luck
on all your deals, believe and achieve!"**

Deal # 4 – Lots, Waterfront and Park Frontage!

The Ingredients
• One lot with 7.4 acres, park and Lake Michigan frontage
• Developed area with city utilities
• Good rental community with business, colleges and recreation

Desired Result
Another simple plan, this one is to locate and purchase property that's ripe for development, but going to tax sale. Buying at these extremely low prices creates instant equity and increased net worth. The lots are held for speculation.

FREE BONUS
Since I don't go in to tax sales in this book and if you want to learn more you can go to www.deangraziosi.com/yourtown/taxsaleinfo to get a better understanding of what they are all about. Also we have complete classes in my Success Academy on Tax sales.

Preparation

- Buy these lots at tax sale, and the cost for all of them totals $5,000.
- Located in developed cities, there are utilities and a potential for development at any time.
- The Jureks will hold these lots, waiting for area growth and development.

Garnish and Presentation

It's hard to argue with success, and these investors are growing their net worth by leaps and bounds. And they're doing it with a great amount of low-risk leverage. With an estimated value of $175,000, this deal results in instant equity of $170,000. The Jureks can sit back and wait for the economy to improve, or for a developer to come in and offer them a nice buyout. Who knows? They may become developers themselves!

STATE OF INDIANA
LAKE COUNTY
FILED FOR RECORD

2009 045784

2009 JUL -7 AM 11: 15

MICHAEL A. BROWN
RECORDER

Prescribed by the State Board of Accounts

TAX DEED

Whereas Joe Jurek did the 2 of April , 2009 produce to the undersigned, Peggy Katona, Auditor of the County of Lake in the State of Indiana, a certificate of sale dated the 11 day of August , 2008 signed by Peggy Katona who, at the date of sale, was Auditor of the County, from which it appears that Joe Jurek in on the 11 day of August , 2008 purchased at public auction, held purchased at public auction, held pursuant to law, the real property described in this indenture for the sum of $101.00 (One Hundred One Dollars 00/100) being the amount due on the following tracts of land returned delinquent in ▓▓▓▓ ▓▓▓▓▓▓▓▓ of 2007 and prior years, namely:

Key# ▓▓▓▓▓▓▓▓▓▓▓▓▓▓▓▓
COMMON ADDRESS: ▓▓▓▓▓▓▓▓▓▓▓▓▓▓▓
The Part of the ▓▓▓▓▓▓▓▓▓▓▓▓▓▓▓
▓▓▓▓▓▓▓▓▓▓▓   in the Office of the Recorder of Lake County, ▓▓▓▓▓

Such real property has been recorded in the Office of the Lake County Auditor as delinquent for the nonpayment of taxes and proper notice of the sale has been given. It appearing that Joe Jurek the owner of the certificate of sale, that the time for redeeming such real property has expired, that the has not been redeemed, that Joe Jurek demanded a deed for real property described in the certificate of sale, that the records of the Lake County Auditor's Office state that the real property was legally liable for taxation, and the real property has been duly assessed and property charged on the duplicate with the taxes and special assessments for 2007 and prior years.

Utensils and Preparation Tips

Joe has contributed a great deal of material for this book in the areas of market research and finding deals. Since all of the students in this book are using one or more of his techniques, I wanted you to be exposed to them early, and keep them in mind as you move through other stories and deal recipes.

I wish I could put more deals from the Jureks in the book, heck I wish I could put in more deals from all of my students. But I want to create a balance of deals, wisdom, inspiration and techniques. Hopefully, by the end of the book, you will agree that we found the perfect balance.

The Jureks Property Location Techniques

By now, you might have some questions: Where can I find properties? What is the best approach? What do I look for to find a good deal? What do I ask when inquiring about a property?

There are various ways to locate properties, more of which you will learn about in later chapters. Once you begin your real estate investing, I'm sure you will add to this short list. Here are a few suggestions to get you started:

- MLS multiple listing service – list web addresses for realtor.com and local links
- FSBOs
- Probate
- Talk to attorneys –divorce / probate
- Word of mouth – tell people you're looking
- Put up Bandit signs, flyers
- Pass out flyers or business cards
- Run ads that you buy homes
- Check Craigslist, Thrifty Nickel or other classified ads
- Unlisted distressed properties
- Investors that will be retiring; may list one property but inquire about others
- Network with real estate agents

Internet Searches

In the Resources section, I'll give you specifics about which real estate search Web sites give the best results for different types of properties. From www. realtor.com to sites like www.trulia.com and www.zillow.com, there are a multitude of Web sites to yield properties for your deals.

I'll also explain in Resources how you can get more information in searches on a local real estate agent's site than you can at www.realtor.com, due to the way in which individual Realtor associations decide on information fields they want to have displayed according to the national IDX (Internet Data Exchange) agreements among brokers.

There's usually something for everyone at each of the largest sites, but there's no site on the Web with everything you need. It's a matter of knowing where to go for the types of information you need. The good news is that almost all of the real estate "portal" search sites allow you to search by all types of criteria:
• Price range
• House or property type
• Number of bedrooms or baths
• Acreage or lot size
• Construction type
• Zip code, subdivision or other area divisions

FSBOs
Some of the best deals you'll make will involve buying homes offered For Sale By Owner, FSBO. Some of the sites we've discussed also display FSBO homes in their searches. There are a lot of these homes out there, as the lower prices in today's markets make it appealing to many homeowners to sell FSBO and avoid paying a commission.

In the Resources section, you'll find an entire chapter on FSBO properties, strategies to locate them, and how to negotiate with an owner selling their own property. There's even a tutorial covering questions you should ask. With FSBOs, you'll want to be organized and have your plan and your list of questions ready. You'll find this plan and specific questions in Resources.

Real Estate Agents
FSBO homeowners have their reasons for not wanting to list with a real estate brokerage. But, as a real estate investor, you don't want to rule out building relationships with real estate professionals.

Think about what they do all day, every day: speak to buyers and sellers. Sometimes there are reasons that a conversation doesn't yield a client, but there's still a buyer or a seller. If you build relationships with agents, at some point, they'll contact you about an opportunity outside of their expertise. Or they may just want to see if you have a someone on your buyer list that would be interested in a new listing they have at a bargain price. Either way, you'll never know about these opportunities if you aren't talking to real estate agents.

In Resources, I'll give you specifics on building these relationships, and how to use real estate professionals on your team. In Lubertha and Bernadette's story, you will see how they were handed an opportunity for a flip deal from a local real estate agent who couldn't locate a property for a buyer.

Signs and Ads for Business

When you get to Greg Murphy's story and deal recipes, you'll be treated to his methods of running ads and following signs to opportunities for lease purchase deals. He uses little or none of his own money, yet builds positive cash flow and profitable resales. It's all about following the ads and signs to the deals, and running your own ads to bring them to you.

Word of Mouth

When Chip and Andrea Weule tell you how they were handed some of their first deals from friends who knew about their investing, you'll be hooked. They make it clear in their story that letting everyone know about what you're doing is like seeding clouds...it rains business.

REOs, Foreclosures and Distressed Properties

This is such an important niche in real estate investing that I've created an entire chapter on it in Resources. Banks make money by loaning money, not by owning houses. Foreclosures are a very negative event for the owners, but create amazing opportunities for the smart investor. You'll read about Joe's foreclosure deals in this chapter, and saw how he stuck to his plan and worked with banks to buy homes at deep discounts.

In Resources, I'll give you detailed instructions, right down to making the phone call to check with a small local bank about REO properties they may have available. The smaller local banks, though they have fewer foreclosures, can sometimes provide better opportunities. Learn in the REO chapter how to approach them, negotiate the best deal, and make them allies who'll call you again and again with new opportunities.

Craigslist

Craigslist is a Web site, but it's not like the real estate search sites. It's a virtual classified ads page for the world. In Jan and Jeremy's chapter, you'll read about Jeremy's use of Craigslist to locate their very first deal as a team. It's an excellent resource, and you'll want to learn how to use it in their section and Resources at the end of the book.

Good Deals Can Fall In Your Lap – But Don't Count on It

You now have a solid introduction to some of the ways in which deals are located. Some will appeal more to you; others will be more effective in your area or for your chosen strategies. The key is to know them all, and select and implement the ones that work for you. You'll get them explained in more detail, right along with the deals they apply to in the student story and deal recipe chapters. Then I'll give you more detail and resource links in the Resources section. Keep reading, as you'll be very glad you did!

Alternative Ingredients and Preparation Tips

Alternatives for the Bank

In several of Joe's offers, you'll see that he offered more than one price and set of terms. You'll not know what the bank will view as the best deal for them, so offering alternatives is one way that Joe made it easier for the bank to accept an offer acceptable to Joe. Each alternative had terms differences and a different price. Joe shares his offer price spreadsheet with us at ***www.deangraziosi.com/yourtown/forms***. Below is a screen shot showing how he enters the basic numbers and the sheet gives him his options:

Calculating Offers

Property Address:

Date:

Asking Price = $ -

My Offers to consider:

	Asking Price		Percent		Offer Price
Offer at 70% of asking price	$ -	x	0.70	=	$ -
Offer at 60% of asking price	$ -	x	0.60	=	$ -
Offer at 50% of asking price	$ -	x	0.50	=	$ -
Offer at 40% of asking price	$ -	x	0.40	=	$ -
Offer at 30% of asking price	$ -	x	0.30	=	$ -
Offer at 25% of asking price	$ -	x	0.25	=	$ -

Price Offered =

+ Carrying costs =

Alternatives for the Deals

With so many different deals and strategies, Joe has probably hit on one or more you'd like to try in your town. In several of Joe's deals, it's clear that he had the funds on hand to carry the deal through to closing, or for acquiring properties at tax sales. If you are wondering how you can use some of his successful deal techniques but you don't have that cash available, stop worrying! In the Resources section titled "Funding Your Real Estate Deals," I'll give you a chapter full of resources for finding money. From helping eager friends and relatives to get far better returns than they're now getting in their savings accounts, to short-term or "flash funding" lenders, there are a great many ways for you to fund deals just like the successful deals Joe has shared with you here.

Tax sales may be handled differently in your county or state, but it's just a trip to the tax assessor's Web site or office to ask questions and pick up instructions. State governments have differing laws on whether or not and how a former tax debtor can redeem their property, so you'll want to get accurate information to use in designing your successful property tax sale buying strategy.

You may find opportunities in your area to do the same. For funding, I'll refer you again to the "Funding Your Real Estate Deals" chapter later in the book. There are lenders and funding methods there specifically structured for commercial properties. There are even government loan guarantee programs for rental properties and office buildings. The FHA and even the USDA are funding deals for multi-family and office properties right now.

In buying this book, you've opened up a treasure trove of information, tools and people resources to realize financial success in real estate investing. Use them and then share your success stories.

Joe and Stacey are so passionate about my books, programs and the **www.deangraziosi.com** *Web site, that they believe anyone can do this if they want to make a difference in their lives and are committed to learning and taking action. Stacey said, "Never let anyone ever steal your dreams, because you can do this. So make sure you take action and Carpe' Diem! (Seize the day)!" Joe said, "This can be the answer to changing your life; Dean provides all the information, tips, techniques and strategies to provide you with a guide map to success. I hope to meet many more new members on* **www.deangraziosi.com**. *You can do it! Believe and Achieve!"*

Your Town Action Items:

- Go to the county courthouse or their Web site and see what's involved in tax sales, how to bid, what rights of redemption are involved.
- Use Joe's tips here and in the Resources section to locate local banks and begin to develop relationships with REO managers.
- Put together your version in your town of Joe's detailed research techniques and tools. Get your maps together, plan your drives, start your filing system.
- Start to research, using the "Funding Your Real Estate Deals" chapter, how you can do deals like those in this chapter with funding resources at your disposal.

CHAPTER 6

LUBERTHA & BERNADETTE
"Persistence pays off!"

Partners begin with hope
and end up with real results!

Dean's Success Students: **Lubertha Cox** and **Bernadette (Sandra) Bruno**

State: **New Jersey, New York**

Occupation: **Home Improvement Specialist** and **Administrative Assistant**

Lubertha's deangraziosi.com User ID:
MyDestiny
Bernadette's deangraziosi.com User ID:
SanBern

This is a story that begins with hopelessness and ends not only with hope, but also with real results. Lubertha Cox felt like she was in a lifeboat on the ocean, stranded without a compass or paddles, lost and searching for an answer. She just didn't know where to turn next; life was about survival, not about enjoyment or fulfillment. If it weren't for one sleepless night in front of the TV, Lubertha might still be stranded in that lifeboat.

Bernadette Bruno knew that she needed change in her life, and that change would require commitment to learn something new. Without change, there was nothing positive in her financial future. Bernadette was sure there was a better life out there for her, and I'm very happy that she was awake that one late night to give me a chance to show her a new path.

This is a story with a bit of everything: two people in different cities, different states, both single parents, both searching for better lives and financial futures. And both, during sleepless nights, stumbled upon one of my infomercials.

Bernadette Bruno in New York

Bernadette couldn't sleep one night, and there I was on her TV screen, talking about life-changing strategies in real estate investment. I'll let her tell you about it.

"I immediately noticed sincerity in Dean's words, not a promise of riches without work, but a promise of knowledge and tools that would get me there if I was determined and made the effort. I had seen other "real estate guru" infomercials and dismissed them as too complicated or promising much more than they could deliver. Dean didn't promise that I'd learn everything in his book, but that I would get knowledge and resources to get started in changing my life with real estate investing."

Bernadette ordered my book "Be A Real Estate Millionaire." It was a small investment for Bernadette to buy my book, and then she bought another one. She spent about the same amount as she would on a decent dinner out. The difference is that the dinner would be over when she left the restaurant, while the purchase of my books was a commitment to changing her life. She took action, and this one small decision was a turning point in her life.

Finding Others to Help When You Need It Most

Reading my books created excitement, but like many of us, Bernadette needed something else to help her get started. She became a registered user on my free Web site ***www.deangraziosi.com***. What she found was more than just information; she discovered people with similar problems, the same dreams, who were generous in sharing exactly how they succeeded. Most new members can't believe the immense amount of information and resources that are provided on my Web site for free. Like Bernadette, they're amazed by how other members share their time to help and inspire and answer their questions.

So many people never realize their potential because they are surrounded by family, friends and co-workers who don't have the same desires or dreams. These people can become naysayers, or as I like to call them, "dream-stealers." They may not want you to fail and be hurt, so they can only see risk and potential failure if your efforts.

This is where my Web site becomes much more than a tool for learning about real estate investing. It's a place where you meet people like you, people share your dream the belief that real estate can be the vehicle that takes you to your destination. Students tell me how thrilling it is to log in and meet this amazing group of people. It is such a caring and giving community, every member understands each other's goals. As previously mentioned, my students call my Web site the "DG Family." The DG family has grown over time and become a community of giving individuals who offer insight, information and advice. I think of it as neighbors helping neighbors. Instead of borrowing a cup of flour or a carton of milk, they are sharing knowledge, insight and information that can change their lives and the community as a whole! So here comes Bernadette, in August of 2008, a new member eager to learn.

Bernadette already knew that the DG family was a tremendous resource because it contained so much information and inspiration. What was hard for her to believe was that it was all free! She continued learning and participating in discussions with others on the Web site. She would often be on the site in the morning or late in the evening, discussing issues with other members, reading their deal experiences, and asking questions.

But still, by July of 2009, Bernadette still hadn't jumped into a deal. Even with all of the support from the Web site, she was reluctant to risk failure. Like others, she felt that financially she couldn't move forward. Saddled with debt and no cash, she was at a standstill. But, she didn't quit, and she did learn something on the site that would make all the difference. She learned that you don't have to do it alone. Other members of the DG family had formed teams or partnerships to achieve success. That's when she met Lubertha Cox on the Web site.

Lubertha Cox in New Jersey

Lubertha's story is one of hardship, financial disaster, and depression. Though she had been in sales most of her adult life, with corporate motivational and sales training experience, financial success just seemed to elude her. Lubertha's life had become an endless daily routine. She believed that there had to be something better out there for her, but hopelessness had taken over.

As a real estate agent from 1994 through 2003, she had some measure of success, with commissions in the pipeline, until September 11, 2001. When the World Trade Center towers collapsed, so did her pending deals.

It's as if the world stopped doing business that day. Her income reduced to zero, she entered a long period of distress and depression. Antidepressants, doctors and sleepless nights became the norm.

At one point, she worked remodeling bathrooms and renovating homes. But the work was physically demanding. So she learned about natural foods, healthy living, and embarked on improving her life. But jobs just weren't coming in fast enough to cover the bills and she had to cut back on expenses, especially the organic and specialty diet products that had been helping her feel better. She couldn't afford medication, so the depression returned. I'll let Lubertha tell you how she turned her life around:

"I had come to the point that I would be on the couch watching TV all night, slipping in and out of sleep. I was very depressed, had no hope for improving my life, and these nights on the couch and lack of sleep were the common. One morning, I woke up on the couch, TV on, and heard Dean's voice. He was talking about changing your life with real estate, and it was different than things I'd heard in the past. The sincerity of his voice, as well as the lack of blown-up promises, made me listen more."

"As I'd been a real estate agent in the past, I knew that many fortunes had been made, but rarely by the agent. I had also purchased books and materials from others promising real estate riches. I didn't finish their books, listen to all the tapes, or watch all their videos, as they turned me off from the beginning. I couldn't visualize being in a position to change my life with real estate investing as, at that moment, I only had $2 in the bank. With only that $2, it was a stretch for me to figure out how to order Dean's book, as I had no credit cards due to a previous bankruptcy. But I called, and they let me do an electronic check. This meant that I had to hurry out the next day to somehow get my account balance up to the $29.95 I needed for that book, 'Be A Real Estate Millionaire'. I returned a designer candle I had purchased a few days before, thinking I just had to have Dean's book. The candle was one of my prettiest, and it meant a lot to me, but I realized by returning that candle and buying Dean's book, there might actually be a real chance to change my life. In May 2009, buying that book did just that."

Lubertha got the book, started reading, and truly believed that there were tools, tips, techniques, strategies and information there that could make her successful in real estate investing. But, as a cautious person, Lubertha believed that she wouldn't be ready to stick a toe in the water until she had learned it all. Still broke, she found the ***www.deangraziosi.com*** Web site and became a daily visitor, sometimes for four or more hours. The site and the people there showed her that she wasn't alone, and that others like her had done it, and were willing to freely share their stories with her.

Lubertha says "*I lived on the DG Web site. With other people like me there 24/7, I found support, discussion and help to build my confidence. I really enjoyed the site, and there I found Indiana-Joe, who was one of my biggest inspirations.* (FYI, Indiana Joe happens to be none other than Joe Jurek). *I wanted to know everything he did and everything he said. Indiana-Joe seemed to be on the site every time I logged in. I swear he probably thought I was stalking him, as I'd be asking him questions almost daily. The problem was that I still didn't have the confidence that I knew enough to go out and do a deal. I kept learning, but not reaching that magic point where I could take the leap.*"

What comes as a surprise to many is that I'm on my Web site daily as well. I love watching students relate to each other, no matter where they live. They are constantly providing details on their latest deal, freely sharing the techniques that made it work. And the other students are excited right along with them. One person's success inspires the others. The DG family is a group of cheerleaders, psychiatrists, and financial advisers. Each one is doing deals in their town, but the information they share works for others in towns thousands of miles away.

Plus, I film a weekly video blog and monthly conference call to keep you on track for reaching the results you deserve. I want to continually provide my students with the latest information, techniques and tools. As I read the many posts on the site, I may find that my students need something new. Then I'll gather as much information on the subject as I can in order to meet the ongoing needs of my students. This way, students have the most current and relevant information available to make informed decisions in real estate.

I watched Lubertha and Indiana-Joe discuss deals, strategies, and problems almost daily on the site. The value of this type of communication is huge. Lubertha's confidence grew as she asked questions and followed real deals through to successful conclusions. There is no substitute for a mentor who is willing to take the time to give you step-by-step instructions and answer questions along the way. This is also why I created the Real Estate Success Academy. It has mentored and educated countless students to excel and make money. That's what my Web site is all about; people helping people to be real estate investor success stories in their town. It was during this time that Lubertha met Bernadette on the site.

Lubertha says: "*Then I met Bernadette on the site, and we began to compare our lives and experience. We had a lot in common, and I realized that what I had to do was to 'get out of my own way' and just get out there and do it. I needed to take what I knew and make it happen. Bernadette helped me to gather the confidence to take the next step, from study to doing.*"

These two people were convinced they had found the way to financial freedom, but neither had yet made the decision to actually try a deal. Bernadette had been on the site for almost a year and Lubertha for over a month when they met. Sometimes we find that the right combination of people is like the perfect combination of ingredients in a recipe, and this is one of those times. These two ladies teamed up and immediately went out and made things happen, and they did it with the very limited amount of cash they were able to scrape together. You'll read their deal recipes and wonder why you haven't already gotten out there and made it happen for you.

Lubertha wants you to know; "*Dean Graziosi has changed my life for the better forever! No more depression and I wake up from a good night's sleep with an upbeat attitude every day.*"

Bernadette says that "*Dean's techniques are simple, and he gives them to you in a step-by-step way. I found other programs and methods too complicated. With Dean and Lubertha, I'm making it happen for me.*"

Deal Recipes # 1 & 2 - $500 In Ingredients Create Amazing Results

The Ingredients
• A REALLY low-priced home
• Flip potential or long term rental positive cash flow
• Motivated sellers or foreclosure properties
• Opportunity in an area not recognized by others
• Rental prospects with government backing via Section 8
• Realtor.com to locate properties in another state

One thing we're learning about our investing team, Lubertha and Bernadette, is that they don't stop if something works once. They do it again. And these two deal recipes prove that a great chef can work in any kitchen. These deals take place in Detroit, Michigan. Considering that Lubertha lives in New Jersey and Bernadette in New York, these two prove that they have quickly developed confidence in their abilities and their teamwork.

Desired Result

They decided on Detroit simply because there were homes selling there for ridiculously low prices. They could have assumed that there wasn't any way to profit in a market that depressed, but they didn't. They didn't let naysayers discourage them either. Just because an area experiences high unemployment, doesn't mean everyone moves away. There are still people living there, and many will need to rent for years to rebuild their credit from foreclosures or bankruptcies. So these two ladies set out to locate potential in a very tough market.

Now, it isn't always just about the market. There's always your own financial situation. Lubertha and Bernadette didn't have a pot full of cash. They had to get creative and look for a market where their small amount of cash could make something happen. Others may decide that $500 might get them an option to purchase a home, or maybe lock up a home for a flip. But, this dynamic duo (as they call themselves on the Web site) decided that they wanted that $500 to buy a home! And that's what they set out to do in Detroit.

Using www.realtor.com, tax assessor's records, police departments, and other city agencies, they searched the Detroit area and located two deals. They checked out the neighborhoods online, looking at crime statistics, surrounding job opportunities and area amenities. Lubertha called a friend in Detroit to go look at the properties, and had the listing broker's photos. By researching crime statistics, as well as population numbers and rental markets, they found these two homes and are on their way to some amazing profits.

Preparation

Deal #1: A Home for Long Term Rental Income

They located a listing by REMAX with these features:
• 4 bedrooms
• 1 bath
• basement

- brick construction
- needing rehab work
- listing price of $900

Their offer of $500 was accepted without any negotiation! They closed on the home on August 21, 2009, and are now doing the work to get it ready for a tenant. With Lubertha's experience, and her brother's help with the electrical and plumbing, the work will cost about $3,000.

Back taxes of $3,296 will bring their entire investment in this home to $6,796. Because they're willing to work with Section 8 renters, they enjoy a list of 13 applicants for rental. They decided to interview and select their applicant closer to the estimated occupancy date of October 15th. Rent will be $800 per month. That's a 141% return on their cash invested the first year! After that, they're collecting $9,600 per year on a free and clear investment. It doesn't get much better than that!

purposes and are not included in the totals.		
D. Name of Borrower:	Lubertha Cox, 82 Steiner Avenue, Neptune City, N Bernadette Bruno, 395 Maple Street Apt. 8, Brook	
E. Name of Seller:	Deutsche Bank National Trust Company, as Truste Loan Trust 2006-1	
F. Name of Lender:		
G. Property Location:	N/A 15381 Birwood Street, Detroit, MI 48238	
H. Settlement Agent: **Place of Settlement:**	Meridian Title Corporation (800) 777-1574 107 Commercial Street, Dowagiac,MI 49047	
I. Settlement Date:	8/27/2009	

J. Summary of Borrower's Transaction			
100.	Gross amount due from borrower:		4
101.	Contract sales price	500.00	4
102.	Personal property		4
103.	Settlement charges to borrower (line 1400)	595.00	4
104.			4
105.			4
Adjustments for items paid by seller in advance:			A
106.	City/town taxes 8/27/2009 to 7/1/2010	2,602.06	4
107.	County taxes 8/27/2009 to 12/1/2009	98.92	4
108.	Assessments		4
109.			4
110.			4
111.			4
112.			4
120.	Gross amount due from borrower:	3,795.98	4

Deal #2: Flip or Fix - A Great Deal

This property in Detroit has two units, each with 2 bedrooms and 1 bath. Listed on www.realtor.com at $1200, they waited until the price dropped to $900, again offering just $500. As with the first offer, this one was accepted without a counter offer! Remember, until these two teamed up, neither had really gone out and started doing deals. Now they're wheeling and dealing with the best of them!

This property needs work, but approaching winter, they decided to immediately re-list it at $15,000 to see if they could flip it for a quick profit. If it doesn't sell over the winter, they plan to do the rehab work and keep it for a rental. After all, they only have $500 in it at this point. They believe it's really worth about $25,000, so the current list price just might bring a buyer. This is possible because they found these two deals at the very bottom of the market in Detroit. Nothing comparable is available in the MLS now.

D. Name of Borrower:	Lubertha Cox, 82 Steiner Avenue, Neptune City, N Bernadette Bruno, 395 Maple Street Apt. 8, Brookl			
E. Name of Seller:	Deutsche Bank National Trust Company, as Truste Loan Trust 2006-4			
F. Name of Lender:				
G. Property Location:	n/a 3242-4 Tyler Road, Detroit, MI 48238			
H. Settlement Agent: **Place of Settlement:**	Meridian Title Corporation (800) 777-1574 107 Commercial Street, Dowagiac, Mi 49047			
I. Settlement Date:	8/27/2009			

J. Summary of Borrower's Transaction				
100.	Gross amount due from borrower:			4
101.	Contract sales price		500.00	4
102.	Personal property			4
103.	Settlement charges to borrower (line 1400)		663.00	4
104.				4
105.				4
Adjustments for items paid by seller in advance:				A
106.	City/town taxes	8/27/2009 to 7/1/2010	1,688.11	4
107.	County taxes	8/27/2009 to 12/1/2009	55.17	4
108.	Assessments			4
109.				4
110.				4
111.				4
112.				4
120.	Gross amount due from borrower:		2,906.28	4

Garnish and Presentation

How do you dress up a dish like this? They took a truly low cost group of ingredients and prepared amazing deal results! We have a couple of cooks with very limited resources to buy ingredients, so they went outside their local town, and prepared their deals in Detroit. If your kitchen isn't suited to the task at hand, find one that is.

Deal Recipes # 3 & 4 - Fewer Ingredients More Technique

The Ingredients
• Motivated sellers
• Sellers not getting results through normal listing process
• No cash required, just a payout on completion

Desired Result
Remembering Bernadette's and Lubertha's stories and backgrounds, we know that they began their two deals with very little cash. They were looking for a way to profit without investing a lot of cash up front. They needed a simple deal recipe, with a reasonable chance of success.

I enjoy sharing "assignment" strategies with my students, as I can see the lights go on when they realize that there's plenty of opportunities to gain control of a property with no money, and even earn money on a closing. These two deals involved being out there, circulating, making calls, and working to build a "buyer list."

Preparation

Deal #3: Assignment of a Residential Rental Home
Lubertha jumped right into the deal process by grabbing the newspaper and finding homes for rent. Many rental homes are owned by investors who want to purchase other rental properties. Wanting to build her buyer list, Lubertha called a man who had a home for rent in the classifieds.

This person didn't really want to purchase other properties, as he had moved out of the state. He did, however, have another home that he would really like to sell. Listed for three years with three different real estate agents, he'd had almost no activity or showings. Based on her market analysis, Lubertha could tell him why: it was massively overpriced. Yes, it's a great property, with a positive cash flow from rental, and a tenant in place.

The seller canceled his listing. Negotiating a 45-day assignment at a selling price of $235,000 with $10,000 to go to our investor partners. Lubertha and Bernadette immediately set out to find a buyer. It's still early in this deal, but as of this writing, the dynamic duo feel extremely confident that they will be able to assign the deal within 45 days.

Deal #4: Real Estate Agent Brings a Deal

Again calling For Sale By Owners and rental ads, Lubertha added prospects to her buyer list. A Coldwell Banker real estate agent renting out her own home placed one of ads. The agent and Lubertha had a nice conversation, and Lubertha put her into her buyer list for future opportunity.

Soon, Lubertha received an email from this agent about a buyer she was working with. This buyer wanted a specific type of commercial property in the area where Lubertha lived. Unfortunately, there was nothing listed that fit the buyer's needs, and the agent wanted to alert Lubertha in case she knew of anything not in the MLS. That's one of the many advantages to getting your name out there as someone who deals in real estate investments. You become the go-to person when opportunities arise.

It happened that Lubertha knew of a rented auto repair shop near her home. The property looked like just what the buyer wanted. Jumping on her bike, (she'd lost her car in her bankruptcy) Lubertha rode over to check it out. Indeed, it looked like just the thing for this buyer. With some research at the tax assessor's office, she found the owner's address and phone number.

There's a lesson to be learned here about perseverance. The owner's wife hung up on Lubertha on her first phone call. She kept trying, finally getting the husband on the phone. As it turns out, he had purchased the property many years before for $50,000. His current tenant wasn't paying rent, so he was highly motivated to just get rid of it. Our team got an assignment at $275,000 and started looking for a buyer.

In the process, it was determined that the property had been a gas station in the past, and would require environmental corrective action to sell. Sounds a little scary. But remember, they are not buying it, they're acting as the middle man (or middle women). Once they found this out, they immediately started renegotiating the assignment and sale price. The agreement is for our investing team to get $12,000 when the property closes.

Remember, they have a buyer prospect on the hook from the real estate agent. But, if that doesn't work out, Lubertha has a second buyer waiting as a backup offer! It is always a great idea to have a Plan B. The more exit strategies that you can consider for a deal, the more options you will have available to complete it successfully. Sometimes the knowledge that you acquire from completing a real estate deal is even more valuable to you in your real estate education than the money you make. What we have here are two deal recipes that are quite simple and require only a few ingredients. But it's the skill and techniques of our investor chefs that make the difference.

Lubertha and Bernadette have become "investment buddies" to help and support each other. It is so inspiring to see my students find others to team with and motivated them. I wish Lubertha and Bernadette amazing fortune, but I don't think they'll be relying on luck to change their lives. These two have taken what they've learned and put it into practice in record time. Like all the best chefs, they show us that even the most mundane and common ingredients can bring about amazing results.

Garnish and Presentation

Again, we see two amazingly resourceful people, feeding on their combined imaginations and common goals, creating great deals out of the most modest of ingredients. When a bump developed with the commercial property, they just went back and renegotiated, changing the ingredients and preparation to suit the new situation. Congratulations Lubertha and Bernadette. Your success shows everyone reading this book that determination and desire trump fancy ingredients and cash in hand.

These two have not made a million dollars nor are they retired from real estate. Are they making cash hand over first yet? No, not really. What I loved about their story is where they came from and where they are now headed. This is inspiration at its finest. I have no doubt the level of success they will achieve. Why? Because they overcame their fears, they didn't let life's obstacles get in their way, they absorbed the knowledge I shared and most of all, took action! Do you have as many obstacles as this team? Whether you do or not, the point is YOU can do this.

When people are lost and looking for direction in life, they can go in one of two directions. They can hide among another group of lost people and they blend in. Or they can seek out those who have confidence and are looking for a better future. At first, this may feel uncomfortable because this group is more focused on the future rather than the pity party the first group is focused on. Confident people may not always know the way, but they are confident they will find the way. You need to believe in yourself, surround yourself with the right people and, sooner or later, you will rise to the life you deserve.

If you want an update from either of these courageous women you can always find them at ***www.deangraziosi.com***.

Utensils and Preparation Tips

Teaming Up – Locating Your Investing Partner

Lubertha and Bernadette have become "investment buddies" to help support each other. They teamed up and are achieving results. It is great how my students can find others to team up and get motivated. These investment buddies can hold each other accountable and both put forth the maximum effort that they can. Often you do not want to let your buddy down when it is time to get together. Thus, you can hold each other accountable and both benefit from knowledge and action.

It's obvious that these successful deal recipes resulted from the partnership of Lubertha and Bernadette. Neither one of them was out there doing deals until they collaborated. So these successful recipes are the result of their combined knowledge, desire and skills . We've seen in their story that Lubertha and Bernadette met on the Web site; you may find the perfect investment partner there as well. Go take a look, sign up, and even lurk for a while if you want. But, at some point, join the discussion, ask questions, or just share your thoughts on how you see your investment business moving forward.

Don't limit yourself to one resource though. Another excellent way to meet others with similar interests is through a real estate investment club. There are hundreds of these around the country, with one or more in your area. In our Resources section, I'll give you links to find investment clubs on the Internet. Most have Web sites where you can check out their membership numbers, meeting dates, and particularly their educational opportunities.

It's not just about finding a partner for your investing. Real estate investment clubs are networking powerhouses. Members aren't only investors. There are mortgage professionals, building and renovation contractors, title company employees, appraisers, home inspectors, and others who make their living in industries and endeavors related to real estate. This group is a vast storehouse of information that you'll use in your investing. You'll get ideas, suggestions, and even referred business from your club's members.

Many investing partnerships have been formed over coffee after an investment club meeting. The synergy of people with the same goal can do wonders. Two investors teaming up can produce results far in excess of what one could have accomplished. Check out the real estate investment clubs in your area, attend a meeting as a guest, and you'll find support and great discussions to help you to succeed.

Real Estate Agents Can Be An Asset

As you saw, Lubertha and Bernadette had one of these deals referred to them by a real estate agent they had called because her home was for rent. They didn't do any business, but Lubertha put her into her buyer list as a possible future customer. Networking with real estate brokers and agents is something that can turn into business for you. Sure, they have their commissions to make, and many times your goals don't mesh. But, agents also know of situations that can't work in a traditional agent representation situation.

Just having a "hello again" relationship with a number of active real estate professionals can mean money in your pocket. Keeping your finger on the pulse of your market, building your buyer list, and watching for opportunities can make you a valuable resource for any real estate agent.

Your Town Action Items:
- Find an investment buddy. Hold each other accountable for your real estate investing.
- Based on what you have learned from Lubertha and Bernadette, identify some key ingredients that you could apply to deals in your town.
- Lubertha and Bernadette found an area of opportunity that may have been missed by others. Identify at least one area of opportunity that may be in your town that others may not be aware of.

- The Web site members inspired Lubertha and Bernadette. If you are not already a registered user on **www.deangraziosi.com**, then register today!
- Once you register, spend an hour or so to familiarize yourself with the site. Contribute to a story by leaving a comment or offering additional insight or information to a topic.

CHAPTER 7

CHIP & ANDREA WEULE

"You don't need money to make money!"

A New Marriage and
A New Financial Future!

Dean's Success Students:
Chip and Andrea Weule

State: Colorado

Occupation: Benefit Administrator
and New Home Sales Consultant

deangraziosi.com User ID:
acinvestments

We often make decisions that impact our future and affect the rest of our lives. Some decisions carry less weight than others, but major decisions, such as finding a career or a soul mate, can bring a tremendous amount of joy. Even before marriage, Chip and Andrea Weule were studying ways to improve their financial future as a couple. Chip, with degrees in mathematics and statistics, and Andrea in business management and marketing, both understood that the best time to begin securing their financial futures was right away, while still in their 20's. Chip had worked in real estate in the past, so he had a decent understanding of how the real estate sales process worked. Andrea was working for a home builder, learning about construction and the characteristics of a well-built home.

Because they had some background knowledge of real estate, the couple tried a few real estate investments prior to getting my book. Unfortunately, they had poor results. This experience made them extremely cautious about real estate as the way to their secure future, but they were still open to it. In spite of their poor results, Chip and Andrea didn't let their first-time negative experience paralyze them to being open to new ideas or taking action. Oftentimes, what we learn from a past mistake benefits us for the rest of our life. If you have made mistakes and learned from them, you should be commended. The only way we can learn in life or change our circumstance is by trying something new. Sometimes we succeed and sometimes we fail, but the experience we gain is priceless. I have failed more times than I have succeeded in life, but that has not stopped me from taking action and it should not stop you either!

As you will see, Chip and Andrea didn't give up. They used their bad experience as an education; they went out and applied that education to their future real estate deals. Though a failure can be painful, it is often one of our most valuable learning experiences.

They attended seminars, read books and studied everything they could find to see how a young couple could work together to invest wisely. But there was still hesitation to actually take the plunge and actively pursue a real estate deal. They still felt they were missing the "how" to do it without losing again.

After getting married, Chip and Andrea went to Las Vegas for their honeymoon. While Andrea was getting ready for their dinner one night, Chip was flipping through the channels on the hotel room TV. There were already pretty sure real estate was the investment course they wanted to follow, so Chip listened for a while when he stumbled across one of my infomercials. He called Andrea into the room and they both sat on the bed and listened. As Andrea put it: *"The longer we watched, the more genuine Dean seemed to be. So, we got on the phone right then and ordered his book 'Be A Real Estate Millionaire'."*

There is more than one major life partnership decision being formed. Not only are Chip and Andrea newly married, they're making another partnership into real estate investing. I like to call these "ah-ha" moments, and it's amazing when two people experience one at the same time. They both saw something in my infomercial that brought about this joint decision, and I applaud them for it. You will too when you see how, together, they create real estate investment success as a newly married team.

The Proverb *"when the student is ready, the teacher will appear"* is fitting here. I am glad that I was there for Chip and Andrea to provide the information they needed and wanted. I am also honored that I can be here for you, too! So let's keep moving with the story.

When they returned from their honeymoon, my book was there on the porch just waiting for them. They read it, and were encouraged by my step-by-step approach to real deals, not hype. *"Dean provided ideas not only to get your mind spinning, but also exactly how to put those ideas into play. Here's how Dean did it, and it made sense. Plus, for added security and knowledge, we joined Dean's Real Estate Success Academy and to us it was priceless. One of the best decisions we ever made,"* said Chip. I'm glad I was allowed to be on the approved guest list on Chip and Andrea's honeymoon. They didn't waste any time, jumping right into their first real estate deal and a wholesale flip to another investor. Plus, here is something that will shock you. As soon as Chip and Andrea joined our Success Academy, they closed on five deals, which gave them all their tuition money back. That's right, every cent!

If, at anytime you would like to talk with one of my trained professionals about our Success Academy training, simply call **877-219-1473**. I believe in you and I want to do everything I can to help you succeed. To prove it, I have a built-in incentive for you to succeed. Once you close your fifth deal, I give you back your tuition money. Yep, give it back to you. I challenge any college to do the same; to give you your money back once you secure a good job based on what you learned in their school!

Recipe #1 – Ingredients in Your Own Backyard

The Ingredients
• Enthusiasm - they were still reading my book
• Action – they didn't hesitate, getting right into a deal
• Announcement of plans to friends and relatives
• Friends who were losing their home to foreclosure
• 2,000+ square foot home, 3 Bedroom, 3 Bath, going into foreclosure
• Bird Dog referral commission payable at sale
• Desired Result

This recipe ties together the enthusiasm of this newly-married couple, who jumped in before they'd even finished my book, and an ingredient that made this deal happen; getting the word out. *"I can't stress how huge it is to let others know what you're planning on doing,"* said Chip.

There is a saying that *"marketing is everything and everything is marketing."* You want to do everything you can to market yourself, from handing out business cards, to posting flyers, to even getting decals on your car. Why not turn your car into a billboard in motion? Can you imagine the amount of people that see your car parked at Walmart? Be bold, be loud and be proud of your real estate investing and one day you might even be financially FREE!

Chip and Andrea immediately started telling everyone they knew that they were in the real estate investment business, and that any help or notice of opportunities would be appreciated. They handed out cards, gave people their email address and talked about their business ventures. It paid off, as they had friends, a couple who were far behind on their mortgage payments and going into foreclosure soon, call them asking for help.

A recent appraisal on their friends' home was $212,000, though they had purchased it for $225,000. The value was clearly declining, and they could no longer afford to make the payments. Though they had attempted to sell through a real estate agent, they couldn't at the lesser value and still pay commissions. A price that would allow paying real estate commissions was too high, so it just sat on the market. Chip and Andrea were new to this game, but they were anxious to jump in and give it a try.

So, the couple set out to help their friends sell their home by locating a buyer or investor willing to pay them a referral fee for bringing the deal. This is about more than helping friends. Of course, it's nice to help friends stop a foreclosure and save their credit. But also, Chip and Andrea can earn money for making the deal happen, the investor gets a good deal and the bank and the local community escapes another foreclosure. Real estate investing gives us the opportunity to create these win-win situations by helping others and ourselves at the same time.
Let's go through the steps of putting together this recipe for a profitable deal with no money invested by our cooks.

Preparation
- All of the best ingredients won't guarantee a great dish unless the technique is right. The difficulty in this deal was the fact that these were friends, they were soured on the system, in trouble financially, and embarrassed to talk to Chip and Andrea. But, they had given up and were moving out, so the Weules made them as comfortable as they could with the fact that they were going to try to help them by locating a buyer. This was a big task, as the foreclosure was looming in the near future.
- They explained the short sale to their friends, and how they were going to try to find an investor who could negotiate a deal with the bank for less than what they owed on the home. A short sale is nothing more

than this: the bank that holds the mortgage realizes that the house is worth less than what is owed on the house. Realizing that getting all their money back is impossible, they agree to short the sale, meaning they agree to take less then the loan amount. What the sale amount goes to is based on comps of similar homes and good negotiating by the prospective buyer. In today's turbulent real estate market, banks are eager to do a fair short sale rather than a foreclosure, since they come out better not having all the fees, additional carrying costs and time lost that a foreclosure takes.

Chip and Andrea started combing the classifieds and looking online for ads placed by investors wanting to buy homes. They found an investor's online ad stating that he specialized in short sales and flipping properties, and that he pays up to a $10,000 bird dog fee to anyone who brought him a deal. They were a little bit nervous about making the call, but they went for it by focusing on what they could achieve. In talking with this investor, they realized he knew a lot more about short sales than they did, so they asked if he was interested in being their mentor throughout the deal. He agreed.

Chip and Andrea arranged a three-way call with the new investor and the homeowners so he could answer any questions they had. The call went well, and they set up a face-to-face meeting with everyone present. Throughout the process, Chip and Andrea learned even more about the contracts and procedures involved in a short sale.

After the owners agreed to the short sale, they signed a form giving Chip, Andrea and the investor the ability to speak to the bank on their behalf. They would contact the bank to negotiate terms for a short sale. The investor contacted the bank, postponing the sale, and negotiating a purchase price just over $185,000. As soon as the price was set, he began to market the property for resale. Because the home was already in great condition, it would show well among the competing properties.

Within two months, a buyer was located for a purchase price of $210,000. After costs of sale, the investor netted about $22,000, and Chip and Andrea received their 20% commission of $4,400.

The end result: all parties made out great. No foreclosure for owners and profits made by the investors.

Garnish and Presentation

This first effort at cooking up a real estate deal made terrific use of the ingredients, and brought them all together for Chip and Andrea to realize a nice profit. Their very first deal they used none of their own money, yet took home a check for $4,400.

Below are actual copies of documents used in this deal. You can find this contract and many others at *www.deangraziosi.com/yourtown*

BIRD DOG Agreement with DTC Home Solutions

This agreement is between ___*Ac Investment Group, INC*___ (hereafter referred to as Bird Dog), and Grundstuck, Inc., alias DTC Home Solutions.

This agreement is pertaining to the purchase and resale of **2997 ▓▓ ▓ ▓ Northglenn, CO 80233 currently owned by** ▓▓▓▓▓ **as of the date of this agreement.** DTC Home Solutions will pay 20% of the proceeds up to $10,000.00 only when and if a successful negotiation and resale of said property is completed. Said Bird Dog shall hold harmless DTC Home Solutions and shall receive no compensation for lost expenses during the whole purchase and resale procedure. Only upon the successful resale of the above mentioned property will DTC Home Solutions pay for the Bird Dog's referral. Should either the sellers: ▓▓▓▓▓ ▓▓ ▓▓ cancel their agreement for sale of said property, or the bank default on their acceptance, or the new buyer not complete the purchase, or for any other reason that the purchase and resale of **2997** ▓▓ ▓▓, **Northglenn, CO 80233** not be completed, this agreement will be null and void and the Bird Dog will receive Zero compensation for referral, nor will DTC Home Solutions receive any compensation from Bird Dog for any lost revenue.

Their comment? *"Getting this check was not only great, but it also gave us the confidence that this stuff really worked! Our minds started racing with all of the possibilities available to us. If we could do this with no money down, then we could only imagine what was next!"*

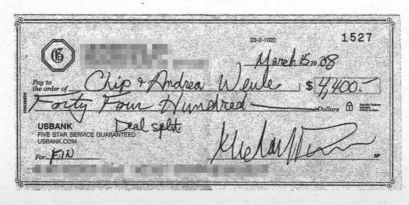

Recipe #2 – Too Many Cooks Don't Have to "Spoil the Soup"

The Ingredients
- Self-directed IRAs (Individual Retirement Accounts)
- Partners to put together the dollar investment needed
- A land development project in Tennessee

Desired Result
Still celebrating their first deal's success and bird dog fee, Chip and Andrea found a new way to free up investment money they couldn't use for anything else they found profitable. They both set up their employer IRA accounts to be self-directed. This allowed them to use the money pre-tax for real estate investing. (They discovered this strategy in their real estate investment club.)

I love it when my students take one of my tools and use it successfully. I really preach the synergy value of meeting with other real estate investors. And I recommend strongly that my students investigate real estate clubs in their area, locate one they like, and network with other real estate investors. You learn a lot, and deals are made among the club members as well. Chip and Andrea did just that, joining a local club and attending meetings regularly.

The desired result for this recipe was for club members to invest as a group in a land development project in Tennessee. The club would become a private money lender, providing funds to the developer to improve a tract of land, increasing its value 20 times.

Preparation
- Provide $5,700,000 in private money to the developer to put into the land purchase, streets, sewers and utilities.

- Take a first lien on the property, so that failure to pay would result in foreclosure and the club having a property worth more than $100,000,000.

- The loan was for a fixed period of seven months, and the interest rate was 50%. This meant that Chip and Andrea would be receiving $39,000 back for their $26,000 investment from their IRA accounts.

PROMISSORY NOTE

$8,550,000.00   Bala Cynwyd, Pennsylvania

October 30, 2007

FOR VALUE RECEIVED, the undersigned, THE MANTRIA GROUP, LLC, a Delaware limited liability company ("Maker"), having an address of 555 ███████████ Bala Cynwyd, Pennsylvania 19004, agrees to pay to TRUST DEED GROUP I, LLC, a Colorado limited liability company ("Lender"), having an address at 6855 ███████████ Centennial, CO 80112, the principal sum of Five Million Seven Hundred Thousand and no/100 Dollars ($5,700,000.00), plus interest in the amount of Two Million Eight Hundred Fifty Thousand and no/100 Dollars ($2,850,000.00) (the "Interest Amount"), unless sooner paid, the outstanding and unpaid principal amount of this Note and the Interest Amount shall be due and payable on the date which is 240 days from the date of this Note.

This Note is prepayable, from time to time, in whole or part, without penalty, premium or fee; provided, however, that prepayments in part may only be made in amounts equal to a Lot Release Partial Prepayment as set forth below, each of which shall include an allocated portion of the Interest Amount.

Garnish and Presentation

This recipe came out of the oven right on time, and was a triumph for planning, cooperation and technique. Their seven month investment yielded 50%, or $13,000. And it went right back into the IRA accounts, so no taxes until later. This proves that having other cooks involved can be a recipe for success. In fact, Chip and Andrea are doing more deals with club members, and loving every one of them. Here are the directions in the IRA for the transactions.

■ Buy Direction Letter (Standard)

*** If faxing, call 303-548-7930 to confirm delivery *** Please mail the original of this form to our office ***

If you will be using funds from other IRAs and/or qualified plans administered by us, please use separate Buy Direction Letters for each IRA and/or qualified plan. You may photocopy this form for this use.

1. Administrator: Entrust New Direction IRA, Inc.
The name of the company that performs record keeping and administration of your plan on behalf of custodian named in IRS form 5305.

2. Name	The best phone number to reach me is:	3. Your Account Number
ANDREA WEULE	▓▓▓▓▓	▓▓▓▓▓

I hereby authorize and direct the administrator and/or custodian, trustee or assigns, to BUY the following asset for my account:

4. Name of Asset

MANTRIA TRUST DEED, LLC

5. Description of Asset

Investment in Mantria Group trust deed

6. Quantity Number of shares, units, etc.	7. Price Price per unit	8. Total Purchase Price Quantity times Price
	$	$ 26,112.53

9. Check made payable to Payee/Seller	OR	Wire Transfer Funds ☒ Wire instructions attached	10. Investment Fax #

Sell Direction Letter

Please confirm via email that this is correct with regards to your payment with Mantria 50 or as you know the LLC to be Trust Deed Group I LLC.

1. FINAL PAYOUT NUMBERS FOR MANTRIA 50:

$39168.80.

Recipe #3 – Twice Baked, Two Homes, Two Recipes

The Ingredients
• Two brand new properties, 1800 sq ft, 2 BR, 2 BA, 2 car garages each
• Long distance research from CO buying in Elk River, MN
• Commercial growth in the area
• New light rail system for better access to the Twin Cities
• Long term rental income
• Refinance for cash out

Desired Result
Chip and Andrea were passing out business cards and informing everyone that they knew that they were investing in real estate. During this time, Chip ran into a friend from high school. They talked for a few minutes, Chip gave him a business card, and they went on their way. The friend happened to call Chip a few days later to ask if he was interested in some bank-owned homes. This was the call that started to change Chip and Andrea's life. Can you see how easy this is?

Chip said he was very interested and his high school friend put him in contact with the bank. The banker informed them of two foreclosed homes that were located in Elk River, Minnesota. The only problem was they lived 1,000 miles away in Colorado. Did they let that stop them!

Once they were made aware of the two properties, Chip and Andrea went into action, doing area research from a distance. They harnessed the power of the Internet to locate all the information they needed for their real estate team and to determine the fair market value of the properties. They did various Google searches and posted ads on Craigslist. The foreclosed homes were on combination lock boxes so they could contact contractors and allow them to enter the home to provide quotes for any work that they would need.

Chip and Andrea gathered prices on comparable homes that sold in the same area within the past 6 months. Andrea also looked at various rentals throughout the area to get a feel of the rent for this type of home. Between the comps for recent sales and the anticipated rental rates, this information provided them with a good picture of the fair market value for the homes in that area.

Their desired result was to buy at a deep discount to keep payments down on the mortgage. Next, they planned to hold these new homes and rent them out for positive cash flow. At a later date, when the market goes back up, they could cash out for a hefty profit.

A second part of desired result was to refinance if the value of the properties would allow decent cash out to pay off obligations and the costs they incurring in setting up their investment business. Knowing that they couldn't possibly manage these Minnesota properties from Colorado, they also would locate and hire a property management firm.

Preparation

First Bake

- Chip loves to keep mentioning the importance of letting friends and relatives in on what you're doing. This deal resulted from a friend's referral, and it became the deal they both say *"made the difference and helped us to turn the corner in our real estate investing business. Once we completed these two investments, we knew that we could do anything we set our minds to."*

- Two brand new, never lived in properties in Elk River, MN were available from a motivated seller. Not only did the two homes have all of the in-demand features, like garages, large rooms, and square footage, they also were in an area with new light rail access to the Twin Cities and a brand new Home Depot and a Walmart nearby.

- When they first acquired the properties, they were appraised at $148,000 each. The Weules had put in an offer for $75,000 each. Based on their research, they believed the homes were probably worth around $150,000, so they decided to offer 50% of what they believed was the fair market value. They worked out a counter offer for $80,000 and the bank agreed to include $1,600 of closing costs in the loan if they made the purchase price $81,600 for each home. By including some of their closing costs in the loan, Chip and Andrea were required to come up with fewer funds at closing time. The two HUD statements were almost exactly alike, so here's a shot from one of them:

I. SETTLEMENT DATE:	05/29/2008		
J.	**SUMMARY OF BORROWER'S TRANSACTION**		**K.**
100. GROSS AMOUNT DUE FROM BORROWER:			40
101. Contract sale price		81,600.00	40
102. Personal property			40
103. Settlement charges to borrower: (from line 1400)		3,938.83	40
104.			40
105.			40
ADJUSTMENTS FOR ITEMS PAID BY SELLER IN ADVANCE			AD
106. City\Town taxes	to		40
107. County taxes 05/29/2008 to 07/01/2008		175.70	40
108. Assessments	to		40
109. Association Dues		9.58	40
110.			41
111.			41
112.			41
120. GROSS AMOUNT DUE FROM BORROWER:		85,724.11	42
200. AMOUNTS PAID BY OR IN BEHALF OF BORROWER:			50
201. Deposit or earnest Money			50
202. Principal amount of new loan(s)		65,280.00	50
203. Existing loan(s) taken subject to			50

- Now the task was to get two loans to get the deal closed. They didn't have the cash for the down payments. Your friends and family can be a great resource for funding your deals if they have the money and if it's a great deal, as this one was. *"We didn't have the cash we needed for the down payment," said Chip. "We called Andrea's dad. He had faith in our new business, so he loaned us the balance of what we needed for the down payment. We agreed to pay Andrea's dad 20% interest but we only needed the money for a few months and ended up paying him around $500 in interest."*

- The couple then worked with Chips' friend who was a mortgage broker and able to locate a mortgage for the properties. With the down payment funds loaned from Andrea's dad, they were ready to close on these deals.

- They decided to hire a property manager, interviewing several until they found the right person. *"While working our way to closing, we started calling and interviewing property managers,"* said Andrea. They decided on Greg, who would manage the properties for 7% of rental income and appeared to be thorough with tenant screenings, and closed on the deals.

- Greg, their new property manager, would show the units, take and process applications and run background checks. They had renters moving into the homes in June.

- With the 7% management fee, $450/month mortgage payment, $125 monthly tax payment, $20 insurance monthly payment and $99/month Home Owner Association (HOA) fees which included general coverage on the townhome, they still had a positive cash flow of around $1,000/month, as they were able to rent them out quickly for $1,150/month each

MINNESOTA STANDARD RESIDENTIAL LEASE

© Copyright 1998, 1999, 2000 by Minnesota State Bar Association, Minneapolis, Minnesota. BEFORE YOU USE OR SIGN THIS LEASE, YOU SHOULD CONSULT WITH A LAWYER TO DETERMINE THAT THIS CONTRACT ADEQUATELY PROTECTS YOUR LEGAL RIGHTS. Minnesota State Bar Association disclaims any liability arising out of use of this form.

The Office of the Minnesota Attorney General certifies that this contract complies with the requirements of Minn. Stat. §325G.31 (1999). CERTIFICATION OF A CONTRACT BY THE MINNESOTA ATTORNEY GENERAL UNDER THE PLAIN LANGUAGE CONTRACT ACT IS NOT OTHERWISE AN APPROVAL OF THE CONTRACT'S LEGALITY OR LEGAL EFFECT.

Landlord and Tenant agree to the following terms.
TENANTS. (Each adult who signs this Lease is a "Tenant.") _____

OTHER OCCUPANTS. _____

LANDLORD. _____
The Premises ("Premises") includes dwelling unit number 10928
at (street address) _____ (city) Elk River MN (zip code) 55330
and garage no. _____, storage unit no. _____, parking stall no. _____.
Term of Lease. (Write number of months or "month-to-month.") 1 year lease
Starting Date of Possession 6/14/08 Ending Date of Possession (if known) _____
Monthly Rent $ 1150.00 Late Fee $ 50.00 Security Deposit $ 3,000
OTHER CHARGES (specify) _____

RECEIPT. Received from Tenant by Landlord at the signing of this Lease:	Amount
FIRST MONTH'S RENT PAID IN ADVANCE Prorated 1150 ÷ 30 × 17	651.67
FIRST MONTH'S UTILITIES PAID IN ADVANCE (See Choices 3 and 4 below.)	
LAST MONTH'S RENT PAID IN ADVANCE	1150.00
SECURITY DEPOSIT PAID IN ADVANCE	3,000.00
FIRST MONTH'S RENT FOR GARAGE PAID IN ADVANCE	
FIRST MONTH'S RENT FOR STORAGE UNIT PAID IN ADVANCE	
OTHER (Specify) Second month's rent PAID IN ADVANCE	1150.00
TOTAL RECEIVED FROM TENANT:	5951.67

Second Bake

- With values of $148,000 each, they were able to refinance with new loan balances of around $100,000 on each property. They used a bank that did not require seasoning. (Seasoning is where some banks require that you own a property for a certain amount of time before you can refinance it).

- The $60,000 cash taken out of the refinance was used to pay their finder's fees, private money loan balance to Dad, some debts they had incurred during the deal, and costs of starting up their new business. After all these costs were paid, they were still able to walk away from this refinance and put $40,000 cash in their pockets! How exciting is that?

- Even after the new loans, their positive cash flow is a total of $330 per month ($165 per each home).

Remember, these images of notes and rental agreements are doubled for

I will make all payments under this Note in the form of cash, check or money order.

I understand that the Lender may transfer this Note. The Lender or anyone who takes this Note by transfer and who is entitled to receive payments under this Note is called the "Note Holder."

2.   INTEREST

Interest will be charged on unpaid principal until the full amount of Principal has been paid. I will pay interest at a yearly rate of   7.500 %.

The interest rate required by this Section 2 is the rate I will pay both before and after any default described in Section 6(B) of this Note.

3.   PAYMENTS

(A) Time and Place of Payments

I will make a payment every month. This payment will be for interest only for the first 120   months, and then will consist of principal and interest.

I will make my monthly payment on the 1st   day of each month beginning on OCTOBER 1   , 2008   . I will make these payments every month until I have paid all of the principal and interest and any other charges described below that I may owe under this Note. Each monthly payment will be applied as of its scheduled due date, and if the payment includes both principal and interest it will be applied to interest before Principal. If, on SEPTEMBER 1, 2038   , I still owe amounts under this Note, I will pay those amounts in full on that date, which is called the "Maturity Date."

I will make my monthly payments at 5690 ████████ SUITE 400E, ENGLEWOOD, COLORADO 80111

or at a different place if required by the Note Holder.

(B) Amount of Monthly Payments

My monthly payment will be in the amount of U.S. $634.38   for the first 120 months of this Note, and thereafter will be in the amount of U.S. $817.68   . The Note Holder will notify me prior to the date of change in monthly payment.

the two properties.

Garnish and Presentation

This "twice baked" recipe is considered by Chip and Andrea to be the deal that actually put them into business. I'm proud of the confidence they showed in their abilities and their effective use of my materials in planning and executing this deal. I would bet to say their confidence and their ability to take action with proven techniques is why Andrea's Dad trusted them with a loan. You to can build that confidence .This recipe

illustrates in several ways the use of my books and training materials:
- They put out the word, and that brought them this deal
- They used family money for funding
- They had the confidence and aggressive attitude to make a low offer and get the properties at prices that made this a great deal
- They used a refinance to free up cash to secure and build on their business

Congratulations Chip and Andrea on putting several strategies into play on one deal to come out with a really fantastic result.

Now let's talk about the trust form of a no money down deal that puts insane money in their pockets and there is absolutely no reason you can't do what they did!

Recipe #4 – Birthday Cake with Ingredient Changes

The Ingredients
- Two 2,200 sq ft homes, with 3 BR, 2.5 BA and 2 car attached garages
- One completed, one just past drywall phase
- A buyer to flip them to just after they were locked up on contract

Desired Result
The good experience in the previous two MN deals came back to benefit them again. The same bank and sellers contacted Chip and Andrea to see if we wanted to buy these two brand new properties. One was finished, and the other close to complete. You gotta be in it to win it...!

Their plan was to negotiate a deal, and if successful, go to their buyer list and other resources to locate an investor buyer to take both contracts on the properties off their hands immediately, before they ever owned them. They wanted to assign these great deals they found to an investor and get paid as the middle man for find and negotiating two great deals. They had already been working on a buyer's list. They utilize several websites such as www.craigslist.com, www.angieslist.com, and Google searches. They even found potential buyer for this property; someone lived nearby and saw the sign they had placed in their front yard.

Preparation
- They had both broker price opinions (BPOs) and comparative market analysis (CMAs) complete on both respective properties. A broker price

opinion is usually performed by a local broker in the area that provides a fair market value price usually to a financial institution so they can have a better idea of the current market value for the property and what they may want to list it for. The BPOs came in at $250,000 for each property. A comparative market analysis is an evaluation of recently sold similar homes in an area. It helps the seller reach a figure for pricing the home. CMAs indicated values of $233,000 each. Both valuations were based on completion of the structures. *Our offer to the bank was for $68,000 each. Talk about a deal, the bank accepted these first offers!"*

- Right away, using an assignment strategy they started marketing them for sale at $210,000, or $105,000 each. Once they found the buyer, they decided on a double close instead of the assignment they first considered. As you can see, it is so important to have more than one exit strategy as you try to get the deal completed.

- The right title company can make all the difference in the world. Chip and Andrea found a good local company that understood what they were trying to accomplish. The title company walked them through every step along the way and they were able to set up a double close without using any of their own money.

- It took two and a half months to find an investor who made some low ball offers. They were able to find the investor by running ads on websites like Craigslist in the local area.

- Finally they settled on $72,500 each, or a total of $145,000.

- *"This didn't leave enough for us to make out on this deal, so we went back to the bank to negotiate. We told them we could get them a close within 10 days, but needed a lower price, settling finally at $50,000 each."* As you will see over and over again in this book, never be afraid to ask. You never know what you may get! The bank wanted to close this deal so they lowered the price to $50,000 each and they were able to close without requesting an extension.

- Chip and Andrea setup the double close so it was conducted the same day at the same title company. They closed on the sale to the investor first and received the funds and then they closed on the deal with the bank and paid the bank out of the funds they received from their investor buyer. A good title company is crucial in any double close such as this.

- It was a double special birthday gift for these two and what a celebration. They were able to get the properties under contract to sell on Andrea's birthday (October 2nd) and then close the deal on Chip's birthday (October 10th).

D. NAME OF BORROWER:	AC Investment Group, Inc.	
ADDRESS OF BORROWER:		
E. NAME OF SELLER:	▓▓▓▓▓▓▓▓▓▓	
ADDRESS OF SELLER:		
F. NAME OF LENDER:		
ADDRESS OF LENDER:		
G. PROPERTY LOCATION:	▓▓▓▓▓▓▓▓▓▓	
H. SETTLEMENT AGENT:	Liberty Title Inc.	
PLACE OF SETTLEMENT:	11108 86th Avenue North, Maple Grove	
I. SETTLEMENT DATE:	10/10/2008	

J. SUMMARY OF BORROWER'S TRANSACTION		K.
100. GROSS AMOUNT DUE FROM BORROWER:		400.
101. Contract sale price	50,000.00	401.
102. Personal property		402.
103. Settlement charges to borrower: (from line 1400)	536.00	403.
104.		404.
105.		405.
ADJUSTMENTS FOR ITEMS PAID BY SELLER IN ADVANCE		ADJ
106. City\Town taxes to		406.
107. County taxes 10/10/2008 to 01/01/2009	620.70	407.
108. Assessments to		408.
109.		409.
110.		410.
111.		411.
112.		412.
120. GROSS AMOUNT DUE FROM BORROWER:	51,156.70	420.
200. AMOUNTS PAID BY OR IN BEHALF OF BORROWER:		500.

Garnish and Presentation

Now, this recipe could have been a bit undercooked. They found that there wasn't a buyer at the price they needed to make this a good deal for them. But, that was just a minor bump in the road for this duo. They just changed the recipe up a bit to adjust for a shortage in one ingredient. Going back to the bank did the trick. They netted about $43,000 after closing costs. Yes, they made $43,000 with no money, no credit and many miles from their house using the exact techniques you can use. Now was it handed to them? Heck no. Did the money pop out of page 187 of my book? Nope. They applied what they learned, were persistent and made it happen.

FREE BONUS
Remember that if you want to learn more about assignment deals, study my previous book at www.deangraziosi.com/yourtown/assignments.

Leftovers

Any good cook will tell you they always prepare more than enough to ensure they are prepared and at times have leftovers. This was the case for Chip and Andrea.

One of the keys to their success was to network like crazy and make as many contacts as possible. Due to this strategy, they have deals that come into their inbox on a daily basis. Isn't it great to know that as time goes on, deals will come to you too? Chip and Andrea have established many contacts and receive lists (bank tapes) of bank-foreclosed properties that they reviewed. They discovered that several of the properties were located in Minneapolis and St. Paul, Minnesota. Previously in the year, Chip and Andrea attended my "Gain the EDGE 2009" event and made several additional contacts and friends. One of those contacts was a fellow DG student named Nathan Biggar. Chip and Andrea knew that Nathan was interested in affordable properties in the Twin Cities.

They sent Nathan the properties in his area and helped him with some of the research. Chip and Andrea assisted Nathan with researching the locations, property taxes due, introduced him to the Minnesota title company they previously used to research any other liens on the properties. Nathan liked one of the properties, so he was put in contact with the wholesaler. Nathan worked with the wholesaler and the title company and purchased the property for less than the asking price. Today, Nathan is now working on rehabbing the property to get listed and sold for a tidy profit. I just think it is tremendous that my students inspire and assist each other.

"Gain the EDGE 2009" Live Annual Event
To learn more about the next "Gain the EDGE 2009" live annual event please visit *www.deangraziosi.com/yourtown/nextedge*. The live mastermind event will inspire you to learn exactly what you need to "Gain the Edge" and make money in real estate. Think "Brainstorm"...think "Mastermind"...think "Gain an Edge"!

The Weule Cookbook

Chip and Andrea started their married life together as a team in the deal kitchen. They studied, took their lessons out into the market, and have been highly successful in cooking up these deals. Remember that four of these properties are in a different state!

It's another case of making another town "their town" for real estate profits. Even better, the last very profitable deal closed on Chip's birthday. Happy birthday!

Utensils and Preparation Tips

Synergy and Deals from a Real Estate Club

One of the Weules' profitable deals came about from their participation in a group investment with the members of their real estate club. There is no way they could ever have been involved in a land development deal of that size on their own. You can do it alone, and you may like that. But, particularly when you first start, learning about real estate investing, what you can learn from the other members of a club will be of value as long as you're in the business.

Not all real estate investment clubs actually do large deals as a group, but there are many smaller deals that result from the cooperation of members. It's networking at its best, with a group of people who all have the same goals and interests. It's a coming together of ideas and a sharing of information and resources that benefits everyone. I can't tell you how motivating it is to regularly meet with others who want what you do. Just talking about deals, successful or not, gets the juices flowing and the ideas and strategies that result are beneficial to all.

Now below I'm sharing some of the information that was shared with me by Chip and Andrea about their IRA investment. I have to say that this is something I have never done; heck I don't even have an IRA. All my investments are in real estate, I barely own a stock. But I know it is of interest on many people at my Web site. So let me share a little information I learned.

Investing With The Funds In Your IRA

A Self-Directed Individual Retirement Account is how Chip and Andrea provided funding for some of their deals. In the "Funding Your Deals" chapter in the Resources section, I'll give you more details on using your retirement account to fund deals, but because it was important in Chip and Andrea's deal here, here's a summary of how it works.

The Right Custodian

You'll need to set up your account, or transfer an existing account to a custodian that allows real estate investment. Most banks and brokerage companies limit your investment to stocks, bonds, mutual funds and annuity products that they handle. But, it's not difficult to find a custodian for your real estate investing needs with a simple Web search on key phrases like "real estate IRA custodian" or "self-directed IRA custodian." Don't shortchange this research, as the custodian holds title to the real estate during the investment. So, you want one who is knowledgeable and experienced in real estate investments.

Purchase and Sale of the Property

Generally, your custodian allows the purchase of raw land, residential properties or commercial structures. As the Weules showed us, you can also invest in larger deals than you can fund alone. They used this ability in working with the club to invest in the land development deal in Tennessee. IRS rules don't allow you to use the property as your personal residence or vacation home though. There are other restrictions I'll share with you in the "Funding Your Deals" chapter in the Resources section.

Operating an IRA-held Property

If you're operating a property for rental, with income and expenses, all of these must move through the IRA account. So, you can't use all of your funds to acquire the property. Leave enough for operating expenses until income is there to offset them. Once you sell the property, the proceeds all go into the IRA as well. Even better, if you can offer seller financing with terms in your favor, the payments all go into the IRA, with all interest income tax deferred.

Alternative Ingredients and Preparation Tips

As you'll find in many of our student story chapters, funding of deals is one of the more creative and variable of the ingredients and preparation techniques of your deal recipe. Chip and Andrea had the luxury of an IRA account that they could self-direct and use to fund their deals. Does this mean you can't do what they've done without one? No way! Separate your thinking...the funding is an ingredient, while the deal is preparation.

You can substitute ingredients in most recipes, and many times actually come up with a better dish. So, how might we have accomplished what these two did without a self-directed IRA? Well, they gave us one alternative right at the beginning. Family money was one of their resources. Throughout this book we talk about using friends and family for funding. In the "Funding Your Real Estate Deals" chapter in Resources, you'll get more detail. But, you need to remember that you're going to become a successful real estate investor, and this means that you'll be displaying to the world your abilities to turn real estate into money. Why wouldn't you want to share your expert skills with your family? They won't look on it as "asking for a loan." They'll be clamoring for an opportunity to share in your financial success by investing their money. When you read Jeremy Zelkowitz's story, you'll see how his father moved from a doubter to an investor when he saw how Jeremy was doing in his investing.

Chip and Andrea's highly successful land development investment wouldn't have happened without their membership in a real estate investment club. Could they have found another group to pull together that deal? It is obviously easier to have access to a group of club members already sharing plans, goals and strategies. But, when you read about Chad Merrihew's successful deals later in the book, you'll find that he goes out and gathers investors as partners. No clubs, just talking to people about opportunities and forming partnerships that work.

Your Town Action Items:
- If you have a retirement account with enough money to fund deals like these, check into how to convert it to a self-directed IRA
- Go out and find one or more local real estate investment clubs. I give you some Web links to find them in the Resources section.
- Tell the world that you're now a real estate investor, and be open to approaching family and friends to allow them to invest and share in your success.

Your Town Tips:

- Form relationships with title companies so that they know what you want, such as the double close.
- Build a professional team no matter where you invest. A little work on the front end will save on problems in the future.
- Network with others at local investment club meetings. Some of the best referrals are through word of mouth.
- As you learn new techniques, you will add to your overall knowledge with real estate investing. Be sure to take action!

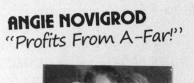

CHAPTER 8

ANGIE NOVIGROD
"Profits From A-Far!"

Florida woman takes big picture approach to markets!

Dean's Success Student: **Angie Novigrod**

State: **Florida**

Occupation: **Real Estate Investor**

deangraziosi.com User ID: **Angie**

Have you dreamed that you are running as fast as you could but, no matter how fast you ran, you weren't getting anywhere? That's how Angie Novigrod refers to her financial situation with her husband Daniel in 2007. To her, they were "hamsters on a wheel." They had more than $20,000 in credit card debt. Angie was going further into debt paying tuition to learn acupuncture, and her husband's income as an attorney was just not keeping up. They had no confidence on a future that included retirement, as they couldn't get ahead enough to put anything back.

Angie had been reading real estate investment books for a couple of years, but never really believed she had learned enough knowledge to do anything with what she had read.

"I loved reading these books, but was left pumped with no knowledge to move forward. It was frustrating."

I have to give them credit, because they kept trying. Angie and her husband attended a real estate investment seminar that came to the area with a lot of publicity. And, if their financial situation was difficult before, it quickly became a lot worse. Beginning with a $500 credit card charge to get started, they ended up getting pressured into another $34,000 in debt for this "real estate riches" program and accompanying mentoring. After the pressure and persistence of the moment and getting back home and talking it through as a couple they decided they wanted out.

In this effort to learn what they needed to improve their lives, they had more than doubled their debt! *"These SALES PEOPLE were GOOD!"* says Angie. They jumped in the car, drove five hours to the seminar provider's headquarters and demanded a refund. Talk about a learning experience!

I believe in the value of paying for solid training. It can cut years of the learning curve, allow you to avoid costly mistakes and find the right path sooner. In this case, Angie and her husband not only spent way more then they should have, but the training and information was not sincere. They got nervous and got out. It was the right thing to do.

Still pumped to do something to secure their financial future, they sat down to figure it out. Angie had been studying hard in her acupuncture classes, as much as six hours a day. Daniel told her that putting that much energy into learning real estate investment should most certainly result in greater success than acupuncture. Angie took that advice to heart. She immediately took several steps to improve their money situation:

1. She withdrew from her acupuncture classes.
2. Going through all of their financial and purchase records, she identified where they were spending money unnecessarily.
3. A budget was constructed to chip away at their $20k in credit card debt.
4. With new spending habits, their situation began to improve gradually, with a small light at the end of the tunnel.
5. They took out a HELOC (Home Equity Line of Credit) on their home, as their credit was good. Daniel's steady job kept up with their new obligations.
6. The plan was to use the HELOC money to finance real estate deals, but now Angie needed to find out how to make it happen.

Now, Angie doesn't want "get rich quick" schemes. She didn't mind some risk, but wanted to manage it and understand the level of risk in her investments. Angie began to look around for books, courses, or seminars that would bring her the knowledge to make intelligent decisions in real estate investment. She knew her complete lack of previous real estate investing experience required that she start with basic, but reliable, information.

She was watching TV one day, and there was my infomercial for my "Be A Real Estate Millionaire" book. I guess I wasn't quite convincing enough, because she did call in, but didn't buy the book on the call. She was in such a "frugal" mode at the time, that she just wouldn't risk even a book purchase without more research. Going to the nearest bookstore, she found my book on the shelf and gave it a thorough look, and in her words:

"This was FINALLY a book that did what it said. Right there in black and white, Dean was showing me a formula to analyze the real estate market! I marched straight to the register and plopped down the cash."

Now that book was a *New York Times, Wall Street Journal* and *USA Today* bestseller. You may even have it. But since then this book and my last book "Profit From Real Estate Right Now" are self-published, I can cut out the middleman and pass along the savings to you.

Back to Angie. That was in April of 2008, and Angie jumped right into reading the book. Daniel tried to do it with her, but realized it just wasn't his cup of tea. Pretty soon she couldn't even talk to him about it, as she had advanced so far in investing knowledge and strategies. Next, she went to my Web site, getting into discussions with other students and investors. Angie is a sponge when it comes to information. She asked questions and learned quickly. She also appreciated the encouragement from others on the site.

"Step by step, I felt more empowered with knowledge and felt that I was getting a firm grasp on what I needed to do and how I was going to get there."

Take a lesson from Angie's orderly approach; her next step was to put some research into play. She wasn't locked into a local mindset. Though they live in Florida, Angie realized that there may be better investment opportunities elsewhere. Taking my lead from the book, she researched areas around the country, taking the big picture approach to markets. One of the other students on my Web site gave her a tip to take a look at the Quad Cities area, which includes the following four cities:

1. Davenport, IA
2. Bettendorf, IA
3. Rock Island, IL
4. Moline, IL

When I say that she did her due diligence, I mean that she thoroughly researched every aspect of the market. She started at state level, and then drilled down to the region and area around these five cities. She looked at everything. Going back in history, Angie found that the area had been heavily reliant on agriculture, taking an economic beating in the farming crisis of the late 1970's and early 1980's. The lesson was a good one, as diversification followed, with the goal of never having one segment of the economy with that much influence on their local well being.

The Quad Cities built commercial infrastructure, encouraged industry, and brought more retail business to the area. Natural features and local sights were improved, and tourism began to grow. With large companies like Oscar Meyer and John Deere, there was a more stable market and diversified economy than ever in the past. From this big picture approach, Angie drilled down to looking at real estate listings and neighborhoods. This was an area abundant with conservative single family homes and she liked it. She quickly realized that there was great opportunity, and decided to go after her dream by putting together a team. Though she'd never set foot in the area, and still hasn't to date she knew that careful selection of a professional team to help her would make it possible to invest with limited risk. She built her team:

- Real estate agent
- Property management
- Insurance person
- Attorney
- Accountant
- Appraiser
- Contractors (roofer, foundation person, etc. Just in case, not needed often)
- Multiple mortgage brokers for residential and commercial loans
- A contact at her HELOC bank for proof of funds letters when needed

Could she have done some of this on her own? Surely. But, Angie didn't want a job. She wanted a support team so that she could leverage her knowledge across many more deals than would be possible on her own. She also wanted to build a business that she and Daniel could run from anywhere in the world, so reliable people had to be in place to make it happen. Part of her decision on team members involved her big picture investment goal. It was simple. Buy long-term rental properties that would provide positive cash flows. Build the inventory until the cash flows would support retirement for Angie and Daniel. Yes, her goals were just that simple.

With her plan in place, Angie selected her team. Her real estate agent is involved in every deal, so this was an important team member selection. She interviewed four or five before she found the right person. Doing deals far from home, she was very careful to make sure that the agent she works with is fast to respond. E-mail and phone contact daily was critical, and when she found a real estate agent who had a handle on communication skills and technology, the decision was made.

"Finding leads for good people to put on your team is easy once you have one good connection or one good team member. A few students on the DG site were investing and doing well in that area so they gave me some names that helped me start my process. Such an amazing resource! Then once I got my real estate agent and felt confident with her, I trusted the recommendations she gave. If you have no connections to the area, you can look online and start calling real estate offices and asking for anyone on staff that would meet your criteria, willing to work, willing to make low offers, able to communicate regularly since you are investing remotely and whatever else you want to accomplish. I surely didn't want some stuffy person that only sold high end homes acting like they were better then me on my team. That was not a fit for me. But with digging, I found a handful of great team members."

Because these would all be long-term rental deals, her property management team was very important as well. She found a husband and wife team that fit the bill. The wife handles most of the property management, and the husband, an experienced handyman, deals with repairs and maintenance. This is important, as we'll see how Angie structures her purchase offers around a pre-estimated amount to repair or rehab a property. This team is an integral part of that process. A great property manager means you don't get calls when the toilet plugs up. When someone wants to move out and break their lease, not your worry, they will handle it. Need to a renter after a tenant moves out? A good property manager works their tail off and gets it filled ASAP. Now you can see why this is an important team member.

Getting the rest of her team set up after having two "A" players was a lot easier. Between her real estate agent and her property manager, she got a list of the best of the best to complete her team.

Insurance person – you want this person or company to be the most competitive on pricing. But also you want someone who is low maintenance. Someone you can call or even e-mail with property information. In fact, your real estate agent or property manager can do that for you. They know they need to send proof to the title company and or bank. If they are missing some information, they are resourceful and find it themselves. Having "A" players on your team can make all the difference in the world.

Attorney – Same thing with an attorney. Once you are this deep with professionals, you will get recommendations. I say look for an attorney that makes you feel comfortable from the first phone call. Someone who has real estate experience in the area you wish to invest. Meaning you don't want a commercial real estate attorney or someone who does huge multiple dwellings when you are going to be buying $40,000 single family homes. Get their fee structure in advance. And once bills come in, see if they charge for every call or give you a fair flat rate for a closing.

Accountant – You may already have one of these in place. If not, make sure you have someone who will take the time to understand completely what your plans are. Someone who will understand the tax laws of the state you are investing in and supports your investing. I have had ultra-conservative accountants who tried to talk me out of killer deals only because they were so structured and scared. I have had deals that accountants tried to talk me out of make more money for me on that one transaction then they make in ten years. So not only get a good numbers-cruncher, but someone who helps add wind behind your sail.

Appraiser – Again with the team you are building you are going to get good advice on who to call for this. Or should I say someone on your team may call to schedule an appraisal. If you and your real estate agent work in unison, do your homework, run appropriate comps and he or she has a feel of the community then you most likely won't need an appraiser to run numbers on a home you are planning on buying. You and your real estate agent should be able to come up with the true price you want to pay, the true value of the property and the value of it after you buy, clean it up and market it. But having an appraiser on your team that you know is fair and honest is a great thing. In most cases, if you get a loan, the bank will want to use their person.

Contractors/Handyman – Let's be honest. The economy has taken a hit on all areas, especially remodeling and building. This is a great time to interview (your property manager or real estate agent can do it in person or you can on the phone). Have a contractor and/or handyman on board and ready to work for you when you get a deal that needs them. Some deals will need small repairs while other deals you may require the work of a contractor. Build your virtual relationship with a handyman so you can trust they will give you honest feedback on the home, repairs and pricing. This could be one of the people you lean on the most for understanding the homes you look at.

Multiple mortgage brokers and/or banks for residential and commercial loans – In most cases, you will just need a residential mortgage broker who has connections with banks and will work at a very fair price. But when you start getting multiple homes, you may have to convert your loans to commercial. Either way, you want mortgage brokers or banks that are excited to work with you and have programs that fit your goals. If you are planning on buying and rehabbing single family homes below FMV and wanting to refinance them in 30 days or less, you need a bank that does not care about seasoning (having to own the property for a certain period) before they will give you a loan. One thing to remember is that if one bank or one mortgage broker says no, that does not mean others will. I have had countless students say it took them 10 or even 20 banks (even Angie) to find the one that fit what they wanted to do. Persistence is everything. What's great about a good mortgage broker is that they will do most of the work; they will collaborate with your real estate agent, your insurance guy, and your attorney or escrow agency.

A contact at her HELOC bank for proof of funds letters when needed – Now you will learn more about there deals in a moment. Angie had equity in her personal home and secured a home equity line of credit (HELOC). Now instead of using that for vacations or new furniture, she used it to fund her real estate deals. What you will learn is that she used this money like cash. With this money available she could make cash offers and close very fast. It was a nice incentive for a seller to go with her lower offer, knowing the cash was there. After buying these homes, fixing them up really fast and getting a renter in there, she would refinance the deals, have positive cash flow each month, and use the banks money to pay back her line of credit. Cultivating a relationship with a representative at the bank where you have the line of credit can only make life and deals so much easier when you need letters or money transfers.

Other key relationship is an escrow or title company. These independent third party companies have expertise in assisting the buyer and seller in bringing the parties and documents together in closing the transaction. Their responsibility is outlined within the purchase contract and they are worth looking into to see what services you may utilize in the future.

"What was nice about the team I built is that they really only make money when I do. So they all had a vested interest to see me succeed. How amazing is that. What other business in life can you get in to, surround yourself with top processionals and none of them are getting paid until they help you get a deal and make money for you. I love this!"

If you haven't figured it out yet, Angie isn't a person who makes snap decisions, or jumps into deals without a ton of research. She took on a bit extra work and built a team. But once it was built, her workload practically disappeared. A couple of months after finishing my book and selecting her team, she found a deal that looked right. Here's her advice in cooking up your deal recipes: *Always know your walk-away price, and don't forget it in the heat of negotiations."* She also has a frequent activity on my Web site using the mortgage calculator and amortization tables to peg her loan costs. This keeps her from errors in her cash flow calculations.

By knowing what she can rent the home for, the current interest rates and the other expenses associated with the property (such as management fees, taxes, insurance, repairs, etc.), Angie can quickly run the numbers to see if the deal would have a positive cash flow each month. To do this, calculate all your expenses and then deduct this total amount from the anticipated monthly rental amount. The amount left over is the maximum mortgage payment you could make each month to break even on this deal. The lower the mortgage payment, the more profit potential or positive monthly cash flow that might be in the deal.

Let's jump right into Angie's first deal recipe.

Deal Recipe # 1 – Duplex for Long Term Rental

The Ingredients
- Duplex with two 3 bedroom, 1 bath units
- Price that allowed cash purchase and repairs paid with her HELOC funds
- Refinance ability to a 30 year loan after repairs to get cash back for a new deal
- Property that would rent quickly with a positive cash flow after financing and expenses
- Instant equity with all costs totaling below market value

Desired Result
Angie wants to purchase properties to rent that are in good neighborhoods, and that she can purchase and repair at a total cost that produces instant equity based on the appraised value. Of course, properties must rent for enough to generate cash flow that justifies the risk and investment in the deal.

She always plans on a purchase and rehab price that can be financed totally out of her HELOC funds. Then she goes out and refinances to get her cash back out for the next deal. This means that the costs for management, operations, and loan costs must all allow for this desired cash flow after the refinance.

Preparation
- Angie's real estate agent located this deal as a regular listing on the MLS (Multiple Listing Service), listed by an individual owner. Her agent knows the exact criteria Angie is looking for and only presents deals that fit in that scope.
- This was her first deal, being a bit nervous so she let her real estate agent teach her as much as possible about the transaction side of a deal along the way.
- However, Angie does all of her own negotiating, telling the real estate agent what she wants to offer and the amount of all counter offers.
- The repair negotiation strategy she employs is a bit different than that used in most contracts. She specifically words her contract such that she can use her own people, rather than a licensed inspector to inspect the property.
- Her property management duo goes in and gives her a report of the condition and the approximate normal repair costs. If a roof or other larger repair is needed, she consults with the appropriate contractor.

- The offer then takes the amount necessary into account in her offer. If there's $10,000 in repairs, she reduces her offer by that amount to begin negotiations.
- This allows Angie to bring in repairs later when dollar amounts are being countered, giving her more negotiating flexibility.
- After closing, repairs are completed and a renter is located. She then refinances to remove her cash for another deal.

It's that last step that got sticky for Angie in this deal. Since this was her first deal, she didn't realize the problem she would face in refinancing a home that soon after purchase. She talked to more than 20 lenders, getting a NO from all, until she finally found one that would do the loan without a minimum "seasoning period." Once she found this lender, he obviously became one of her team members for financing.

Garnish and Presentation

The numbers:
- $85,300 purchase price
- $10,000 rehab costs
- $1,500 monthly rental income projected
- $101,000 appraised value
- $5,700 instant equity
- $570 per month in positive cash flow

It's easy to see that once Angie gets her money back out of a deal, it's time to repeat the process. After all, this recipe results in cash in her bank account every month, and she has all of her HELOC cash back in the bank and ready to do it again.

J. SUMMARY OF BORROWER'S TRANSACTION	
100. GROSS AMOUNT DUE FROM BORROWER:	
101. Contract sales price	85,300.00
102. Personal property	
103. Settlement charges to borrower (Line 1400)	367.00
104.	
105.	
Adjustments for items paid by seller in advance	
106. City/town taxes	
107. County taxes	
108. Assessments	
109.	
110.	
111.	
112.	
120. GROSS AMOUNT DUE FROM BORROWER	85,667.00

200. AMOUNTS PAID BY OR IN BEHALF OF BORROWER:	
201. Deposit or earnest money	1,000.00
202. Principal amount of new loan(s)	
203. Existing loan(s) taken subject to	
204.	
205.	
206.	
207.	
208. Carpet allowance	300.00
209. Rent prorate	93.80
Adjustments for items unpaid by seller	
210. City/town taxes	
211. County taxes	
212. Assessments	
213. Tax prorate	1,006.64
214.	
215.	
216.	
217.	
218.	
219.	
220. TOTAL PAID BY/FOR BORROWER	2,400.44

300. CASH AT SETTLEMENT FROM/TO BORROWER	
301. Gross amount due from borrower (Line 120)	85,667.00
302. Less amount paid by/for borrower (Line 220)	2,400.44
303. CASH FROM BORROWER	83,266.56

Deal Recipe # 2 – Triplex, Some Conversion to Excellent Rental

The Ingredients
- A triplex, two each 2 bedroom, 1 bath units and one 1 bedroom, 1 bath unit
- Purchase and rehab costs within available HELOC funds
- Ability to convert one single bedroom unit into a two bedroom
- Instant equity and rent potential with a positive cash flow after refinance

Desired Result
Just as in her first deal, Angie's desired result is for long-term positive cash flow in renting out the three units. By setting up to add a bedroom to one unit, rental potential would be better, and cash flow increased. Also, her plan is to refinance and take the cash back out of the deal to do another.

Preparation
- This is an REO listing, so the dealings were with the bank.
- Angie lets her real estate agent do the legwork, but all pricing and negotiations are done by Angie, including conversations, if required, with the bank.
- Once the property is purchased, an entry door is blocked off and moved, two doors added, and a communal entry added as well. This allows the additional bedroom.
- Because of a city ordinance related to the rehab, the refinancing was more expensive, as the loan had to be commercial, with a 20 year amortization and a 5 year balloon. Yet the numbers still made sense to go forward.

Garnish and Presentation

Despite the commercial loan that added monthly costs, this deal still produced a positive cash flow of $360 per month after all expenses. Not a problem, as there will be opportunities to refinance again later, and the other numbers really shine for this deal:

- $67,000 purchase price
- $8,700 rehab cost
- $75,700 total invested
- $1,725 monthly rental income
- $110,000 appraised value
- $34,000 instant equity

J. SUMMARY OF BORROWER'S TRANSACTION	
100. GROSS AMOUNT DUE FROM BORROWER:	
101. Contract sales price	67,000.00
102. Personal property	
103. Settlement charges to borrower (Line 1400)	337.00
104.	
105.	
Adjustments for items paid by seller in advance	
106. City/town taxes 11/10/2008-06/30/2009	161.91
107. County taxes	
108. Assessments	
109.	
110.	
111.	
112.	
120. GROSS AMOUNT DUE FROM BORROWER	67,498.91

200. AMOUNTS PAID BY OR IN BEHALF OF BORROWER:	
201. Deposit or earnest money	3,000.00
202. Principal amount of new loan(s)	
203. Existing loan(s) taken subject to	
204.	
205.	
206.	
207.	
208.	
209.	
Adjustments for items unpaid by seller	
210. City/town taxes	
211. County taxes	
212. Assessments	
213.	
214.	
215.	
216.	
217.	
218.	
219.	
220. TOTAL PAID BY/FOR BORROWER	3,000.00

300. CASH AT SETTLEMENT FROM/TO BORROWER	
301. Gross amount due from borrower (Line 120)	67,498.91
302. Less amount paid by/for borrower (Line 220)	3,000.00
303. CASH FROM BORROWER	64,498.91

Angie's planning and research paid off again in this deal recipe. As she continues to refinance and remove her cash for more deals, Angie continues to build her monthly positive cash flow toward that retirement she plans for Daniel and herself.

Deal Recipe # 3 – Single Family REO for Premium Rental

The Ingredients
- Single family REO home in good neighborhood
- 1008 sq ft, 3 bedroom, 1 bath
- Instant equity and positive rental cash flow required

Desired Result
What does a great chef do when a recipe is a resounding success and the restaurant is booked every night with people who all want to try it? She keeps cooking it of course! Angie has managed to combine the right ingredients, items she's located through careful research, and prepare her deals with the outcome of a perfect dish every time. This one is no exception, and even results in an amazing instant equity amount for the cash invested.

It's an REO, and her strategy was to purchase at a deep discount, rehab at a reasonable cost, and rent it out for a premium, as it's in a great area. (Remember you will learn all about REO's a little later.)

Preparation
- Negotiating with resolve, and using the repair costs for leverage, Angie buys this property for $48,000.
- Again, she funds the entire deal from her HELOC funds.
- Even while repairs were still being done, they were marketing it for rent.
- Though a short period of seasoning will be required before refinance, it's not tying up too much of her cash.
- Refinancing comes in for a 30 year fixed loan, and she again takes out all of her cash.

G. PROPERTY LOCATION:	H. SETTLEMENT AGENT
Davenport, IA 52804	
	PLACE OF SETTLEM
	Davenport, IA 528(

J. SUMMARY OF BORROWER'S TRANSACTION		
100. GROSS AMOUNT DUE FROM BORROWER:		4(
101. Contract sales price	48,000.00	4(
102. Personal property		4(
103. Settlement charges to borrower (Line 1400)	592.00	4(
104.		4(
105.		4(
Adjustments for items paid by seller in advance		
106. City/town taxes		4(
107. County taxes		4(
108. Assessments		4(
109.		4(
110.		41
111.		41
112.		41
120. GROSS AMOUNT DUE FROM BORROWER	48,592.00	4:

Garnish and Presentation

This deal recipe presents like a fine platter of sushi, with flair. With an appraised value of $102,000, and costs to rehab of $12,000, Angie ends up with instant equity of $42,000. We're talking equity of 68% based on her $48,000 purchase price! It cash flows positive at $337/month, financing costs included.

Recipe # 4 – REO Single Family Home for Family or College Student Rental

The Ingredients
• Single family, 4 bedroom, 2 bath home, 1264 sq ft with a 2 car garage
• Dual rental possibilities, either a family, or university students
• Instant equity and positive rental cash flow

Desired Result
At the time of this writing, this deal is moving toward closing and repairs haven't yet been done. Because her team gave her advance notice, Angie negotiated a price that covered the $15,000 she needs to replace the roof, paint and make other minor repairs.

She did her homework as usual, running the numbers and determining what her monthly expenses would be. Then she determined if the anticipated monthly rental rate would be enough to produce a positive monthly cash flow if it can rent quickly. The amount of the cash flow will depend on the renters. It is expected that a family will pay around $1,100 rent, while university students would rent it for $1,300 per month. While repairs are being done, they'll be marketing the property for rental.

Preparation
• Negotiated with the bank for a discount price
• Necessary repairs and roof issues were used to negotiate a lower purchase price
• Once closed, the home will be refinanced to pull out her cash for yet another deal

Garnish and Presentation

Purchased at $55,000, with repairs of $15,000, this deal will still provide instant equity of $10k to $15k based on the appraised value of $80k to

$85k. When rented, after all costs including the loan, cash flow should be between $362 and $540 per month. The low number is for occupancy by a family at $1100 per month rent, while the higher number would be for the $1300 per month rent paid by university students.

Recipe # 5 – Single Family Listed Home in Good Rental Area

The Ingredients
• Single family home, 4 bedroom, 2 bath, 2304 sq ft
• 75% finished basement and a 2 car garage
• A price well below appraised value
• Repair costs that are in line for a total cost that produces great instant equity
• Desirable area, with few rental properties, so a great rental opportunity

Desired Result
Locate a property in a highly desirable area with high rent income potential as an "executive rental." This will require good research,

but also a little luck and some very hard negotiating. It will require a motivated seller, as positive cash flow required to justify the purchase price will require a deep discount purchase. There are specific zip codes or areas that Angie is targeting. There are sometimes even specific subdivisions in these communities that would be seen as a "high-end" rental.

Preparation
- Angie would have her real estate agent target these specific subdivisions in her target areas of choice. Angie had her agent search the MLS for key phrases in these desired areas indicating value. For example: "under appraised value," "short sale," "pre-foreclosure," "foreclosure," "REO," "bank owned," "corporate owned," "motivated seller," "relocating," "estate sale," "probate," "second home," and "vacation home."
- Angie could also track other indicators on homes in her target area of interest such as days on the market, price reductions and if the home is "vacant". Time and expense can often motivate a seller.
- The asking price was $200,000, so first offer was made at $169,000.
- Counter offers continued down through $190k, with final agreement at $180k.
- This deal is currently on its way to closing.

Deal Garnish & Presentation

This home is appraised at $255k to $260k in value. With $20k in estimated repairs, Angie is still looking at instant equity of around $55,000. In this upscale neighborhood, this home, as an executive rental, will bring in from $2250 to $2500 per month. Once the refinance is complete, the expected positive cash flow will be $445 to $670 per month.

Getting Off That Wheel

Angie and Daniel no longer feel like hamsters running in a wheel. They are well on their way to realizing their retirement dreams with the cash flow from this first year of investing. It's an accomplishment I want to congratulate them for, and I take a great deal of pleasure in telling you that Angie is looking right now at approximately $144,000 of net worth increase and equity, and monthly positive cash flow from rentals of $2150. Wow!

Utensils and Preparation Tips

Research
When you get to the Resources section, you'll want to check out the material on market research. You can see that Angie availed herself of a great many sources to research a market where she didn't live. From real estate data to business information and development plans, she learned as much as possible before searching for a deal. I'll give you some resources for state and local chamber of commerce sites in the "Knowing the Market in Your Town" chapter. Angie went back into history for the Quad cities, and she saw developing trends in diversification of local industry and business. Realizing that the state and the Quad Cities were both acting in concert to spread their economic base and avoid too heavy of a reliance on one industry, she made the decision that growth in the area would follow.

Funding Her Deals With a HELOC
If it is an option for you I think it is a great one. I talk more about this and other ways to fund your deals in that chapter in Resources, but seeing it put into action here should inspire you to check out this very useful financing tool. And it doesn't have to be your home. In the "Funding Your Real Estate Deals" chapter, I give you reasons why your family and friends would be happy to help you with deal funding. They can increase their return on investments, and some of them may have a lot of equity in their homes. If they can get a HELOC at a rate several percent lower than you're willing to pay them for short term funding, why wouldn't they jump at the chance? If you're buying properties with all cash, you can even give them more security with a lien on the home. It's a true win-win situation.

Building a Team
Especially when you're investing far from home, a carefully selected team is a definite asset. Angie told you how careful she was in her selections, and they've served her well. In the Resources chapter "Building Your Real Estate Team," I'll give you more detailed information and tips for putting together a team of professionals all dedicated to your success. After all, your business is bringing them business; another win-win situation for all.

REO Listings
Several of Angie's deals involved REO (Real Estate Owned) properties held by banks and lenders. You'll find that to be the case in several other

student chapters, and very much so in Joe Jurek's story and deals. She did her homework, and her own negotiations with these banks. You've seen Angie's concentration on good research, and dealing with bankers and REO asset managers requires that you be on top of your game and the local market. The REO chapter in Resources goes into this specialty niche thoroughly, and once you've read it, you'll know how to find them, contact the bank, and negotiate great deals.

Alternative Ingredients and Preparation Tips

Angie brings out a new form of funding deals here, using a home equity line of credit. Of course, if you don't have a lot of equity in your home, this wouldn't work for you. Also, these types of loans have become harder to get in many areas, and charge higher interest rates. Angie tries to get her money back out right away, paying back the HELOC, so that's not a huge concern.

But, if you don't have this funding option, don't let it stop you from putting Angie's deal strategies to work for you. Using resources I give you in the "Funding Your Real Estate Deals" chapter, I'm sure you can find an alternative funding method. Hard money loans are good for short-term funding, and you may find that to be a good way to go. They are more costly, but you have those costs figured into the deal as costs of doing business. If the deal is still profitable, or cash flows well as a rental, then use the funding resource that makes it happen.

Another thing Angie did was to go outside of her town to find opportunities. She went pretty far outside. First, do thorough research on your town, as it's always nice to be where it's happening when you're doing deals. But, if there just doesn't seem to be enough opportunity in your town, then do what Angie did, and go out and find "your town for deals."

Your Town Action Items:
- If you have significant equity in your home, contact local lending sources to shop for a HELOC with the most flexible terms.
- If you don't, do any of your close friends or family members have that kind of equity? You can pay their setup fees, and they don't owe any money unless you do a deal, for which you'll reward them with a nice return on their short term investment.

- Do your local research to locate opportunities. If they're few and far between, start widening your search area until you find "your investment town."
- Whether local or farther away, start building your real estate investment team.

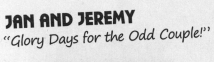

CHAPTER 9

JAN AND JEREMY
"Glory Days for the Odd Couple!"

Partners use craigslist to
score a great deal!

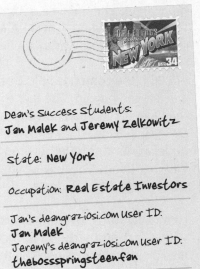

Dean's Success Students:
Jan Malek and **Jeremy Zelkowitz**

State: **New York**

Occupation: **Real Estate Investors**

Jan's deangraziosi.com User ID:
Jan Malek
Jeremy's deangraziosi.com User ID:
thebossspringsteenfan

We have all read about partnerships that have formed in the past from Sears and Roebuck to Roy and Walt Disney. But have you ever wondered how those partners first came together? Was it by chance or maybe even fate? Whatever the reason, Jan and Jeremy are two great guys that had a passion for real estate and they found each other on my Web site at ***www.deangraziosi.com***. Today we are going to meet the "Double J" team of Jan and Jeremy!

Jan's Story

Jan Malek's story is one that many in their 40's and 50's will readily recognize. Let's see if Jan sounds like you . . . twenty years ago, you completed your education and found a job with a large company. Working hard, contributing, and adding value to your employer's business would usually move you up in the ranks, with promotions, pay increases, and a growing retirement account. But, that was then, and this is now.

Jan's first real estate experience was 20+ years ago, when his father passed away. Going home to Connecticut, he structured a purchase of the home from his mother that put him into an ownership position while helping her with income down the road. It was his first experience with "creative financing," and he loved this home he grew up in. And he stayed in it until it was taken away.

In 2004, the company he'd been working for 18 years was taken over in a leveraged buyout. The fact that he had a profitable territory as an area manager for this company gave him a feeling of comfort, even with new ownership. One Friday evening, he decided to go to the office to do some paperwork, and found his regional manager there with a box packing with her things. As he was sympathizing, Jan found that there was a box on his desk, too.

Like many of us, over the years he'd "improved" his home and lifestyle with a first and second mortgage, and some credit card bills as well. In his 50's, another position like the one he lost wasn't available, and things just continued to get worse. Finally, he and his wife Beth had to file bankruptcy, and they lost his childhood home. The sheriff who delivered the eviction notice was a lifelong friend. He says that it was a terrible time but *that we were so far at the bottom of the barrel that there was nowhere to go but up."*

Beth has always supported everything Jan wanted to do, and he began to look at real estate investment as a business to change their financial future. Watching the infomercials of a popular real estate guru "about 150 times," Jan never saw enough there to convince him that he could go out and do it. Going into 2006, Jan saw one of my infomercials. He watched it 3 times, and ordered my book "Be A Real Estate Millionaire." Then he ordered my "Think A Little Different" audio series.

Jan isn't afraid of hard work, and he knows nothing gets handed to you. He went straight to my Web site, joining discussions, meeting other investors and learning as much as he could. He also joined the Real Estate Success Academy, using the last of his 401k account. Studying for hours every night, he believed that the answer was near, but still wasn't ready to jump into active investing.

"There was something about watching Dean. I wanted to believe in him. It was something about his mannerisms and the way he talked. I just knew that this guy was on to something. And, I have no problem telling

anyone today that, next to marrying my wife and having kids, joining Dean's program is the best thing I've ever done."

Jan was on my Web site every night, studying for hours. It wasn't all joy and inspiration for him. He was experiencing frustration watching others posting profitable deals. One of my successful students, Matt Larson, was a frustration and education for Jan. Only a frustration because Jan wanted to do the deals Matt was doing and sharing on the site. Jan's not a shy guy, and he was able to express some of his frustration on the site and to Matt. *"Matt doesn't let you cry on his shoulder, and he told me that I was the only one standing in my way,"* is how Jan describes it.

The tough talk was needed, admits Jan, but it wasn't enough at the time. His site visits had been going on for about a year, with no attempt at a deal, when he finally gave up and left the site for two or three months. His wife Beth watched his frustration, and convinced him to go back to the site in the fall of 2008. He just decided finally that it was time to *"quit feeling sorry for myself and jump back into the game."* So, it was back to the books, mentor materials, and the Web site.

Another new thing Jan jumped into was membership in the Central New York Real Estate Group. He'd been reading in my books and on the Web site that real estate clubs are great places to network and learn. He considers this decision as second only to buying my books and materials in helping him to succeed as a real estate investor. *"The knowledge I gain in this club is priceless,"* Jan said. *"The other investors, 19 of them, are not big wheels with a lot of money. They're a great mix of small investors who I can identify with and learn from."* The largest of these investors has eight properties. They do all types of deals, flips, rehabs, buy-and-hold, and are a great resource in learning strategies that work in the local market. The mortgage broker Jan works with is also a member. He considers this to be a great asset, as they talk frequently, and he can bounce ideas off him at meetings.

Now, Jan was getting more motivated, and decided to try a deal. He teamed with a contractor friend to make an offer on a home that needed renovation. They never got an acceptance, and there was no deal, but it was an icebreaker for Jan. He was finally doing something and it felt good. While this was going on, he was still on the site. He knew there were people teaming up after meeting on my site, but his cautious side made him slow to warm up to anyone on the site.

One day he received an e-mail from Jeremy Zelkowitz, introducing himself and suggesting they talk about teaming up on a deal. This is where an interesting dynamic in New York State comes into play. I'll just quote Jan, as he put it this way: *"Jeremy lives in Brooklyn, and upstate people generally aren't fond of city people. So I blew him off. It would have been even worse had I known he was only 18 years old!"* Forty years difference in their ages seemed to be a big hurdle to a business relationship.

Jeremy didn't give up, continuing to e-mail Jan, and eventually asking him if he wanted to team up on some deals in the Catskills, where Jeremy's uncle lives. His uncle had expressed an interest in real estate investing, and it seemed like one way to get started. But Jan was adamant that he only wanted deals near where he lived. But still, they kept communicating by e-mail.

One day Jeremy e-mailed him with the question *"How close is Mohawk, NY from you?"* Well, Jan let him know that he could see Mohawk from his front porch. Jeremy had located a property on Craigslist, and wanted Jan to go take a look at it. *"It didn't scream buy at me, and was a bit rough, but it was worth consideration."* He let Jeremy know, and the response was *"Make an offer!"* Now, Jan's cautious side jumped up again. After all, they had no agreements, in writing or otherwise. They weren't partners…yet.

Jan was interested though, and asked Jeremy if had financing. *"I have money in the bank and I want us to make an offer,"* was Jeremy's quick response. So, Jan was in a decision dilemma. He had been working with real estate agents trying to locate a property, but few wanted to deal with him when he mentioned "creative financing." Now, here's this kid using Craigslist wanting to buy a house right now.

Jan went over his options and the strategies he really wanted to use in his market. His cautious side makes him really picky about deals. He also realized that locating properties that belong to older people with no or low mortgages provides the greatest opportunity to use owner financing. This is particularly true in his area of upstate New York, as there aren't really that many foreclosure and REO properties. In fact, a recent report stated that his area had one of the lowest foreclosure rates in the country. Many properties are over 100 years old, and have been in the family for generations.

But, that doesn't make the market right for flipping, as the older population and the fear of job loss makes it difficult to buy and rehab to flip. The selling prices usually don't rise to a level that makes flipping profitable. However, the rental market is good, and Jan wanted to buy and hold local rental properties that he could self-manage. Contacting older residents with no mortgage, or a very low one, Jan finds that explaining the tax advantages of owner financing helps him to convince them to offer creative financing.

Life is all about decisions, and Jan can make them well. He teamed up with Jeremy, and their first deal recipe is an impressive one. People on the Web site call them "the odd couple." Age and background differences don't mean a thing to these two, as we'll see in their deals. In fact, Jan considers his silver hair an asset in getting this first deal. More on the details of that deal soon.

Jeremy's Story

Usually when you see two stories presented this way, they're about two different versions of the same story, with some different opinions as to the real story. Now we see why this "odd couple" has hit it off so well. Jeremy's story of how he and Jan came to work together is right in line with Jan's, though from a very different background and perspective. He did laugh when he heard that "upstate people" weren't that fond of city folk, an attitude he says doesn't flow in the other direction.

Jeremy's childhood was one of a working class family in the city. His mother is a secretary, and his father a cab driver. Jeremy took their work ethic out and accumulated around $30,000 in savings doing catering, shoveling snow, and any other job that an 18-year-old could get in the city. His parents, concerned about his future, were very negative about the idea of his investing those hard-earned savings in real estate. *"Everything that you see on TV is a ripoff!"* was their view of my infomercial.

The infomercial is where Jeremy first met me. It was another late sleepless night, and Jeremy says *"Though I'd seen others, I got a different feeling when I saw Dean that night. Something about the way he spoke told me that there was substance to what he was telling me. I ordered his book in January of 2009. My parents have worked their whole life, and they're still renting. I wanted to change all our lives for the better."*

Jeremy read the book and went straight to the Web site to see what it was all about. On the site, he met Jason Lassiter. Jason had an assignment deal that was in trouble. If he didn't get some funding fast, the deal would be lost. This wasn't a bad deal; the expected funding just didn't come in. Jeremy isn't one to hesitate if he sees an opportunity. He wired $28,000, almost all of his savings, to the title company Jason was using. Over the weekend, he got a check back for $29,000 after the deal closed. Jeremy will be quick to tell you that you can't shovel enough snow in a weekend to make $1,000. His first real estate investment deal was a wonderful success!

All the while, Jeremy was on the site, reading, learning, and meeting other investors. One of those investors was Jan. Jeremy has an uncle that lives in upstate New York, not too far from Jan, so he started a conversation with an introductory e-mail. We know from Jan's story that he was hesitant to team up with anyone, even before he knew Jeremy's age. But, it's funny how Jeremy puts it: *"Once we got a deal going, and I drove up there to meet him, I realized I didn't know anything about him. He could have been a psychopath!"*

Since Jan is a normal guy, no bad things happened. In fact, Jeremy was humbled by how Jan's family *"embraced me like I was a part of it."* This meeting was to walk their first deal together. Jeremy found it on Craigslist, and Jan did the initial walk-through, and negotiated with the owner. Once they had a commitment from her, Jeremy came up to take a look and meet his new partner. Here's how their deal recipe came together.

Deal Recipe # 1 – Cash Flow and Owner Financing

The Ingredients
• 2 story 4 unit apartment building Jeremy locates on Craigslist (You will find more about finding on-line deals toward the end of this chapter)
• All 1 bedroom units
• Rents totaling $1800/month
• Older owner with a very low mortgage
• With the right owner financing, a nice positive cash flow
• Utilities included in rents, but averaging very low year round

Desired Result
Jeremy's use of Craigslist is something that Jan didn't expect, but it turns out to be a great way to locate deals. When Jeremy indicated he could

swing the down payment portion of this deal if the price was right, Jan's plan was to purchase at a discount to the asking price of $102,000, with owner financing for long enough to get a refinance loan. They would continue with existing tenants, and at a positive cash flow based on the existing rents, utilities, and the ultimate mortgage payment.

Preparation

1. The homeowner was asking $102,000, and expressing from the beginning that she didn't want any part of owner financing.
2. Price negotiations weren't that difficult, with a settlement on $78,000 as a purchase price.
3. The financing was the hard part. Three more times, the owner refused to discuss any kind of owner financing.
4. By the fifth approach, Jan convinced her to work with them. The deal was to close with $12,000 down, and they would take over her payments for 12 months, with an option to go to 15 months before refinancing.
5. When the refinancing is arranged, they'll be getting a loan for $80k, and paying off the seller with a balloon note of $66k. This leaves them $14,000 to use for other deals.

Garnish and Presentation

This apartment building will easily appraise at $102,000, leaving our team with $24,000 in equity. Here's the breakdown on current cash flow:

- Income from rents is $1800/month
- PITI payment on current loan is ($759.13)
- Average utilities total is ($300.00)
- This gives them a monthly positive cash flow of $741 or $8892 yearly.

Their plan is to bank the positive cash flow every month for the first 12 months, giving them a nice cushion for the unexpected. Once they refinance and pay off the seller, they'll have that money and the cash generated in the refinance to do other deals.

Deal # 2 – A New Home for Jan's Family

The Ingredients

- A desire to own a home again after losing theirs in bankruptcy
- USDA backed loan program
- 3 bedroom, 1.5 bath ranch home with a pool
- Encouragement from his new partner Jeremy

Desired Result

Actually, before Jeremy's encouragement, there wasn't a plan. Having lost his childhood home in bankruptcy, Jan was resigned to renting for a while. Besides the credit hit, no cash is a pretty big hurdle to home financing in today's lending market. At least that's what he thought. But, he did his research and found a way.

Preparation

1. Jan's real estate agent knew he was looking, and contacted him to come see a home that seemed right for Jan's family.
2. The asking price was $80,000. Jan offered $65,000, and they accepted it just before their first open house.
3. Jan was using a USDA (United States Department of Agriculture) backed loan to get into this home with no money out of pocket.
4. $500 earnest money deposit was made, and there is $393 in other fees, totaling $893 out of pocket...at least until closing.
5. They get all of their out of pocket back at closing!
6. They locked in a rate of 5.50% for 30 years.

Garnish and Presentation

I just can't stand it. I have to back up just a bit and remind you of Jan's story. The job layoff, bankruptcy, losing his home of many years, and no real job prospects out there for a 58 year-old account rep. Wow, how do you come back from that? Jan did, by reading my book, studying, and most of all, using my Web site to get encouragement and more information. Oh, and let's not forget his partner, Jeremy.

So, Jan is about to close on his new home, and he isn't investing a dime out of pocket. Because he negotiated a good price, there's some instant equity in there as well, even though he didn't put up any down payment. It just doesn't get any better than this! I'm proud of this odd couple. Their "glory days" have not passed them by, they're being written as we speak today! Now Jeremy and Jan are the Boss!

Jan and Jeremy Going Forward

I asked Jeremy his thoughts on doing more deals with Jan. I can't say it with any more feeling than Jeremy:

"I know that both of us will be millionaires. I feel it. We have each other's back and promised to help each other to become a millionaire. We're a team, and I don't want to see that change...ever."

Needless to say, Jeremy's mother and father have a very different view of his investing now. In fact, his dad wants to get involved to see if he can have a better retirement than he'd dreamed of before. Jeremy's uncle also called to say that he'd like to be involved. Jeremy's team is growing, with immediate family, and his extended family at Jan's home. This odd couple has a bright future together.

Utensils and Preparation Tips

There are several important lessons to be learned from Jan and Jeremy's story. The first; "never judge a book by its cover." If Jan did not like Jeremy because he was not from "upstate," or was young, then Jan could have missed an opportunity of a lifetime. Keep a positive and open mind; don't ever let negative thoughts cloud your judgment.

As I have said before, you never know what someone else has to offer; whether it's a future partner, part of your team or even a seller. Believe that everyone has something to offer or knows someone that can assist you. The question is whether they will open up their "treasure chest of knowledge, networks and contacts" and share them with you? I have known countless business people with a wealth of resources who usually wear a t-shirt and jeans. Can you imagine how many people may have missed an opportunity working with these folks due to the way they're dressed? Judge no one; believe in everyone!

Another important lesson: know what others have to offer. One party might have the knowledge while the other has the resources. The great thing about partnerships is that people can come together and compliment each other's abilities.

A final lesson: youth are better connected with our technology-filled world, from social media to the ever-expanding universe of the Internet. Think about how far we have come in the past several years. When I was in high school in the late 1980's, mobile bag phones were "totally awesome dude!" Later, the brick cellular phones were "wickedly sweet." Today, they're much more than just a phone, aren't they? So as you move forward with your real estate investing, be open-minded, accept technology and embrace others who can help you better understand what's possible in this ever-changing technological world.

I want you to be an explorer, let's just start with a comfortable chair and an Internet connection. While most of us could not fathom life without the Internet, I bet our grandparents would have never imagined that something could trump the television for grabbing our attention on a daily basis.

There is so much information at our fingertips. When it comes to real estate, we just have to know where to look! Of course, I know that you have already found **www.deangraziosi.com** and this may be your home base for real estate knowledge and inspiration, but let's take the journey out there and visit some other destinations and ports of call!

Exploring On-line Auctions

In today's down real estate market, there are many homes that are being foreclosed on that the banks are taking back faster than they can handle. A bank may even have a backed-up inventory of homes they need to process and get back onto the market. More and more banks are turning to auction companies to liquidate their inventory. Previously, you would have to go to a large convention center and bid on the properties of your choice. Today, automation has made the process as comfortable as bidding from your kitchen table! You may want to look into auction companies for a potential deal.

There are several major auction companies where you can locate more information on their Web sites:

- AuctionZip (www.auctionzip.com)
- Hudson and Marshall (www.hudsonandmarshall.com)
- RealtyBid (www.realtybid.com)
- Real Estate Disposition Corporation – REDC (www.ushomeauction.com)
- Williams and Williams (www.williamsauction.com)

You can visit these Web sites and view properties by zip code or state. You can even register to receive auto-notifications of when properties are listed or auctions are coming to your targeted market areas.

Most of the auctions have open houses two weekends prior to the auction. You might even be able to view the property through a real estate agent; it just depends on the area. The key is to exercise your due diligence and know what you are bidding on. You have to run the numbers; what the fair market value of the property in its current "as-is" condition, what repairs are necessary, and the after repaired value once the improvements are completed. Often properties do not have the utilities on and, in colder climates, winterization of the pipes could have caused plumbing issues. I have purchased several homes that were "winterized" and later found broken/cracked pipes or that radiators with a boiler were the heat source.

Your Town Tips:

- Have your real estate agent search for any listing in your target area for the word "auction." Often I have found new leads or auction companies through MLS listings that state "the property is now up for auction, please contact xyz regarding this property."
- Look for smaller auction companies in your local area and get on their mailing list for future auctions in your area of interest.
- Drive your area and look for auction signs. People who know you're in the real estate business can see signs and contact you about a potential lead. We call these people bird-dogs because we may give them a small cash fee for each lead they give us.

Remember, to be successful with an "auction" it takes "action" and the only this that could be missing in this formula for success is "u".

Craigslist

Jan is at least one generation older than Jeremy, but in using the Internet, they're even farther apart. He uses it, but would never have thought about using Craigslist to locate a property. Jeremy, on the other hand, gravitated to Craigslist before other real estate specific search sites. He had used it to buy and sell things, and saw that homes were for sale. Jeremy is quick to point out the types of real estate listings he sees regularly on Craigslist:

- Real estate agents
- For Sale by Owners
- Every age group
- Motivated and desperate sellers
- Owner financing is frequently mentioned

Jeremy also posts to Craigslist that he's an investor who can help owners sell their homes, receiving inquiries that could be deals at some point.

When someone moves out of one of his or her rentals, the first thing Jeremy does is to post the rental vacancy on Craigslist. The last time, he got 20 applicants the first day and they were able to raise the rent!

A tip we picked up early from Greg Murphy on using Craigslist is to explore all the listings because some of the real gems could be in the older listings. These older listings may have more motivated sellers. I would recommend contacting each and every ad that you may have an interest in their property. To save time and effort, create a standard e-mail for your initial contact.

```
Hello,

I saw your recent ad on Craigslist for the property
you currently have for sale in _____. Is the
property still available? If so, could you please
tell me a little more about the property and the best
way to contact you with additional questions. Also,
if you happen to have any other properties you are
considering selling, could you please let me know
about these as well? Thank you for your time and
assistance.

- Jeremy 555-1212
```

Can you imagine having sellers tell you about a few other properties that they may consider selling? Can you say package deal or owner financing? It gives you the inside scoop before others even know the property may be on the market. The key is networking and you are about to find the power of the virtual world of real estate. This is a great way to locate the unlisted hidden gems!

The power of the Internet allows you to scan hundreds of properties and communicate with more sellers in a few hours than if you called and meet sellers in an entire week! You can also ask the following:

• "If I had all cash and could close quickly, what is the best price you could accept?" You may not have all cash, but you may find out how flexible they are.

- "I like your property but another less expensive property may make more financial sense for me, is there a way you could provide owner financing?"
- "How much of a second mortgage could you hold?"
- "Is there anyone you know who would willing to provide a loan and make a great interest rate? We could make this a win-win for all of us."

The Local Newspaper – The Online Edition

You never want to rule out any potential sources for a deal. Be sure to checkout your local newspaper online. Most motivated sellers may only decide to list their home on the Internet edition rather than appearing in the printed classified ads. Some sellers may only run their ad for a short time say Friday through Sunday. Be sure to check out these online classified ads for the potential latest and greatest deals in your local area.

The Power of a Catchy E-mail Address!

We have discussed several topics in the book already such as getting people to respond to our ads or our "call to action." I like handwritten bandit signs that you can post with a phone number or even a flyer with a little tear-off numbers at the bottom of the flyer. But if someone is driving or in a hurry what if they don't have a pen? Here is a way to generate leads for free! Create an e-mail address for inquiries that's easy to remember. This is a way to reel in the "Internet-savvy bandits." Use something catchy and easy to remember like fastcash-close@yahoo.com. These ingredients will get you on your way. Just stir up some interest with signs or flyers, simmer in your local area and watch the leads pop to your e-mail!

Becoming a Sponge to Soak Up the Information

I believe there is benefit in everything we do each day. We might not see the current benefit, and we may never realize where a simple conversation can lead. As you contact people to inquire about their properties, be a good listener, cultivate a relationship and soak up as much information as you possibly can. You may not be able to work out a deal for this property, but you can gather information and contacts from each seller. This potential seller may have a few good and even great contacts such as bankers, handymen, and contractors or simply know people who do odd jobs like painting or landscaping.

Both Jeremy and Jan have a great story to share. People will help other people that they like and can relate to. Many seasoned investors would be inspired by Jeremy's drive and ambition at such an early age. These same seasoned investors will also be inspired by Jan's determination to start a new career after being laid off. The key here is to never let anything hold you back; what you see as a potential disadvantage could really be utilized to your advantage!

Targeting Your Best Demographic

Jan's favorite strategy works best when a seller has a lot of equity or a paid off home. As his area of Upstate New York is made up of older communities, these are usually people in the "boomer" or older age groups. Getting them to offer owner financing is made easier when they have a large equity position. When Jan shows them the difference in all cash placed in the bank at 3% and owner financing at two times that or more in interest, it's not too difficult to move them toward doing the deal, even at a lower selling price.

This niche market strategy serves them well, and you may find that something similar will work for your real estate investment business. Once you define your niche, study it, and find the best way to market to your targeted buyer or seller. Throughout this book, you're reading about student deals that work for them and seeing that they just keep doing the same thing again. Why change what works?

USDA Loans

The U.S. Department of Agriculture has a home loan program. You'll have to check if it is available in your area, as it was designed to help borrowers in more rural areas where other lending options might not be available. I'll give you the details in the chapter on "Funding Your Real Estate Deals," but the high point is that they'll let you finance up to around 103% of the appraised value of the home. That's right, more than it's worth. So, if you can get into one at a good price, and maybe negotiate some of the closing costs with the seller, you can actually move in with no money out of pocket.

Alternative Ingredients and Preparation Tips

Is there an alternative to Craigslist for finding motivated sellers? Of course. There are still the tried-and-true classified ads, eBay, local bulletin boards, neighborhood newsletters, and even church periodicals. If you don't have a Craigslist that covers your area, then use any or all of these other tools to locate your sellers. Remember what Greg Murphy does? He doesn't just watch other people's ads, he runs his own which bring him buyers and sellers almost daily.

Actually, if a Craigslist does not cover you, you're very likely to be eligible for the USDA rural loan. That's a great tradeoff! But if you can't get that loan in your town, it's just a temporary hurdle. "Funding Your Real Estate Deals" in the Resources section will provide literally hundreds of funding sources for you. With the FHA and other government stimulus activities, it's not difficult to get financing if you just do the research.

Jan mentions that his strategy of owner financing works best with older owners who have a great deal of equity in their homes. Could you adapt a bit of Greg Murphy's lease purchase strategy to your market as an alternative? As you read these student stories and their deal recipes, compare ingredients and preparation techniques, you'll find that they cross over, and can be used in other recipes with scrumptious results!

Your Town Action Items:
- Check to see if Craigslist covers your area. If so, test various searches using keywords and phrases that can make that great deal jump out at you.
- Check out other auction-related Web sites on the Internet.
- Create your catchy e-mail address for those Internet bandits!
- If you're still hesitating, maybe you're a Jan in need of a Jeremy. Go to my Web site and join the discussions, ask questions, and meet other investors. You never know where your investing partner might be.

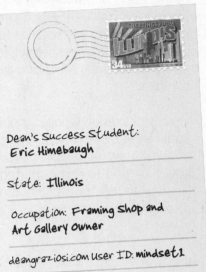

CHAPTER 10

ERIC HIMEBAUGH
"Down but not out!"

Dean's Success Student:
Eric Himebaugh

State: Illinois

Occupation: Framing Shop and
Art Gallery Owner

deangraziosi.com User ID: mindset1

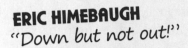

Art Gallery Owner locates
Real Estate Gems!

It starts with a dream, a goal, or just a desire for something more in life. The willingness to do what others won't do so that, one day, you can do what others dream of doing. You work long hours, take large financial risks and give it everything you can. Family and friends may not understand why you work as hard as you do, but you have a vision and are committed to your business. The entrepreneurial spirit is alive and burning in many individuals. We're a country founded on entrepreneurial spirit. Being self-employed, and owning our own business, is a common dream, you might even say is the American Dream. Eric Himebaugh, 30 years old and living in Moline, Illinois with his wife Beth, is one of those entrepreneurs. And the couple had made progress, with their own art framing and gallery business. But, it's tough out there. Customers want more for less and suppliers are providing less for more. One of the first casualties is discretionary spending. And, unfortunately, artwork is not a necessity of life.

Eric and Beth work long hours to keep their business afloat and it's been an exercise in just barely making it in. With all the challenges business owners face today, the couple are to be congratulated for even keeping the business open. They also realized that retail, especially discretionary retail, is too dependent on other economic factors. Looking for something better, they bought a few real estate books, and even attended one guru seminar for $500. They didn't mind the investment, as it was supposed to be the launching pad for their future success. Lifting off from that launch pad was a bit more expensive than they originally planned, as they then paid $25,000 for a series of real estate investment courses from this same company.

Taking courses on wholesaling, Eric poured time and resources into study and market research. But, though the courses were long on motivational material, they were short on real-life experience and instruction. It didn't take him long to realize that they were wasting their time and money. He wanted the "nuts and bolts" to go out and do real deals. And it was discouraging to spend money and not end up what he so desperately wanted.

It was at this time that Eric had a chance meeting with Matt Larson, one of my top students, a great guy now a good friend. Matt offered to spend some time with Eric, providing encouragement and advice and sending Eric to my Web site. Until then, Eric had no idea that there was a place like this, with real people doing what he wanted to do. And they were honest, helpful, and offered amazing advice! Sharing their successes and their mistakes was invaluable, finally, here were those "nuts and bolts" he'd wanted! This was exciting to Eric, and ordering my book "Profit From Real Estate Right Now" seemed a small investment to keep moving forward in his real estate investment education.

You can't call Eric a procrastinator. He read my book in just two days and soaked up every bit of information he could. Finally, he found those nuts and bolts he wanted, and it changed his approach right away. Previously, he didn't have cash for investing and his focus was on trying to do bird dog deals or flips that would get him in and out without a lot of cash. Now, he was excited about the idea of applying what he was reading, buying homes outright, refinancing them and holding them for rental income. I met Eric in person in the Quad cities, and he told me that he got more from my book then he got from the $25,000 program he bought. Now that's a compliment!

Going right to the basics of creative financing, Eric approached his father to offer him an investment opportunity using funds from his IRA account (which was not making much or any money at all.) Some of my materials caught his attention, especially the rule that allows removal of IRA funds for up to 60 days without a penalty. The strategy he explained to his father was to cut an aggressive deal on a home, pay for it cash with IRA funds, rehab it quickly, then refinance to get the money back into the account.

If he could locate a home with reasonable rehab costs, cut a really deep discount buy, then there would be a new value after repairs that would allow refinancing with enough cash out to reimburse the IRA before a penalty. His father jumped on board, and now wishes he had more time to become an active partner. So Eric had a funding resource; now he had to locate homes he could buy at a price that would make this strategy profitable. There was a bit of a learning curve in this part of the story.

Eric wanted to use our 25:1 ratio low-offer blast. He needed the perfect real estate agent to help him with that. Now that the bug had bit him, he was networking to get the right people on board to help him achieve his goals. So he found a real estate agent and together, they immediately started making deep discount offers on a lot of properties. By a lot, I mean hundreds! He had read that he might make 25 or more offers before getting a contract, but his ratio at first was zero deals with more than 100 offers. To make matters worse, the real estate agent decided that there wasn't enough opportunity in the relationship to justify the time invested in all of these offers. So, no more real estate agent.

The problem: Eric was not following all the pieces in the 25 to 1 strategies. If you would like the exact 25 to 1 strategy that Matt Larson used to become a millionaire and so many of my successful students have used, check it out in my last book, Profit From Real Estate, or go to ***www. deangraziosi.com/yourtown/25to1.***

One update to that strategy. More people are now competing for the low priced homes that hit the market. So here is a little secret that works extremely well: don't always target the cheapest houses on the market when using the 25 to 1 strategy. Look for houses that are overpriced and have been on the market for a long period of time. Many of these people are just asking so much that no one is making offers. Therefore, your offer competition is minimal. Here is where you can negotiate, make a low offer, be one of their few offers and possibly scrape up a great deal other investors missed.

Again, we see the value of my Web site and the sharing of ideas, strategies and information among the members. If you go there today, you'll get to tap Eric's experience and learn from his mistakes. And he admits to mistakes. Few of us who are really ready to act on what we know can get by without mistakes. But, as Eric says, you learn as much or more from your mistakes as you do from your successes. So, Eric will help you here by sharing his errors with you.

Mistake # 1 – Scatter Gun Approach to Offers

Eric realized he was throwing out offers on too many properties with little chance of a counter offer. He admits to offending a lot of homeowners who had their properties listed. As he was using a real estate Web site IDX (Internet Data Exchange) search utility, he could see all of the listings of all real estate agents in the local MLS association. But what he realized was that seeing every listing wasn't the same as seeing all of the information about every listing. Getting over his loss of confidence when he lost his first real estate agent, Eric found another one. This time, he asked her to send him reports of listings that had the full information, the same listing detail that real estate agents have. This gave him a priceless piece of information: the owner's name. Now he could see which listings were REOs, which properties were held in trust, and all estate sale properties.

By focusing on properties that would have more pressure for a sale, he could cut the number of offers and improve his chance of success. He'll tell you today that his ratio is approaching 25 to 1, not hundreds before a deal. He never offers over 60% of asking price or value, whichever is less. By being careful to have a reasonable estimate of repairs, negotiating a great front-end purchase price would leave him with a home ready for refinancing at its increased post-repair value.

Eric shows us how mistakes are great learning experiences. Far from feeling discouraged, he made money and knows he will never make those mistakes again. You gotta be in it to win it!

Deal Recipe # 1 – Estate Home With Problems

Ingredients
- 2 bedroom, 1 bath home, 1150 sq ft with a one car garage
- Motivated sale situation, couple had died, and heirs wanted the cash

- Greater negotiation power because of foundation problems discouraging other buyers
- Even with foundation issues, repair costs would leave adequate value for refinancing

Desired Result

Simple plans are best, and this one's no different. Eric borrowed the money to purchase the home from his dad's IRA account. Once he closed on the deal, he would immediately make the repairs, get refinancing based on a realistic appraisal, pay his father back, and rent the home out for a positive cash flow.

Because he would not purchase unless he could get the home for around half its true value, he was confident the appraisal would get the money back into the IRA, free up some excess cash, and create a mortgage that would still generate positive rental cash flow. This is where Eric is kind enough to share with you how the end result didn't quite match the plan.

Preparation

- Using the MLS search utility, and getting full detail listing reports from his agent, Eric located this property for sale by the estate. He assumed that the heirs would have an interest in getting it sold as quickly as possible, getting their cash inheritance.
- Listed at $68,000, Eric made his initial offer at well below that, and negotiated a final purchase price of $36,000. He wanted to present a strong presence during the negotiations, so offered $5,000 in earnest money from the start.
- The heirs were not from the area, and just wanted to liquidate the property to complete the settlement of the estate.
- The foundation issue was mentioned in the negotiation. Eric wanted them to know that it was a problem for buyers, and he was willing to overlook it, thus a lower offer.
- Once they closed on the home, the refinance was completed, with a $57,000 loan, paying back the IRA and sealing in equity of $23,000. This was a great first deal, yet there were a few unexpected issues that were a great learning lesson.

Mistake # 2 – Not Getting the Whole Story From the Refi Bank

Eric is charitable to the bank in this regard. He says it's his mistake, and that it's one with great educational value. The bank doing his refinance had some new policies, and one of them cut the cash out on the first deal. While he had an appraisal of $80,000, the bank had done an estimate of value prior to the appraisal. That value was placed at $72,000. Current policy required that they use their estimator's value, rather than the appraisal. Though he still had enough to take care of the IRA reimbursement, Eric didn't get to take out the cash that he wanted for another deal.

Eric's attitude is that it was a lesson learned. And he's quick to tell others to sit down with their lender and be sure that all of the terms of a financing transaction are exactly the way they understand them. It's not fun to find out your check at closing is a lot less than you expected. And that's when Eric found out, at the closing table. Prior to any closing the title company usually prepares the HUD-1 closing statement. It is a good idea to request a copy of the closing statement at least 24 hours prior to closing. Any errors or adjustments are easier to correct because you have more time to get it done. I spent a lot of time in life with a simple "ready . . . fire" approach, sort of what Eric did. He was so excited that he got a deal for 50% off using our techniques that he "ready, fired!" The older I get, the more I want to make smart choices, so I added one really important variable to my approach: "aim." So now it is "ready, aim, fire!"

Mistake # 3 – Not Doing Your Homework for Repair Costs

Doing extensive plumbing work twice, at an extra cost of $1,500, wasn't in Eric's plans or estimates. He located a contractor handyman who did all kinds of repair and rehab work. This contractor had a couple of rental homes himself, and had the experience to do the work needed on the home, including the plumbing. But, they were in Rock Island, not Moline, where they had experience. The plumber didn't check codes, and though he did a good job on the piping, the city inspector failed the home because they used the wrong type of pipe. Eric's positive attitude about learning experiences stands him well, because he certainly could have been upset about this situation. Instead, he did the work again with a licensed plumber in Rock Island and still made this a really nice deal.

Eric was moving really fast to start a new life, and he has done an amazing job, with a few small mistakes on the way. The biggest mistake he could have made was not starting at all or letting little bumps in the road stop him from realizing his potential in real estate. One way to avoid these mistakes is to re-read Angie's chapter on how she created her "A" team of real estate professionals taking her time, cultivating referrals and asking hardcore question to make sure all the people on her team were the best of the best.

Garnish and Presentation

Despite some mistakes, Eric's overall plan was solid. As a first deal, it's hard to be critical, as he came out with $23,000 in equity, paid back his father, kept some cash, and has a positive cash flow rental property generating $125 every month over costs. I think he did phenomenally well, and kept a great attitude, even through a few setbacks. I also really appreciate the way that he's helping others by telling them about his errors as well as his triumphs.

Deal # 2 – Foreclosure to Rental Home

The Ingredients
• REO property in an area good for rental properties
• Opportunity to buy at well below appraisal value
• Home ready to rent without a lot of repair or rehab

Desired Result
Eric had pretty much the same goals with this property as he did with Deal #1. He needed to purchase at a deep discount, then refinance at value for a nice difference. Here's where he has some advice for you. Eric didn't get the appraisal he hoped for on this property, though it was still a profitable deal. It seems that the bank rotated through a list of three appraisers, and he was unlucky enough to get the most conservative of the bunch.

Eric learned from this, saying that he'll research how a bank handles appraisals, and the appraisers they use in the future. *"It's all about adjusting your offer to the risk involved,"* he says. If he can't control the selection of appraiser (and you almost never can) Eric adjusts his offers to take into account the worst-case situation. Today, most banks are using appraisers on a rotating basis. You can be professional and polite when they come out to do the appraisal. I find that if you are friendly and offer the appraiser a summary of all the improvements and important aspects of the property, they will usually be grateful for the information. I have even provided a drawn layout of the property with room dimensions, just to save the appraiser a little time and effort. The appraisers have to capture information and take a lot of notes, so if you can make their job any easier, they may be able to remember more of the positive aspects of your home in their final report.

Eric had some more valuable advice for you: if you plan to hold the home for long-term rental, be sure that you do your best to have a renter ready the moment you close. He advises to make the home more appealing than the competition and advertising early for renters. He isn't happy with holding a home, paying taxes, and sitting on equity when the cash isn't flowing. Also, banks and appraisers like to know what the home has rented for. A nicer home that commands a higher rent could have a positive effect on the appraisal.

Eric felt that it was important that he share where he messed up in his learning curve. But he said it is more important that you know that, even with all he learned, that when you use a proven strategy, buy a property for a huge discount, and you what to do with it, it's not about if you win or lose. It's really about how big you win.

Preparation
- Assuming a value of over $80,000, a deal was negotiated to purchase the home for $45,000.
- Even with a $70,000 appraisal, Eric has about $20,000 in instant equity in the home.
- He had a renter lined up for immediate occupancy

Garnish and Presentation

Even with his appraisal problem, Eric ended up with a positive net worth adjustment of around $20,000. He has the home rented out with a cash flow of $325/month paid back his dad's IRA in full and still left the refinance table with a few thousand dollars in his pocket after everything was paid. So, he's sitting pretty, and he learned some valuable lessons for his next deal. Sometimes the most valuable thing may not be the cash you put in your pocket, but the knowledge you gained from doing the deal. The knowledge you acquire today will benefit you in the future on countless deals. Anytime you can make a tidy profit and learn from the deal consider it a double bonus.

Utensils and Preparation Tips

Locating the Right Deals With Fewer Offers

Eric admits that his first approach created a lot of offers, some resentment, and no real deals. So, he refined his approach and built a solid relationship with a real estate agent. Though he could search the MLS listings, he couldn't see the most important piece of information: the owner's name. To locate distressed properties, he needed to see bank or trustee names. So his real estate agent set him up to receive listing reports with the owner names and full detail. This really helped Eric. He could now focus on making offers on the properties most likely to be available at deep discounts. I'll give you more detail on this in the "Building Your Real Estate Team" and "Finding Deals" chapters in Resources.

Repairs and Contractors

Eric is giving you valuable information by sharing his mistakes. He didn't make his expected profits on one deal because of extra costs in re-plumbing the home. This was a combination of using the wrong contractor and lack of knowledge of the building codes in a town he hadn't done work in before. In the "Valuation, Repair and Renovation" chapter in Resources, I'll give you much more detail in assessing structure condition, and even links and books on construction estimating. It isn't that you have to do it all, or know it all. But, having enough knowledge to catch mistakes, or to see when you're not getting the whole story, is something you really need.

Alternative Ingredients and Preparation Tips

Though the lower appraisal didn't make Eric happy, he was able to refund his dad's IRA. Remember that IRA accounts have been mentioned several times as funding sources for my students' deals. Could Eric have handled funding differently? Sure. When you read the "Funding Your Real Estate Deals" chapter in the Resources section, you'll see several different ways to get short term, or "flash," funding to carry you through from the purchase to refinance. Other options would have been more expensive for Eric, but they're out there if you need them.

Your Town Action Items:

• Check into how you can best locate estate property, just as Eric did in his first deal.

• Make a list and file of probate attorneys and bank trust departments in your town that handle probate real estate.

• Make a note to learn who the local appraisers are, who is known to be liberal and who is the most conservative. Then see which banks use which appraisers.

CHAPTER 11

CHAD MERRIHEW
"Time To Live Your Dreams !"

Dean's Success Student:
Chad Merrihew

State: California

Occupation: Youth Pastor

deangraziosi.com User ID: cmerrihew

California Pastor is Proving Age
and Location Aren't a Problem!

In life there are some things we just can't control. We have to deal with the cards dealt to us and make the most out of each and every situation. How we handle those difficult situations determines who we are or who we may become as a person. Chad Merrihew is 24 years old and living in Southern California. He's in one of the toughest real estate markets in the country. Are you in your 20's or even your teens and worried you may be too young or not have enough resources to invest in real estate? Or are you older with more life experiences and feel you live in a better place to invest than southern California? Whatever your story, age or zip code may be, you are going identify with Chad's story. It will solidify that this is for you.

Maybe you're in Florida, Arizona, California, or another hard-hit state. You've watched home prices tumble, or even drop like a rock. People all around you are losing their homes to foreclosure, and the financial news doesn't seem to be getting any better. At times, it is better to just go on a news "diet" and not even listen to the nightly news or read those depressing articles in the newspaper. Chad will tell you that it can't be any worse than his area of California. Yet, using none of his own money, he's done more than 20 deals. Some homes he flips, others are held for rental with positive cash flow. They're profitable, and he's done it during the worst of times in one of the worst areas of the country.

Chad is a junior high pastor in Costa Mesa, California. He's been work-ing full-time for a year and loves it, although this wasn't his original plan when he was attending college at the University of Oregon. As a business entrepreneurship major, the plan was study in London for a year. He'd set it all up, was ready to move, but his world changed before he could leave. With a friend in the car, Chad was in a serious accident in October 2005, flipping the car five times. Chad was in a coma and his friend almost died. When he came out of it, Chad describes his life as "a bit of a mess." *"The next three months were really hard. I had lost some short-term memory, and was struggling with what was next for me in life."* He experienced doubts about his future and why he was even allowed to live. He couldn't carry a full class load at college, so dropped out of some classes. As he'd canceled his living arrangements expecting to move to London, he had nowhere to live either. Going abroad was no longer an option for health and financial reasons, so there were tough decisions to make.

There wasn't any real background experience to move Chad toward real estate investing. Many years before, his father had purchased some land in southern California, making money on it from a long holding period. The only other real estate deals his father had done were the purchase and sale of the family homes. Chad's step dad owns one investment prop-erty in which cash flows well. And his grandfather made a little money on some land deals in the 90's. So there really wasn't a family history in real estate investment that brought it to the forefront when Chad was trying to figure out his housing situation.

Chad wanted to stay in school, but needed a place to live. He went to his father for advice, and his dad told him to just buy a home to live in while in school. He was fortunate in that the family had created a stock account for him in the past, and it held about $17,000 that he could use to get into a home. Not being one to dally, Chad did some basic real es-tate research and went out to look for a home right away. *"I didn't know much,"* he says. He bought a home for $180,000 with an FHA 3% down loan. Renting part of the home out to roommates, he got his first educa-tion in cash flow. By his own admission, Chad lucked into a positive cash flow, even though he hadn't done any research into the costs of owning and maintaining the home, nor had he studied rents in the area. But he was making money on the rents, so why not do it again?

To understand how Chad attacks his real estate investing, here's what he has to say about risk and fear: *"I've always been a guy who operates in the red zone with a high risk tolerance. Most people written about in history had huge failures, but overcame fear and tried again to succeed. I never let fear rule me, and I take on the risk that's necessary to succeed."* This is obvious in his one attempt at day trading the stock market. He lost $12,000 before he decided there had to be a better way. Chad doesn't consider real estate an asset unless it's generating cash flow. Just holding it doesn't make it an asset. Actually, he is blunt in calling owning a home a liability if it's costing you money instead of bringing in a positive monthly cash flow.

Now that you know Chad a little better, let's talk about the next home he purchased in college. Remember, he hasn't bumped into my material or me yet. He's just a college guy who had a lucky first experience in buying a home and decided to go out and do it again. He found one he could buy with 10% down on a 30 year loan, and from his dad borrowed the $20,000 he needed for the down payment and closing costs. Even with paying his dad back at 15% interest for two years, he managed a $250/month cash flow. As he had set a goal to buy a property every year until graduation, he ended up with one more, owning three, all generating cash.

How would you be rating your success if these were your deals? They all resulted in positive cash flows, but Chad is critical of his process. *"My cash flows really weren't as good as they should have been. I went into these deals with no exit strategies and no real market knowledge. Three years later I was locked into these deals without a profitable exit strategy, and I could have, and should have, done better."* This self-criticism would help Chad after graduation, as he knew that he wanted to continue investing in real estate, but he didn't want to repeat his mistakes.

After graduation, Chad decided that a career as a youth pastor was his dream. He knew that the salary would be low and that this passion didn't align with his financial goals. Real estate investment would be his vehicle to achieve his financial dreams while he pursued his dreams in the church. *"I believe that a lot of good can be done in the world with money. I want to help others with my money, do good in the world, and even give up my salary at some point if possible."* With these lofty goals, Chad set out to learn more about real estate.

When it all comes together: Attending a real estate conference in September 2008 in Los Angeles, Chad met a friend who knew Matt Larson, one of my top students who now is well-known by many in the investing world. He is also now one of the in-house mentors for my success academy. Another friend at the same conference gave Chad a copy of my book. So Chad heard about Matt, the he was student of mine and used my techniques to transform his life, and got a copy of my book, all at the same time. Talk about convergence!

Chad's friend sat down beside him one day and told him "I have done you a monster favor." His friend had called Matt Larson, telling him about Chad and his goals. Being a great guy and wanting to share his newfound techniques, Matt invited Chad to fly out and meet him in person, learn from him, and actually do a deal together. Matt gave Chad a basic education in what he'd learned in my classes and materials, and offered to find a property for him in Illinois. This becomes our first deal recipe from Chad. We'll take you through it here, but let's take a moment to describe Chad's strategy as it evolved over time and how he pursues deals now.

Chad locates investors to form partnerships. He never uses his own money to fund deals. He is able to do this because of his confidence in following a proven strategy. If you think there is no money out there to invest or create partners, you are wrong. Chad has them lined up, even in Southern California.

Chad is relentless, always making offers far under asking price, sometimes making 150 offers to get one deal. The other partners fund the deals, while Chad locates them, does the research, and gets them done. The profits from a flip or the monthly cash flow profits are all split among the partners. In meeting with potential investment partners, Chad has heard just about every excuse for not getting involved. Here are some of the most common:

1. **Too Good To Be True –**Even a good friend of his from college was too afraid to get involved, as he believed there had to be something wrong with a plan that made money the way Chad's did. *"It's just fear"* is Chad's take.

2. **It's Too Risky –** This is when people display their lack of tolerance for risk, and come up with some amazing examples of the terrible things that could possibly happen. One man asked, *"What if we buy an investment house and a hurricane blows it away and the insurance*

company goes out of business?" Bizarre excuses happen, people don't sign up and continue to live their lives with few prospects for financial security.

3. **More Money With Do-It-Yourself** – In one investment meeting, the question was asked, *"Why don't we do what the real estate agent does and do the repairs too? It's just more money in our pockets."* This man didn't sign up either, because he saw dollars going out of his pocket to others that he wanted to keep. The problem is that you severely limit the number of profitable deals you can do if you're hammering nails or delivering contracts. Chad doesn't only leverage money; he leverages his time as well.

4. **If It's Not Close-By** – The best deals aren't always in your backyard. Chad is doing deals in other cities and states, and doing quite well. This is another risk-avoidance thing, as there are many who decide not to become involved if they can't walk into the home and see it first hand.

5. **What's the Return on Investment?** - A basic lack of understanding of the numbers is another factor that keeps people from joining partnerships for profit. While holding money in savings accounts earning 2%, they still can't understand the value of rental property cash flowing at 12%. For some reason, that doesn't seem like enough.

The "Right" real estate agent is so important- Chad went through three agents to find the perfect one. I did an empowering conversations interview with him and his agent and it was easy to see why Chad chose him. He is the type of real estate agent all investors want.

FREE BONUS
If you have not already seen it, I have included a clip of my video interview with Chad's real estate agent so you can see what a great agent looks like. Go check it out at *www.deangraziosi.com/yourtown/findagent.*

Here's what makes a remarkable agent: He or she can…

• Be your eyes and ears in your local target market.
• Has pulse of not only what is happening in your local area but also the ability to gather information and quickly provide details when needed.

- Present offers and close deals.
- Know which mortgage brokers get the most deals done in the market today and have an extensive network of professionals to refer.
- Offer insight and information when asked.
- Get offers presented quickly and ensure they do everything they can to close the deal.
- Know that to make money, you need to make money first.
- Understand that time is money and of the essence.
- Understand that at times you need to be aggressive.

Now you know Chad's basic operating plan and how he approaches real estate investment without using his own money. For those who can get past those five or so negative dream-killer thoughts, Chad locates great deals and gets them through a profitable flip or long term rental with positive cash flow every month. So, let's look at Chad's very first deal after meeting Matt Larson.

Deal Recipe # 1 – Using Other Peoples' Money in a Long Distance Deal

Ingredients
- 2 Bedroom, 1 Bath home in Illinois
- Good rental potential
- Commission to Matt to locate the property
- Deep discount purchase price
- Loan from a friend until refinance
- Repairs and costs in line with value

Desired Result
Chad would borrow money from a friend on a short term loan in order to pay cash for a home. By inking a really low purchase price, necessary repairs still makes for a positive cash flow rental. Chad would also had the commission to Matt for finding the home, so all the numbers worked for this deal to generate monthly cash. The home would ultimately be refinanced to pay off the money borrowed to make the cash purchase. Sound like a familiar strategy?

Preparation
- Matt locates a home in Illinois that can be purchased for $34,000, with expected value after repairs of $70k.
- Matt's fee for bringing the deal is $2,000.

- Repair costs are $6,000, with $1,000 in other expenses.
- Legal and closing are another $2,000, bringing total cash out at closing of $45,000.
- A friend has loaned Chad $50,000 at 12% interest with a balloon pay-off in 12 months.

Garnish and Presentation

This deal actually ties together several concepts used by many of my students. Matt earns a commission for locating deals, a favorite strategy of students who don't yet have the cash to fund their own deals. Though Matt's net worth is such that he can do pretty much what he wants, he still likes these quick turns for a nice commission without risk. And Chad gets a profitable long-term rental he would never have found on his own.

We see how Chad uses friends and family for temporary funding, creating a net worth infusion and a long-term positive cash flow investment. The home is rented for $675/month, with $575 of it going to cash after expenses. He's not paying payments on the $50,000 loan, just interest until he pays it off with the balloon, so the refinancing will take care of that with a profit to boot, as its value is $70,000.

Deal Recipe # 2 – Moline, IL Duplex

Ingredients
- One two bedroom one bath unit with about 500 sq ft
- The second unit is a small studio
- All brick construction and in good condition
- Wholesaled to Chad
- One unit in neighborhood already owned, so systems/team in place
- Instant equity with good rental potential

Desired Result
To purchase another property in a familiar rental area, and take on his aunt as a partner. The property would need to be purchased at a deep discount with instant equity. It would need to cash flow enough at the beginning to allow refinancing later and continued positive cash flow.

Preparation
- Home appraised at $65,000, and was purchased for $40,500
- Other costs:
    - $5,000 assignment fee
    - $4,000 in renovation costs
    - $1,000 in travel expenses
- This resulted in an instant equity of around $15,000
- Chad's aunt acted as his investor, putting up the $50,000 necessary to do the deal, and allowing Chad to get it done with no money out of pocket
- With rents of around $850/month when both units are occupied, they have a nice cash flow until later refinancing
- They expect to maintain a positive cash flow after the refinance, and they'll use the money they pull out for another deal
- Because it was in the same neighborhood as another of Chad's properties, his team was in place; property management, contractors and the bank.

Garnish and Presentation

Not only did Chad get to help his aunt realize a better return on money she had invested elsewhere, he got this deal with his expertise and connections, and needed no money out of pocket. His experience in the neighborhood made it an easier research project with less risk. He and his aunt plan on more deals as soon as they can get the cash out of this deal with a refinance.

Deal # 3 – California is a Market of Opportunity

Ingredients
- An REO property in Riverside, CA
- Tough market with a motivated bank owner
- In 2004, home would have sold for around $400k
- 3 BR, 2 BA on a 13,000 sq ft lot
- Home is 1,000 sq ft
- Great neighborhood with solid rental potential if flip didn't work

Desired Result
Chad's plan for this home was to buy at a very deep discount, do some rehab work, and then flip it for a nice profit pretty quickly. The backup

plan was to rent it out if there wasn't a buyer that would bring the right offer. Again, he wanted to put in none of his own money, but make his share of the investment be his abilities, knowledge and connections.

Preparation

- Chad's investor partner in this deal was a commercial investor who wanted to buy and sell REO properties. He would put up all of the money, and Chad would get the deal done, rehab completed, and find a buyer.
- Their offer was for a cash closing in 14 days with a $10,000 deposit.
- The REO bank really wanted to move this home, and took their offer of $100,000.
- Rehab and other costs totaled about $30,000.
- They put it on the market at $175,000, and had a bidding war with 10 offers, the winner buying the home for $182,000.
- The whole deal, from purchase through rehab and sale, took less than 60 days.

Garnish and Presentation

This one is one of Chad's best. He was dealing in his own hometown, with no assignment fee to someone else. He still got it done with none of his own money. Profit was around $37,000 after expenses and in only 60 days. His investor was quite happy, and they've now bought 13 units in 8 months together.

Utensils and Preparation Tips

Friends and Family for Financing

Too many of us have taken to heart the old cautions about neither lending to nor borrowing from friends or family. And there's a lot of value in this advice when the borrowing or lending isn't a business transaction that benefits both parties. Too many of these types of loans are made for discretionary purchases and with little or no interest paid to the lender. It's not hard to see why these loans can end up with hard feelings.

The difference we see in Chad's use of his father's funds and those of his aunt and his friend is the generous interest rate he pays. Actually, they may have been offended if they weren't offered this opportunity to turn their 2% savings return into a 12% to 15% return. Don't automatically assume that you're going to offend your family or friends if you approach them for funding. It's not a loan, it's a business investment that's better than most any other.

Forming Investor Partnerships for Funding

Chad doesn't use his own money, no matter how many deals he does. Building a track record of good results gives him credibility when approaching investors to partner with him in deals. Once he gets past the naysayers and those who have too much fear to get involved, he builds a partnership that funds his deals, and allows him to take his share of profits without a cash investment.

Throughout this book, my students and I give you so many ways to adapt your life and your finances to fit strategies that will bring you success. Partnerships and other peoples' money is just one of many techniques. Remember: we all have assets around us, even if it is just our determination and drive. Find and use your assets to everyone's benefit. As we discussed in Jan and Jeremy's chapter, do not be too quick to judge. You may be searching for private money and not realize that people, relatives or neighbors actually have cash ready to invest.

Using Bird Dogs to Find Properties Anywhere

Chad would never have located some of his best deals without Matt. If there isn't enough opportunity in your town, or you're in a dry spell in locating deals, don't let that stop you. Using my Web site, a number of students have worked with each other in this type of relationship. You are looking for a deal, and there's another student on the site living in a town where there's a great deal waiting. All you have to do is get to know each other and trade information.

You should also let the world know what you're doing and that you pay commissions to those who bring you deals. Advertising in the newspaper and on Craigslist that you pay "bird dog" fees will generate phone calls from people who know about opportunities. They're out there, and eager to bring you deals for a fee. Since you're only paying this commission if the deal closes, you just factor it into your negotiations, with no risk. It's like being a huge corporation with your own sales force out there bringing you deals every day.

Alternative Ingredients and Presentation Tips

Can a 24 year old do 20 profitable real estate deals in one year without using his own money? Chad did it. And do can you. If you don't see yourself talking to potential partners to finance your deals, then maybe you'll be like Jan or Lubertha and find a partner on my Web site. Or take the Weules' approach and invest with your real estate club. There's synergy and power in groups when all of the people involved have the same goal.

Think of your family and friends as a group of potential partners. Why wouldn't you invite them to participate in your prosperity before taking in others? Maybe you have co-workers or business associates who have low-yielding investments and would welcome an opportunity to dramatically improve their returns. Your group of partners can be anyone, from anywhere. All you have to do is open your mind to the probability that you know several people who would like to take this trip with you.

Stories and Recipes – What Have You Learned?

Since Chad is the last of our student chapters and deal recipes, let's look back for a moment at what you've learned.

You're not alone – Just a trip to my Web site will introduce you to a bunch of amazing people, all sharing their stories, deal details, strategies and frustrations. There is no substitute for discussion with people just like you.

Opportunity takes many forms – Just think back to the many strategies these students have used successfully. It's amazing how many ways you can make money with real estate. It's not just buy low and sell high. In fact, you've seen a number of ways to make money without ever buying or selling one property!

You're not a shark, but a lifeboat – Some people get the idea that homeowners in trouble are always taken advantage of by investors. You've seen here, with people like Greg Murphy, that you can help a homeowner in distress, someone who just wants a way out with salvaged credit and no foreclosure. There's nothing wrong with a profit if you're giving them what they desperately want. He's helping people who are going both ways, out of a home with a problem, and those who want into a home, but have credit or down payment problems.

Funding is not a problem – In every student chapter, you've seen very different ways of funding deals. For every funding resource you don't have at your disposal, there are several that take its place. Read and use the "Funding Your Real Estate Deals" chapter in the next section to make it happen for you.

Any other town can be "your town" - When you can't find the best investment opportunities in your town, you can adopt a town. Several of these students have shown you how they've done deals far from home, and been highly successful. It's a big world in miles, but a small world in communications with today's technology.

Your financial situation means nothing - The stories told by Greg, Lubertha, Bernadette, and others show you that bad credit, no cash, or upsetting financial situations are not a barrier to success. You can do this!

Your Town Action Items:

- Make a list of potential people you may be able to partner with in your area.
- Interview to find your perfect real estate agent, one with the pulse of your market and who will help take you where you want to go.
- Scout your area and others to determine what's best for your investing activities.
- Always have a plan B.
- Meet new people and network with real estate professionals; a world of opportunity awaits.
- Never tell yourself that you can't do something, such as finding a down payment for a killer deal. Ask how can you do it, listing 5 to 10 solutions to any problem you may encounter.

CHAPTER 12

GARY AND JILL CERIANI

"Proof you can make money anywhere!"

Dean's Success Students:
Gary and Jill Ceriani

State: Florida

Occupation: Real Estate Investors

deangraziosi.com User ID: gceriani

Retired couple dominates in the sunshine state!

There are places that people dream about living one day. When they have enough of the snow and cold, they long to pack up their belongings and move south to a warmer climate and leave the snow shovel and winter jacket behind. Most who live up North dream of making that move but never do. However, that's not true about Gary and Jill Ceriani.

Gary and Jill decided to move to the sunshine state and never looked back. Since getting my book, they have completed 17 deals and have made over $507,000 in profit! All in the state with supposedly the worst real estate market, with an all-time high rates of foreclosure and unemployment. Even Mickey is not getting as many visitors! So you ask, "Dean how could this be? Did they really do all this after getting your book?" Absolutely, positively.

I was so impressed by what Gary and Jill had accomplished that I flew to Florida to meet them in person. Yes, this couple is living the life of their dreams, all because of their real estate investing. Gary and Jill are now retired from their day jobs; they get to take a one-month vacation each summer with their 12-year-old son. How great is that? You can't measure what that time is worth! Jill gets to spend time riding one of the several beautiful horses they own. Gary gets up when he wants and never has to work 7 days a week as he once did when they lived in New Jersey. Most of the other parents and neighbors wonder what is their secret. Well, today will tell you; there are no secrets. Just a passion to succeed and a "can-do" attitude.

As you read these stories, you're already comparing yourself to one of the students, aren't you? You can relate to their dreams and even some of their challenges. Here's a little background on Gary and Jill, so grab a plate and jump right in to this buffet of information!

Gary owned a heating oil company in New Jersey and Jill worked in customer service. When Jill was pregnant 12 years ago, she decided there had to be more to life. She told Gary she wanted to try real estate. Without much guidance from anyone, they bought their first home. It was a duplex they got a great price from an older gentleman who really wanted out. They cleaned it up a little and did a refinance. They ended up with $10,000 cash out of the refinance and had a $300 a month positive cash flow. This experience showed Gary and Jill the power of what real estate could do! I believe it can be an epiphany for people on the 9 to 5 treadmill. You work so hard at your job every day, every week, every month and every year, only to realize a 3% raise. Why not make your own opportunities by finding some killer deals that can help you accomplish some tremendous things?

This was a turning point in their lives. At the time, Gary was working 7 days a week and on call 24 hours a day. They had had enough and wanted to enjoy the birth of their first child. They decided to create a plan that would change their lives.

So one day, they decided to sell it all and move to sunny southern Florida. The money they got from selling everything allowed them to get in to a nice home and have some money to live on. But they knew that would not last, they had to do something. They continued with what they knew worked: real estate.

Gary admitted that he is "old school," and figured he had to learn it all on his own. And this couple was doing pretty darn well without my guidance. Gary told me that, in real estate, you have to think like an entrepreneur not a 9 to 5 worker. You have to take educated risks. Over-analyzing only causes you to do nothing; that won't work in real estate. You need to be prepared, do your homework, but once it is a good deal and you know it, you have to move!

One day, Gary called Jill in to watch the TV show about my book. He had always been skeptical about stuff on TV, but loved the fact I was talking in real terms. *"You seemed like a guy I could learn from,"* Gary said. He took a gamble and ordered my book; a gamble that would change Gary and Jill's life forever!

That is when the Gary and Jill team kicked it in to high gear. He found newer, cutting-edge ways to do what he had been doing, he learned more about foreclosures, and became a guru in smart marketing and negotiating tactics. In fact, Gary felt so confident of what he was learning that, using one of the creative funding techniques, secured a home equity line of credit on their home and used it like cash. *"That's when things started to take off,"* he said.

Even though Gary was "old school," he still had enough vision and confidence in me that he jumped on the first opportunity made available to him.

These two had always made a strong team as parents and investors, but now their roles really started to define themselves. Have you ever noticed that some teams form naturally? As members work together, roles become better defined as each member begins to excel in their area of expertise. For those teams that don't come together so naturally, others need a coach for direction. My Success Academy has coaches that can assist you in your team-building efforts. To find out more call **877-219-1473**.

Back to our story. Jill was on the computer every night searching Web sites to get the most information on available properties. Jill would search for deals every night after their son went to bed, looking for out-of-town owners, agents that were out of the area, and basically anything they thought was an eminent deal. And she loves doing it.

Your Town TIPS:
- Based on your area, do a little research and discover what your niche might be. For Jill, it was locating the out-of-town owners and real estate agents that were out of the area.
- Visit your county courthouse. You will be amazed at the vast amount of information that is made available to you.

Gary and Jill mostly focused on 2 to 3 bedroom, one-story ranch houses built in the 1960's, 70's and 80's for snowbirds (people who migrate south for the winter). They bought them for $25k to $75k, did a quick rehab and flipped them fast for a nice profit. Just like having your griddle filled with pancakes; you have to know when to flip them so they don't get burned!

Gary said the biggest secret to their success was that they bought for a insanely low price and then sold it for sort-of a low price with a profit in the middle. They wanted to make sure they could sell their homes fast when they were done, so they were willing to make a little less. This way, they were able to replace the money they used from their home equity line of credit.

After reading my book, Gary was pumped about working with foreclosures; he said it all just made sense. So Gary and Jill went on a "foreclosure hunt," buying vacant lots that were in foreclosure or a bank-owned REO (real estate owned). We will discuss REOs in greater detail later.

With their line of credit and profits from previous deals, the Cerianis now have cash to buy troubled deals. A little cash can go a long way as you discover REO's, foreclosures, desperate or motivated sellers. Gary and Jill saw an opportunity and they were in a position to jump on it.

While using my newfound techniques, Jill and Gary attended my live "Gain the EDGE 2009" event that took them to an even a higher level. Gary said the event was just tremendous and provided so much information and *"knowledge is power!"*

"You just have to bite the bullet and go for it. Don't over analyze. This is not a get rich quick program; it's a lifestyle for fulfillment," Gary said. *"Learn to be a problem solver. Don't focus on the problems, learn to find solutions! This is real world proven systems and techniques."* Let's see how Gary and Jill found some of those great deals.

Recipe #1 – "The $100k + Deal!"

The Ingredients
- Action – they didn't hesitate and over analyze, they got right into the deal
- Leveraged their Home Equity Line of Credit (HELOC)
- Located a probate opportunity
- Had a vision and saw a potential that others did not see

• Hired a builder to build a spec home
• Sell the home for a potential profit

Desired Result
This recipe starts by taking a plain vacant lot and turning into a desirable dish. Gary and Jill purchased a vacant lot that was in probate by leveraging the funds from their HELOC and hiring a builder to build a spec home on the land.

Preparation
The vacant lot was originally listed on MLS and Jill watched it daily for months. When the sign was taken off the lot and no longer listed on the MLS, Jill researched county records at the courthouse to get the owner's name. She found that owner of the lot lived out-of-state, and they sent him a letter.

Okay, let's take a look at some of the keys. It is important to watch your market to know what is happening with properties of interest. Look for price drops and time on the market; these are the ingredients for a motivated seller. A seller's motivation can change on a daily basis, so always be ready. Jill was ready, when she saw the owner lived out-of-state, this potential deal screamed "opportunity."

Turns out, the discouraged property owner just wanted get rid of the property, so the Cerianis bought it for $18,000. Some owners simply don't know what to do with their property. You become a solution to their problem! Because the Cerianis bought this lot for such a low price, they built a spec house they could sell really cheap and still make a profit. Notice how Gary and Jill had a plan and an exit strategy even before they started. This is a crucial step with any deal; knowing your exit strategy helps you craft better offers with maximum profit potential.

Garnish and Presentation

Once the spec house was built, they marketed the home themselves, pricing it according to their recipe of buy really low and sell sort of low.
The first person that looked at the home loved it, made a lower offer and left. This prospect lived out-of-state and had other houses to look at. Gary knew no other house the prospect looked at would be as new and affordable, so he waited until end of day, called potential buyer and said, "I know you went looking and probably didn't find anything as nice for

that price." The woman agreed, they settled on a price of $252,000 and a deal was made. It had been on the market for two days.

The profit they realized on the deal was over $100,000. They purchased the vacant lot for $18,000, hired a builder to build the spec home for $130,000, and sold the home for $252,000. Way to go, Gary and Jill! That's more than most couples make combined in one year working traditional 9 to 5 jobs.

Your Town TIPS:
- Take an inventory of all resources that you have available to do deals. Even if you have limited resources, a can-do attitude will go a long way in this business.
- Determine your exit strategy before you make an offer.
- Learn how to do research on your areas of interest.

Recipe #2 – "The Credit Card Deal!"

The Ingredients
- Leveraging funds from credit cards
- The ability to multi-task on more than one deal
- Network, network, network!
- Be creative and "think outside the box"
- A pinch of "how can I make this happen?" problem-solving skill

Desired Result
While in the middle of building the above-mentioned spec, the Cerianis were presented with an amazing opportunity, brought to them by the seller in a previous deal. This is a great example of how word-of-mouth can be a powerful marketing tool.

Sometimes, all the burners on your stove are going and there's no more room for any more pots. However, you have to prioritize, even if you have to rotate your pots.

Gary got the call about a house he knew they could make money with. The had just one problem: no more money left in their HELOC. It was all tied up building the spec house. But it was a deal that Gary and Jill do not want to pass up. "There's no way we were missing that deal," said Gary. It was a winner and they had to buy it! Now they needed to find the money.

Preparation

The Cerianis had this golden opportunity, but had to focus on finding a solution rather than worrying about not having the available funds. Jill thought he was nuts, but Gary took all their credit cards and secured $80,000 in cash advances. Because many of the credit cards had 3 to 6 months with minimal or no interest, this should not be considered bad credit card debt. Bottom line, Gary had an exit strategy and was leveraging an asset for a much bigger payoff.

Garnish and Presentation

They bought the home for $71,000 and worked as a team to renovate it in about 2 weeks. (They leveraged the $10,000 for repairs from their credit cards). At that time, Jill's father was ill, so the Cerianis did not market this home for sale on their own. They listed it with a real estate agent. A short 8 weeks from the day they bought it, the house sold for $135,000. After repaying all the credit cards and expenses, they made a profit of over $50,000! Now that's a way to use a credit card. Pretty impressive for a few months of work, isn't it? I bet the folks around the water cooler back in New Jersey still can't understand why Gary left his job to pursue real estate investing.

You may wonder, "How did they know it was a good deal?" They know because of their own research; Jill is online everyday, getting sold comps (not list prices) from their real estate agent. They get the "sell fast value" or "SFV" as we coined it earlier. Gary and Jill realized that they wanted to move the property and make a profit.

With homework and the right knowledge, you can build security and have confidence to go out there and do it! Also, remember that we are providing to you a "buffet of options" with a tremendous selection, something for everyone. It's up to you to fill your plate and come back as many times as you want!

Your Town TIPS:

- Know your market and research the comps for sold properties in your target areas
- Network and let everyone know your name and that you're in the real estate game!
- Try to be organized, multi-task, and have great time management

Recipe #3 – "The Unadvertised Deals!"

The Ingredients
• Find the homes that are for sale without a sign
• Network, network, network
• Pass out as many business cards as people will take
• Gather your information and make an offer to a motivated seller

Desired Result
Jill would often drive around local neighborhoods, looking for garage and estate sales. She wasn't looking for cheap dishes or cassette tapes, she wanted to talk to the owner to see if the house was going to be for sale soon.

Preparation
Jill wants to find the homes that are not advertised by a "for sale" sign. This way, you can really limit your competition on any deal. The key is to network with a wide variety of people and find the deals that others wish they knew were out there.

Garnish and Presentation

From an estate sale that Jill stopped by, the Cerianis ended up buying not one but two homes from the owner who lived out of state. From stopping this one estate sale, Gary and Jill made $18,000 in three and a half weeks on two homes they bought with HELOC money. It gets even better: while they were starting to renovate these two homes, someone stopped by and bought them both!

Gary and Jill have perfected their niche. They go to county clerk's Web sites to find where tax bills are sent, how much was paid for home, what is owed, if taxes are paid, see if they are in foreclosure, and more. As you can see, information really is power! Search your county clerk's office Web site by Googling "court county clerk's office" for your local county. You may be amazed at how much information is available to you at your fingertips.

This couple has done tremendously well with their deals to date but they are always looking for new opportunities. They have been researching probates and have developed a passion for them. Jill loves out-of-area owners and out-of-area real estate agents. The out-of-area real estate agents don't have the pulse of what is going on in other markets, making it easier to negotiate a deal. The out-of-area families that are involved with probates are most eager to sell and receive their cash.

Unlike most people you may have read about in the book, the Cerainis did not build a huge team. As a couple, they love doing the renovations themselves, so they try to buy homes they know they can handle fixing up. If they have to go into deeper repairs, then they go to their "next level" repair team.

As far as real estate agents, they barely use them. The couple has had great success marketing and selling their own properties. Since they stick with buying really low and selling sort of a low, they always have a great product that is less expensive than anything on the market. By not having a real estate agent, it lets Gary and Jill sell their homes for a lower price because there will be no commissions paid.

As for deals, you never know when a seller's motivation will change. A deal they involved a 2 bedroom, 2-bath home with a 2-car garage with 1600 sq. ft. of living space. It was owned by an older gentleman from Massachusetts. His daughters handed the home and listed it at $79,000. Gary and Jill offered $52,000 and it was rejected. Then one month later, they received a call from the agent. Family members were fighting, they wanted it sold ASAP, and the Cerainis offer was now accepted.

I like to call these "boomerang" properties. Just throw the offers out there and you will get a few of them that come back to you a few weeks or even a few months later!

It is always important for you to keep on the pulse of the market and see opportunities before others do. Gary and Jill said their market has changed. Their new strategy for going forward is to focus on properties that have been on the market for a long period of time rather than fighting to get the less inexpensive properties where competition is now at its highest level. I am sure Gary and Jill will continue to thrive in the Sunshine State.

Your Town Action Items:

• Visit garage and estate sales to see if you can discover any opportunities on properties.

- Determine your target area for investing, get to know the market and determine what would be the sell fast value (SFV).
- Look into possible financing options such as HELOCS or low interest credit cards. Remember, there are many no-money-down techniques, but you need to have other options for those deals where you need to act fast.

CHAPTER 13

Becoming the local real estate expert in your town!

Let's continue our journey to discover deals in your town and local market area. The following question comes often: "This is all great information that I am learning, Dean, I know there are deals out there, but how do I locate the deals in my town?" Congratulations! Now you're thinking about creating that action plan and how to get it started. You're on the right track; the following resource chapters will provide a combination of content, exercises and information.

In the next chapter, we look at how to find properties, from Web searches to newspaper ads. This chapter will teach you how to learn about your local market, who your buyers and sellers are, where they want to live, and trends that can make all the difference in your profitability. It's not necessary that you use all of these resources, but knowing they're out there is important. Let me say that again. It is not important that you use every resource, it's important that you know they exist.

I bought a significant number of properties in Iowa and Illinois without having to do much research. Why? How? Because my partner and I took the hired an amazing real estate agent with a pulse on the area we were investing in. She knew all the comps, what was selling, what was not. She knew what a good deal was and when a great deal popped up. She could tell us what that house would sell for right away as well as what the rent would bring. We hired right and the benefits are massive. And the best part is that your real estate agent only makes money when you make money. So let's learn how you can add the right people to your team to do it right.

I often talk about having the right tool for the job. When you start a project, you bring a toolbox to the job site. You may not use all the tools all of the time, but at least you have them if you need them. So as you read, keep placing those tools of knowledge in your toolbox. You never know when you may need them.

When I was young, I would often claim that I didn't like broccoli. My grandmother would often say, "Dean, how do you know you don't like broccoli?"

I would reply, "I know I don't like it."

"Have you tried it before?" she asked.

"No."

"Dean, do you like chocolate chip cookies?" Gram asked.

"YES! I love chocolate chip cookies!"

"How do you know you like them?" was gram's question.

"I've had them before!"

Gram said, "You tried them and know you like them? What if you never would had tried a cookie?" asked gram.

"Okay, okay, I will try the broccoli!"

This conversation taught me a valuable lesson: you have to try things that are new or different. At times, you'll just find broccoli but other times you will find your next chocolate chip cookie!

Your Town Tips:
- Each day we learn from what we do, what we try, and what we experience. Part of our process includes the lessons we learn and discover along the way.
- The lessons we learn today will prepare us for tomorrow and guide us in reaching our goals.
- Okay, we are now ready to jump in and tackle this market analysis. Preparation is the key to getting started. Picture running a race. You line up and will hear: "READY"......"SET".......GO!"

Your market area can be defined as the area where you want to concentrate your investing efforts. You may not think there are any deals here. So let's talk about how to find a deal in YOUR town!

So, let's talk about your town, your neighborhood and your local area.

There are deals everywhere; we just have to create our plan to find these deals in your town, right? Are you ready? Great, let's get started!

First, we will look at a general plan for your area to assess your market. As we determine the market analysis, it will help to determine what types of deals you want, such as flip the home, assign the home, or buy and hold the home for a future stream of income.

When looking for deals, most people look in their exact area because they feel comfortable. The key to remember is that you do not have to find deals in only the homes you would want to live in. Thus, what I mean is that a good deal is not only the type of home and price range you currently have.

For instance, if you happen to live in a typical middle-class home, you may believe that you need to look at middle-class or high-end homes to find a deal or future rental. A key here is to see what others do not see! You may find great deals in a neighborhood with lower-priced homes. You want to find homes that will appeal to the people because of their affordability. Every area has homes that are in different price ranges and we are going to do the analysis in your town to assess the different homes and the different price levels. Your goals will determine the home you purchase in your town or a town near yours. Thus, the analysis is important to determine where your treasure is how to get there.

Your Town Tips:
- Select a price range of homes to keep on your radar, that you track, watch and begin to learn the market.
- Do not only focus or concentrate on your price range of homes that you currently live in or the homes you want to live in. The deals that you complete can be in any area or any neighborhood.
- Remember you do not have to live in the neighborhood where you choose to invest in real estate.

Market Overview Questions

Let's take a look at your local market areas. By answering the following "Market Overview Questions" it will provide a better idea of your local area real estate market.

You can jot down these questions and your answers to organize the beginning of your market analysis process. We also have these forms at the Web site at ***www.deangraziosi.com/yourtown/forms.*** As you review and gather information, we use the term "town," but many find that they're answering these questions for subdivisions, neighborhoods, multiple zip codes, or other areas inside or around their town. Do this exercise for every area in which you may want to invest.

What is the major zip code?

This will help you in searching the Internet real estate sites for properties. Get a zip code map of your town or investment area and make notes about the general real estate makeup of each one. One might be heavily industrial or commercial, while another may be completely single family residential.

What zip codes border your town?

It's always fun to locate a really profitable deal just a block outside of the area you had targeted. Don't let your success be restricted by too tight of a focus.

What types of properties are in your town?

Just jot down the property types you may want to consider, such as condos, single family detached, duplexes, multi-family, town homes or apartments. Note which one you need to learn more about. As an example, if you don't know the town's zoning treatment of duplexes, you'll want to get that information.

What nicknames are given for parts of your town?

Does your town have specific nicknames of the local area, such as north side, east side, west side or south side.? I know a friend of mine in Chicago would often talk about the neighborhoods by nickname such as the Loop, Bucktown, Andersonville or the Gold Coast. Get to know your area and the nicknames that may be associated in larger cities.

How many of each property type are for sale now?

Go to Web sites that have all of the local listings, and search by type, recording the number on the market right now. More on using Web searches for property data and listings is in the next chapter.

Determine property use by area.

By identifying areas by the primary property use, you may turn up opportunities. Is an area mostly homeowners with very few renters, or a high percentage of renters? Jot down an estimate of the percentage of rentals to owner occupied homes in areas.

Where are property types concentrated?
Either by name or mapping determines areas heavy in any one property type, such as condos or apartments.

What are general price ranges by area and type?
Many times condos and single-family homes are in the same area. Knowing the price ranges relative to each other can yield opportunities. There may be buyers out there who want to live in a trendy area of single-family homes, but can't afford it. Knowing about condos at lower prices can be a big advantage for you.

What are the prevailing rents in your town?
Knowing what rents are by property type, size, bedrooms, etc. will help you to recognize a profitable investment in a home or multi-family property.

By area, what's most expensive, least expensive and average price?
Knowing the highest, lowest and average priced properties in your town or a smaller area or subdivision will help in valuation later.

What are the pricing patterns in your area?
Try to look for patterns such as pricing being different in certain areas of the town. For example, are the properties in the north side of town more expensive than maybe the other parts of the town?

What are ratios of owner occupied vs. rentals?
What is the average ratio between owner occupied properties and rentals? A good real estate agent or a property management company can probably tell you an average and where the higher concentration of rentals are located. Based on these areas, look at the rents that you can charge.

Where are the properties advertised?
Prepare a list of where properties are listed in your area: magazines, newspapers, on-line, bulletin boards, etc. Be specific and check these areas frequently. Often you can even have a family member assist you by picking up those "free home books" the next time they make a trip to the grocery store.

What is the ratio of FSBO properties in an area?
You can't be exact here, but get a general idea of how many For Sale By Owner properties are in an area as compared to listed properties in the MLS.

Don't worry about writing all of these questions down, as reminder we have created a form ready to write in the answers to these and more questions about your town's real estate market. Here's a piece of that form, and you can get the whole form on my Web site at ***www.dean-graziosi.com/yourtown/forms.***

Market Overview Form Data Gathering for Your Town	
Question	**Complete your answer**
1. What is the zip code(s) of your town or city?	
2. What are other town's zip codes that border your town or city?	
3. What are the types of properties such as condos, townhomes, single family homes, duplexes, multi-unit apartment buildings, etc. in your town?	
4. Does your town have specific nicknames of the local area, such as north side, east side, west side	

Your Town Action Items:
- Complete the Market Analysis Overview form
- Find 3 FSBO properties this week and call on them.
- Determine what price range are the most plentiful
- Determine what price ranges sell the fastest

Your Town Tips:
- Contact specific rental properties that are advertised in your local area.
- Separate the properties by zip code in your town if there is more than one zip code. Inquire to the landlords about their properties.
- A key to inquire about for the local market is what features make "their" rental property more special or unique over other properties. This will allow you to see what they view as important. It could be school systems, near parks, near expressways not being located near railroad tracks, etc.

CRUISE NIGHT AROUND YOUR TOWN

Let's go cruise around your town. The purpose of the cruise is to try to see things you have not seen before and become more familiar with the streets around your neighborhood. Pretend this is your first time here and you're taking in the sights as you drive. If you drive by a mini retail mall, did you ever notice each and every business? Which ones did you miss? A local street map always comes in handy. If you want to drive the area and look for some FSBOs, then take the road less traveled! These roads may only be a few blocks long, a one-way street or have a dead end, but they might contain the hidden gems you are looking for!

You can also print out maps at the following Web sites:
www.mapquest.com
www.maps.google.com
www.bing.com/maps

Your Town Tips:
- Purchase a street map of your area to easily locate streets in your local area and discover patterns of property listings in your as you may decide to put a dot of where homes are currently listed in your local area.
- You local city hall or the local real estate agent could even offer a free map of the area or have a map available for a nominal fee.
- When driving your area, always be aware of what is happening in each community or specific blocks of your town. If you notice an area has several large dumpsters where people are doing rehabs, this could be an indication of an area that may be a little more attractive for a real estate investment or deal.

Your Town Activity Action:
- Take a map of your local area and put small little dots where the current homes are located for sale. Do you see a pattern or cluster of homes? Clusters of many homes in a certain area can indicate motivated sellers or an issue in that area. Thus, learn about the area and it checks out good, then start in that area. The more sellers that are not selling create more motivated sellers.
- As drive through your neighborhood and notice different properties, be sure to complete the Rehab Tracker form, the FSBO form, and the Rental Tracker form.
- On future drives, try to complete the Cruising Game and guess prices of new listings

Rehab Tracker Form

As you drive through your neighborhood, you may see other properties being rehabbed with dumpsters in the street or yard. Complete your rehab tracker notes form to keep track of current rehabs in your area. If you have time talk with people, you may even meet the owner. The owner could be an investor and become a future buyer if you locate deals in the area. Or the property owner could be a valuable resource to network with and share contractor contacts. Many rehabs in a certain area could result in an area of town becoming more desirable in the future. Thus, you may be able to pinpoint the hot part of town for investments.

FSBO form

Complete your For Sale by Owner (FSBO) form as you drive your neighborhood. You may see a "Take One" box or canister tube by the FSBO sign. If you do see the "Take One" box, I often take two; one copy for my notes and a clean copy for my file. Thus, you will complete your FSBO form with the property address and phone contact information. Then, when you get home, you can call on the FSBOs you have located while driving the neighborhood.

Rental Tracker form

Complete your rental tracker form as you see "For Rent" signs while driving your neighborhood. You can write down the street and contact number and then call when you get home. This information may provide a better idea of where most of the rental properties are in your town. You may also begin to see patterns where certain areas of town can command higher amounts for rent. Also, these landlords could become a great resource to network with for information or could even become a future buyer.

The Cruising Game

As you check out the area, your goal is to become familiar with properties and the range of price they may be selling in. When you see a new listing, play a little game by trying to guess the asking price, size of the home, etc. This information can be verified later but over time and after looking at several properties, it is amazing how you will become better at this game!

Free Magazines, Home Books, Thrifty Nickel, and Craigslist

While you are cruising around town, stop off at a few gas stations or supermarkets. Often by the exit doors of these businesses you will find free home listing books of the properties in your surrounding area. You may even find specialized books such as waterfront properties, or FSBOs. Pick up whatever is available. Also pick up the free local newspapers, such as the Thrifty Nickel.

You are not looking for anything specific, just casually look through each of these resources. Then go online to www.craigslist.com and look in your local area for properties for sale. Once again, you are only casually looking to just see the amount of properties in your area. You never may have had an idea that there were so many properties for sale. As more properties come on the market, it may motivate sellers to make price adjustments on their properties.

Your Town Action Tip:
In the future, when you go through the free magazines, look for ads for other professionals that may become part of your network. Often real estate attorneys, mortgage brokers, etc. will advertise in these publications.

Print Media for Research

Answering those market overview questions will involve a great deal of reading and combing through print publications. Whether newspapers, home magazines, or specialty real estate publications, there is a lot of valuable information in print. By valuable, I mean information that helps you to put together a "big picture" view of your market. Also, you can really get a firm grip on areas that are likely to thrive in the future based on items in print about local activities and initiatives.

There simply is NO unimportant information! Everything you learn is going to give you an edge in locating great real estate deals. What you'll find out very quickly is that there are far more opportunities out there than you ever imagined. You just didn't recognize them before, because you didn't have the knowledge and tools you're learning in this book. Once you start looking armed with this knowledge, you'll be presented with a great many more possible investment situations than you can research in depth. Using these techniques, you can quickly rule out the less lucrative, and concentrate your valuable time and efforts on those that have the greatest potential.

News That Yields Opportunity

If you're constantly reading local real estate related articles, you will learn about areas in favor, possible problem high crime areas, or new parks or green belts that will make an area more appealing. What about new mass transit, or extensions of existing routes and services? If a subdivision out 15 miles suddenly gets tacked onto a light rail route, would it be more in demand by buyers, or renters? The same could be asked if a widening of a major highway corridor is announced. If you're trying to evaluate two similar investments, knowing that one is about to become an easier and faster commute could make the difference.

Your Town Tip:
• Often local cities, towns and counties have press releases and they may even post committee meetings on their Web sites. If your local area posts these committee meeting minutes (such as the zoning committee or city council), review the minutes of the meetings to find gems of new or developing information. It may not be news covered by the local paper, but the news of recent approvals could be some great information you discover because of your extensive research effort.
• Also, a good source is to see if your area has an Economic Development committee. Their entire job is to promote growth and bring in new projects, so see what they are up to.

National print media shouldn't be ignored either. Newspapers and magazines that write about national real estate trends have the resources to commission surveys that can tell you something about your market. Recently I read an article in a national magazine that mentioned cities are learning that people want more walking or local mass transit and less driving, particularly when it comes to getting to work. Some cities are looking at large abandoned commercial sites, or obsolete local government facilities for conversion to residential areas. These sites are in and around the urban areas where the jobs are. Using less expensive gas, getting a little exercise, and spending more time with family instead of work travel is appealing to people today.

You might say the fact that it's already in the news makes it old news as far as taking advantage. Don't believe it. If you're keeping up with discussions in your town about possible major urban redevelopment, you're ahead of 90% of the general population. Knowing that a new park and dedicated residential area is about to be developed to replace a government facility is important. A home that becomes available, whether listed, a FSBO, or an REO may be just outside this new planned development. You just may pick up a healthy profit by doing a rehab on an REO that's about to be a block from a new green belt or higher priced new homes.

Real Estate Brokerage Ads Tell Us a Lot

Pay attention to the advertising done by major real estate brokerages. Check out the keywords and property description phrases they use. It isn't always industry jargon. They deal in property sales in all areas every day. If a broker is really playing heavily on "perfect executive home" for one area, you might want to take a look at a rental income property there. Real estate agents will tend to market the features they're most asked about in an area. They'll push the most desired features in their newspaper and homes magazine ads. When you can locate a deep discount buy with the features that are being touted in an area, you may just have a gem of a deal recipe in the making.

This approach works on the selling side as well. If you're flipping a home, or selling a rental you've had for a while, take a look at the real estate ads for the area. Again, these brokers work with buyers and sellers every day in that area, and they know what amenities are in demand. It's free research, but it's valuable to know that the home you're flipping has a feature that's in demand right now in that area. You also may learn that a minor project or inexpensive remodel job can net you more than the cost because it's in demand and not present in the competing homes.

Don't forget new homebuilder and subdivision ads. Builders try to keep up with the very latest features that homebuyers want. Also, if the homes are affordable, you may see some features that you can incorporate in a remodel that will help you sell or rent a home faster and for a better price. Check out new subdivision ads, and builder features, comparing them and looking for trends in materials or amenities.

- *Bedrooms:* 4
- *Baths:* 2.5
- *Living:* 1
- *Garage:* 3.0
- *Optional Finished Basement:* Yes

Home Lifestyle:

- Working From Home
- Movie Buff
- Outdoor Living
- Cooking and Entertaining
- Focus on the Family
- Big Game Players
- Formal Dining

Description:
Features include: Tile floors, granite tile countertops in kitchen, berber carpet, upgraded tile in all the bathroom, central vac system, speakers throughout the home, front and rear yard landscape, built ins throughout.

Visit Today!

Homes for Rent Ads for Market Information

Knowing your market inside and out, including the prevailing rents in each area, will help you to identify potential profitable purchases. If you know that 3 bedroom homes in a certain area or neighborhood are renting at the top end of the price range, you will be far more likely to recognize a profitable deal in a home when it comes up for sale in that area, and has three or more bedrooms. You'll become very good at looking at the home's asking price and converting that into your costs to own. It's just one faster step to see if prevailing rents would result in positive cash flow.

If you really like to keep up, watch for how fast certain properties disappear from the rental ads. Or make a friend or two in property management companies. If your real estate investing team includes a property manager, ask them to keep you current on what renters are demanding and paying more for. It could be really valuable information to know that renters are requesting a small third bedroom for a home office much more than a washer and dryer. Or, you realize that a couple of rental condo or apartment projects seem to have far fewer vacancies than others. Check them out to see what's different. Whether it's location, price, or amenities, it's valuable information for your business.

Taking the Caravan Approach to Learning Your Market

Why do real estate agents do weekly or monthly caravans, going through all the homes listed in an area? They know that it's in their best interest to promote their listings to other real estate agents, but the tramping through the homes is also to their benefit. They see features, learn similarities in homes in an area, and get a feel for relative pricing by walking through these listings. Non-real estate agents are rarely allowed to go on these caravans, but you have a great resource for similar results.

You have "open houses." Whether it's a FSBO seller showing off their home on their own, or a professional real estate agent sponsoring an open house, these homes are inviting you in for the purpose of attracting possible buyers. You should take advantage of every one that you can. Pick up the literature that they're offering, and fill a file cabinet with it if you need to. Whether you have an interest in a home you visit or not, what you learn about it is valuable. Take notes, make a file folder for each property, and put flyers and literature into it. File them by area, neighborhood or subdivision.

If you have no interest in this home, why go to the trouble of filing information on it? At some point in the future, you're likely to have an interest in another home in that area. You can pull out your file and refresh your memory as to the features, size and details of the home you visited, and compare them to the one you're looking at. As far as this use of your files, it will be far more valuable to you if you also followed up when they sold to note the selling price in your file. Think about one day seeing a 3 bedroom, 2-bath home for sale at a listed price of $210,000. It's two blocks away, and very similar to, a home you visited as an open house a few months ago. You pull your file, and look at the contents, discovering that they're very similar, but the other home sold for $245,000. This could be a great deal in the making!

Your Own Caravan Approach for Market Research

We previously discussed getting a feel for your market by just going out on the town for a cruise around town. We're learning about our town, and the properties that will be our business in the future. We'll talk about actually searching for properties in the next chapter, but for now, it's about learning your town's real estate market.

Map out your drives, so as not to skip whole streets or neighborhoods. Those short streets, one way streets or streets that are the "roads less traveled" may contain some real potential gems to look into. Since most people do not drive that way, they may never see the for sale signs for properties in these areas. Take it slow, and pay attention to things like the location of parks, sidewalks, shopping, schools, and employment. A good approach is to print a map of your route for this drive, taking notes on it as you go. This can then be filed in your neighborhood sorted filing system we just discussed. Over time, you're building a detailed neighborhood profile, ready to pull out and use in a first-look assessment of a potential investment. If you're into technology, the new Microsoft Live Maps and Google Maps are both offering street level views and very detailed satellite views of areas. You can pull up an area you're about to drive through and print the street map, then the detailed satellite view as well. As you drive, you can mark reference numbers on the maps and write notes for those numbers for your file. This doesn't have to be a chore, but even a couple of notes about something like a few homes in the middle of a mostly commercial area could yield an opportunity later.

Take these drives like you would if you were new to the area and considering moving there. We definitely take a closer look when the result will be the purchase of a home for our family. Driving through as a potential new resident, you'll see things as your future tenant or buyer will see them. Write down your impressions in your map notes. Every bit of information is helpful later if you're considering a deal in that area. You'll be thanking yourself when you pull out that file folder and find a ton of information before you even go out to drive by a potential property.

There's No Substitute for Market Knowledge

The more information we can learn on a subject the better decisions that we can make. Keep learning as much as you can about real estate and how different things that happen in your area may impact your local market. The knowledge you obtain will continue to open new doors of opportunities for you. Never stop learning about your town, business trends, who's moving where, what subdivisions are hot and in demand. If you are like most of my students, you'll love your new real estate investing business, and this won't be work for you. It will be fun, and it will give you the opportunity to create win-win deals by helping people along the way!

In this chapter we really touched on the grass roots way to know your local market. I believe there is no better way to get a feel for what is going on in your area. But know this, like I mentioned before, a relationship with a great real estate agent can be worth its weight in gold. He or she may be able to tell you in a snap what the FMV of a home is and what the SFV is (Sell Fast Value), what neighborhoods are desirable and which ones are not. So building a solid team is just that important and you will learn that soon.

And if you want to go really deep on knowing real estate cycles, you can find a section in my book "Be A real Estate Millionaire" that goes into great detail, explaining how local and national factors influence real estate cycles. Check it out at ***www.deangraziosi.com/yourtown/factors*** to get that section of the book for free.

CHAPTER 14
Finding Deals

I hope you've tried some or all of the methods for learning your town's real estate market in the previous chapter. Though you can just jump out there and try to find deals, it's a lot riskier if you do it without general market knowledge. In fact, that's a quick way to learn that something was "too good to be true" the hard way. The knowledge you gain from walking through an exercise can be priceless.

So, you've developed a solid overview of your town, where people are moving to, and where they're moving away from, as well as what they are buying and renting in the way of features. Now it's time to go out and find a deal. In the student stories, you saw how these methods were used to close profitable real estate deals. In this chapter, I will give you the how-tos of those techniques. Depending on timing, your target customer or property type, or just your preferences, you'll use more than one of these techniques to find your next great deal!

Web Site Real Estate Listing Search Sites

The Internet has become a dominating force in the marketing of real estate. Listing sites are everywhere. What's very important to your invest-ment objectives is to know where you can find ALL of the opportunities out there. And, though many major real estate Web site portals lead you to believe that they have all of the listings, none of them do. Each has value, but you'll want to use more than one Internet resource for locat-ing properties. You will probably even develop your favorite sites that you believe give you the most information and leads for your area. Be sure to be consistent and setup your routine to check for new listings. Sometimes if you are the first one to find and call on a deal, you can get it locked up faster than your competition.

Realestateagent.com
The largest site, realestateagent.com, says that it has them all, and if you mean all of the ones that Realtors list, then it does come close. The National Association of Realtors run this site, and the listings you find there are a collection of all of the local member associations around the

country. But, recently a few local associations, some quite large, have withdrawn their listings from the site. So, ALL listings aren't there. Another thing to know about realestateagent.com is that it takes the local MLS listing data and breaks out what the site wants to display.

Listings are sorted on this site by a number of criteria you select. You will also be looking at paid ads for real estate agents. This doesn't mean the site isn't one you should use, as Lubertha found properties in Detroit on it while she lived in New York. I believe the site is very helpful for investigating markets you are interested in.

I often find new real estate agents in other areas by their number of listings. For example, if I am looking into a property in New Buffalo, Michigan, 49117, I can search listings under zip code 49117 and locate all listings for that zip code. I then group the listings by agent and/or office and see which agents have the most listings for that area. These agents usually can save you the most time and effort because they have a pulse of their local markets. Thus, if I ran across a home in New Buffalo Michigan and I live 2,000 miles across the country, I could locate the local expert to provide very helpful information on the area and their local market. However, you can also look for local MLS IDX sites, as well, and we'll talk about those next.

Local Realtor MLS Search Sites
MLS, Multiple Listing Service, the Web sites for members of the National Association of Realtors, made an agreement with IDX, Internet Data Exchange, for their listing information. This means that any member who wants to (the vast majority do) allows their listing info to be displayed on their competitors' Web sites in an IDX search. So, if you're searching, you're seeing all of the area listings, not just those of the listing broker whose site you're on. You still won't see FSBOs, and you may not see foreclosures, unless the bank lists with a local real estate agent. But, if you want to see listed properties, these sites are pretty comprehensive. There's usually some kind of disclaimer on the site and some version of the IDX and Realtor logos.

The limitation here is that each MLS decides which information fields are allowed in an IDX search. Many times, less than half of the available fields of information are displayed. You'll generally end up on these sites with a Google or other search on "**the town** real estate" search phrases. Please don't forget to use the tool that my team and I created for you at www. totalviewrealestate.com.

In Eric Himebaugh's story, he told us about getting a local real estate agent to send him MLS printouts of what the agents see. He wasn't able to get all of the information he needed from the IDX search page. In his case, it was the owner's name, but it could be any of a number of important fields of information. I know of rural MLS that doesn't give you the acreage in their IDX listings. Think about that, as you could be trying to compare two homes in a listing search and can't figure out why one is much more expensive. In this area, it could be because one is on a quarter acre lot and the other is on 10 acres.

You have to remember this is all done for a reason. If you had all the information, then you may not contact the real estate agent's site that you saw the listing on. They want you to contact them so you can become a client. This does not make them bad; they are just trying to create business. When building your investment team, it may not be a bad place to start looking for the right real estate agent if you don't have a lead or referral from someone you trust. Also, remember, that you can work with more than one real estate agent because you never know who is going to be your "A-team" player.

The fact is; there is a lot of information missing. But it can be a great way to start and narrow down your list. Whether you establish a new relationship or have a current one with a real estate agent, asking him or her to give you detailed information on any properties you are interested in should be a piece of cake. Remember, once you build your "A-team," your real estate agent will be doing most of the legwork and searching for you for free. This is the power of leverage. We all have 24 hours in a day; most of us just use and leverage our time differently. The more professionals' time you can leverage by having them assist you with your investing efforts, the more time you will have available to locate more leads.

Also, if you would like, your real estate agent should be able to set you up with an automated alert system. They put in your search criteria of size, bedrooms, price range, etc. Then the system sends you e-mails of the reports as new listings come on the market, and many will also send you price and status changes. It can be pretty exciting to see deals in your inbox everyday that are close or fit your criteria.

What's a "status change," and why would you want them? Again, it's important information about your market to know what's happening, and a status change from "Active Listing" to "Sold" will alert you to contact your agent and ask what it sold for. Print out the listing, and note the sold price on it for your file. You're building your own "comparable solds" price list. What about a status change from active to "withdrawn" or "expired?" This means that the period they signed for has ended and they didn't renew their listing, or they pulled it off the market early. I have bought more then one property that was newly expired. The sellers were fed up that it did not sell and more motivated than ever at that point to sell. Many times, the seller will go out looking for a new real estate agent and while they are looking, it's a good time to contact them. In some cases, since their contract has run out, they no longer have a sales commission to pay and your savings at that point could be huge. I bought my dad a home exactly this way. You also want to look for price changes as well, this combined with someone have a listing with the terms "motivated seller" or "must sell," may lead to a great opportunity or a homeowner who's given up and is in trouble with their mortgage. It is important to remember that the timing of your offer could be everything!

Web-focused real estate agents will usually have a prominent link or button on their IDX search page to alert you to the fact that you can save your search and get these automated alerts. You're not using up their time, though you may get some junk e-mail marketing once you're in their system.

One more thing about these automated alert systems that make them extremely valuable. Real estate agents, even in slow times, have a lot of things going on. They do have a "hotsheet" report in their MLS system that alerts them to new listings, status and price changes, but most of them don't look at it every morning. In fact, many of them don't go over it even weekly. What does this mean for you? You're getting information in your e-mail inbox that they haven't yet seen. You know about significant price changes before most agents do!

I know this has helped one investor with an amazing buy in a resort and vacation home market. She was receiving these automated alerts for homes priced under $200k, a really tough price range in this market of high-end ski resort vacation homes. There were a few foreclosures listed by agents in the MLS, but they didn't generally hit the market as bargains, as the banks know the market well. She just watched her alerts, and particularly one home. This home was an REO, and it had sold for well over $200k to the owner who lost it in foreclosure. It listed at just over $200k. She just waited and watched. It went through five price drops before it hit her magic number, and she called the agent who set up her alerts and said, "Time to make an offer." Now, this was on the day the price change was made, and they got that offer in immediately. It took several days for most of the local agents to see it on their "hot sheets," and several more days for them to contact their prospects that might have an interest. In that time the deal was locked up at $120,000! All the others could do was submit backup offers, four of them in fact.

You're going to learn a number of ways to locate profitable real estate deals in this chapter. But when you can get set up with an automated alert system to bring possible deals to your e-mail every day, why wouldn't you? By setting your price and other criteria tightly, you can limit your alerts to a narrow range of possible properties that won't take up a lot of your time to check over the listing report.

Homegain.com
Homegain is a site that allows you to search by state and local areas, and their listings include some MLS listed properties, new homes, and foreclosure listings. Homegain also has a search function just to locate agents in your areas of choice. You can get reports and information anonymously from multiple agents, and then select the one you want to do business with.

Trulia and Zillow
These two other sites have grown quite sizeable and popular. They have real estate agent-entered listings, syndicated listings, new homes, some foreclosures and some For Sale By Owner listings as well. They also have real estate agent advertisements. Zillow has a comment function where viewers of listings can enter their opinions of the listing.

ForeclosureAlert.com
You can't argue with the value of a listing of foreclosure properties to the real estate investor. When banks are holding properties, their goal is to get them off the books, offering value and opportunity to the investor who locates them and knows how to work the foreclosure market. ForeclosureAlert.com offers one of the most comprehensive listings of foreclosure properties in the world. And, with your ability to search by more than a dozen criteria and location fields, you can zero in on bargains like a laser.

This site will give you daily foreclosure alerts for properties right in your backyard. Locating the right property as early as possible has made fortunes for many real estate investors. Even if it's not priced right when first listed, this site makes it easy to follow the property, timing your offer when the price hits that magic number you've been waiting for.

Other very large and popular real estate search sites also market themselves as one-stop resources. This simply isn't the case; they don't have them all. I want you to know this, because there isn't a one-stop resource. Even the local real estate broker sites that advertise all of the MLS listings do not have FSBO homes, and many don't have foreclosures. Over time, you'll develop your favorite resources on the Web, and you'll use more than one.

Don't forget to try out www.totalviewrealestate.com. It's an amazing site to help you research, view, get comps and so much more all in one place and it's free.

FSBO Ads Can Be a Gold Mine

As far as print media and FSBO homes, the Thrifty Nickel and newspaper classified ads are both great resources. The owner selling on their own will usually place ads in any and all inexpensive advertising media. There won't be detailed information, considering that they're paying based on words or lines used, but you'll get alerted to homes that aren't listed, and may be available at nice discounts to value. It takes some time to scan these ads every day, but it can bring you many profitable opportunities. Some sellers will use their classified word or line allotment carefully, mentioning the best features of their home with their contact information. Using what I've mentioned already about gaining market knowledge, you'll be able to quickly identify FSBO homes with the right features in the areas where you want to invest.

Craigslist, as we learned in Jan and Jeremy's story, brought them their first deal, and it was a highly profitable 4 unit rental. Jeremy considers the FSBO listings on Craigslist to be one of his most valuable tools for finding deals. Because it's free, the cost-conscious for sale by owner seller considers it a great place to show off their home. And, you may pick up on desperation or motivation to sell in their ad wording. FSBO sellers are so important, and the ways we deal with them so specialized, that I'm devoting a full chapter to this subject later. So stay tuned!

Craigslist and eBay

We mentioned Craigslist in relation to FSBO properties. But there are others listing homes for sale there and on eBay as well. Real estate agents use Craigslist a lot, with some sites offering automated syndication to these sites when an agent fills in their listing information and uploads photos. Because of the popularity of Craigslist, every individual, bank, or estate trustee may find it an easy and free place to advertise real estate.

And, when you read next about homes-for-rent ads in print, just extend that thought to Craigslist as well. It's a huge resource to locate rental properties. As you've read in my student's stories and deal recipes, a great many purchases and resales as well have come from an initial contact with a person advertising a rental. Craigslist allows you to localize and search quickly with your criteria for price, bedrooms, and other features.

Homes for Rent Ads Bring Sellers and Buyers

When you're reading the deals in this book, several of my students tell you that they found the home they purchased by calling on "home for rent" ads in the paper. Why would you call to buy a home that's for rent? There are a great many landlords out there who are just plain tired of that role. There are also landlord owners who haven't taken good care of their properties, and they're experiencing lower rental income and more repair issues. They have been called by my students and responded happily to an expressed interest in taking their landlord problems off their hands.

Lubertha Cox told us how she found an agent when she called a landlord. This resulted in a buyer referral later. Greg Murphy calls on rental ads to find homeowners who are in trouble and would really just want to be out from under their home and mortgage. They haven't been able to sell it, and now they may even be having trouble renting it for enough to pay the mortgage. Once he locates a distressed or tired homeowner, he offers them a lease purchase deal that almost nobody turns down.

You are a real estate investor running a business. It's going to work for you to tell them that on these calls. Even if they really want to keep the property for rental, they may be perfect for your Buyer List. If it's working for them, they may like the idea of buying another property. You really don't care which way this conversation goes, as you have a way to help them whether they're in the mood to buy or sell. Every name you add to one of your contact lists, whether it's buyers, sellers, bankers or other investors, is a potential deal in the making.

Divorce Attorneys

How many attorneys does it take...? We've all heard the jokes. But, it only takes one to hand you a profitable deal. Get to know the attorneys in your town. Those who handle divorces are important resources. In divorce, there is usually a need to sell the home and other real estate to divide the marital assets. Neither spouse has the cash to buy the other out, so selling is the only way. Cultivating relationships with divorce attorneys can get you in the door before they list with an agent, obligating them to a commission that raises the listing price. I know one investor who does quite well with this strategy. She has a number of divorce attorneys who appreciate her ability to buy homes, or to find a buyer quickly. They don't have any problem calling her with an introduction to their client to talk about selling the home without that agent commission.

Probate Can Be A Very Profitable Niche

Did you know that there are many times more properties in probate at any given time that there are foreclosures? Many, many more. And I'm not talking about having to cold call a grieving relative either. Developing relationships with probate attorneys, bank trust departments, and doing research at the courthouse can yield probate property purchase opportunities. With so many properties in probate all of the time, you can build a nice pipeline of deals just by developing strategies to get in front of these attorneys and estate representatives as early as possible.

Think about the motivation. Those handling the estate, whether an attorney or a lay person appointed as a personal representative, want to liquidate the assets, pay off debt, and divide up what's left among those set to inherit the remainder. And the heirs, many of whom aren't even local residents, just want to see it all over with as well. They may be waiting on a significant amount of money when the probate is settled. You bring value to the table as an experienced investor with a buyer list. Contacting the estate's administrator, the estate's executor or personal representative doesn't require talking to heirs, only the person tasked to get the property sold.

Catching them before listing with an auction house or a real estate agent gives you an edge. You can offer them a faster sale without commissions. The estate representative gets their job done and the heirs get their checks. Because the home is generally the most valuable asset in an estate, most debts must wait for payment until it's sold as well. So, here you are, the investor buying or bringing a buyer to the table. You get the property sold, allowing the bills to be paid, and the heirs get their inheritance. Everybody wins.

If you would like to learn more about probates I have included a free bonus link below for you to watch a segment from my Live Edge event that give you quite a bit of information. ***www.deangraziosi.com/yourtown/ probate.***

Your Town Tip:
In certain counties, the local newspapers are favored to run the official legal notices required for foreclosures, auctions, public notices, etc. See

if there is a local newspaper in your area that favors these "legal notice" listings. Most attorneys in the area would probably be aware of these types of publications.

Run Your Own Ads

Whether in Thrifty Nickel, the classifieds, or online with eBay or Craigslist, running your own ads is one of the most effective tools you'll ever use for finding properties. Remember the success Greg Murphy had? You can model that and put your own twist on it. Let's just think about who's out there reading these ads:

• For Sale By Owner sellers
• People in trouble with their mortgage
• Pre-foreclosure owners that are highly motivated
• Asset managers with foreclosure properties to sell
• Estate representatives selling property out of probate
• Buyers with poor credit looking for a way to own
• Tired landlords who would just as soon sell and end rental headaches

If all of these potential clients are reading ads in print and on the Web, what might catch their attention? You're an investor who can help any or all of these people. Just saying so is going to bring you business. Greg Murphy told us about running ads that let troubled homeowners know that he could save their credit and help them avoid foreclosure. That's the selling side. Then he ran ads for tenant buyers that advertised "Bad Credit? I can put you in a home now." Or, something like "Rent-to-Own with no credit check." There are a number of ways to word ads that will get you a phone call or an e-mail from a buyer or seller with special needs.

The "I Buy Houses" ads you see everywhere are there for a reason. They work. You never know how long a person in mortgage distress may have been thinking they have to do something. Then, one day they just decide to take action, and it is frequently because they saw an ad that they'd seen many times before, but just weren't ready. Placing ads that run regularly in the same places will work for you. When the need gets great enough, they go to the place where they remember seeing ads that offered help. You need to be there.

If you would like free examples of ads used by my successful students, I have set up a page for you at *www.deangraziosi.com/yourtown/ads* - use them as a foundation and modify them to fit you, your local market and your desires.

Flyers and Business Cards

These are grouped together because they have a common goal; having your contact information in a permanent form that someone will hold for future use. Whether you produce a flyer targeting asset managers and leave it at banks and lender offices, or you give your business card to probate or divorce attorneys, you're placing your business presence in their hand and hoping they'll hold on to it until they're ready to take action.

I'm sure you can find a dozen resources to design and print flyers and business cards, and there are many great ones online, allowing you to use a color printer to do the flyers yourself. One inexpensive online source for business cards is OvernightPrints.com. You can use their design tools online, or upload your own custom business card at reasonable prices and have them in a few days. The key is to use these marketing tools once you have them. Flyers and business cards should be with you at all times, and can be useful just about anywhere:

- Tacked to local bulletin boards
- For rentals, college bulletin boards are great
- Leave flyers with banks, lenders and trust administrators
- Cards and flyers left with attorneys are productive
- Some investors put out flier boxes as bandit signs
- Leaving flyers among magazines in just about any waiting room
- In high traffic neighborhood places such as grocery stores, laundromats, pizza parlors, bowling alleys or delis
- Even include you business card when you pay the bill at restaurants, but remember to leave a nice tip to be remembered.

Your Town Action Steps:
- Can you think of specific area in your town to leave business cards or flyers?
- What other high traffic areas would get visibility for you?
- What other people do you meet on a daily basis that can help you for future leads? Could it be the bank teller, grocery cashier or the receptionist at the local dentist office? Build your list and watch for more new leads!

In today's world of high-tech and the Internet, it's easy to overlook the old tried-and-true marketing methods that still work. In fact, when you look at Jan Malek's target seller, an elderly person with significant home equity, you're far more likely to come to their attention with one of these tools than on the Internet.

I have included some example of flyers and business cards on the same page as above that had ad examples. If want examples, go to **www. deangraziosi.com/yourtown/ads.**

Driving Around and Seeing Signs

Joe Jurek, Greg Murphy and other students I meet tell me about driving around and looking for signs. Joe talked about signs that were too small and in windows, instead of prominently displayed in the yard. Those are opportunities, as fewer people will take action, or even see, these signs. Fewer callers on their sign will cause the seller to pay more attention to your call.

Every trip you make to the hardware store, for groceries, or to work is an opportunity to see a brand new for sale or for rent sign. I know one investor who doesn't like to take the time to write down the contact information, especially since they are driving a lot for work, seeing new signs every day. They bought the least expensive digital camera with a good zoom lens they could find. They pull over for just long enough to shoot a close-up of the sign, and one of the homes. Now, they've captured even more information than they would have with a pencil and pad. It may seem a bit outdated with all the technology we have today, but a taking a different route to work each day or a nice Sunday ride with the family can prove to be extremely profitable if you have your eyes open and ready to spot a deal.

Real Estate Investment Clubs

Several of our student stories mention real estate investment clubs. The Weules did an amazing group investment in a major land development with their fellow club members. The Weules truly can't say enough about how valuable investment clubs have been to their success and they joined as many as they could locate in their area to network with as many people as possible. Other students tell us that they learn a great deal from their fellow members, and some get referral deals from them. Other students have built their entire buyers list through real estate clubs. When a group of people gets together regularly to talk about their shared interests, there is always value to this "meeting of the minds." One of your first local activities should be to seek out the real estate investment clubs in your area. Almost all will allow you to attend one or more meetings to get a feel for the club before you have to join or pay dues.

Though you may find them in the Yellow Pages, it's more likely that an Internet search with your town name and "real estate investment club" will locate them. Here are some resources to help as well:

http://www.reiclub.com/real-estate-clubs.php
http://www.creonline.com/real-estate-clubs/

You can also contact real estate professionals such as real estate agents, attorneys, title companies, escrow companies, and property management companies, to inquire about investor groups in the area. Some of the best groups may be discovered by word of mouth or referral. The information you gather from a few calls can make the difference for your future.

You'll find that joining one of these clubs will be one of the most valuable things you can do early in your real estate investing. First, it will be about learning and meeting people who can help you. Then, it will become a networking resource to turn up team members for all of your activities, as well as locating deals.

There are also smaller groups of informal real estate clubs. As you meet investors and real estate professionals, inquire about any investors they may know whom you could network with. I had one of my students tell me that there were no formal groups near his area, but he did find two different small groups that would meet one a month for coffee. They were not a formal club, just a few of the area investors that wanted to meet to share information. You never know where some of the best contacts or leads may come from, so be sure to follow-up on every opportunity you may discover.

Your Real Estate Agent

And last but not least the real estate agent, Realtor or broker (all do the same thing with different levels of credentials) that you will be working with. This could be one or more until you find the person that fits you perfectly. In Chapter 18 we will go deeper on finding the "right" one for you. You should be able to leverage your time by having the right real estate agent call or e-mail you regularly with great deals that meet your target market areas. They will do all the research, make sure it is a good deal, in the right area and should strive to have a vested interest in your success!

It's All About Working Multiple Strategies

You may use a couple of the "finding deals" strategies here all the time, and very successfully. Or, you may use several, or even all of them. The key is to realize that no single strategy will bring you all of the best deals out there. Using several will get you access to more buyers and sellers. None of these are expensive, though you will need to budget to run ads in print media. If Craigslist is in your area, you may want to focus on placing ads there before spending for print. Don't dismiss any of these techniques out of hand. If you're getting plenty of deal opportunities with a few of them, that's great. But if you would like to turn up more possible deals, or maybe more profitable deal types, then keep trying methods here until you find the ones that work best for you "in your town."

Remember Rome was not built in a day. With all the information you have taken in up to this point, you may be feeling a bit overwhelmed. So have all my students who have had success. The important thing to me is that you are a "doer" and you are taking your first action step. Start off with small goals. Look at Craigslist for 10 minutes a day and call on 3 properties a week. Or contact a real estate agent to receive automated e-mail each day so you can look at deals in your area and write down the ones you like.

Kaizen is the art of one tiny step and one tiny accomplishment at a time. Basically even a 100 mile foot race starts with one step at a time. Set smaller goals, pat yourself on the back when you accomplish them, and move on to the next one. Once you start accomplishing these small goals the path opens up, your confidence grows and you are migrating towards your first deal, your first accomplishment and your first check. You can do it, I promise you that.

CHAPTER 15
Funding Your Real Estate Deals

Whether you're flipping a pancake or a house, certain tools are necessary to get the job done. With a pancake, it can be the right refrigeration to chill the batter, or the right oven to get the cake to rise. In real estate investing, an extremely critical tool is the financing to carry a deal through to completion. The more options you have available for financing the more deals you might be able to complete. So if you run into a short stack or full stack of deals, you will have the financing available to eat up as many deals as you want. It is very important to note that we said financing not "available" hard cold cash!

The old saying that "it takes money to make money" may be true in many cases, but definitely not in real estate. And it definitely doesn't have to be "your" money. This is where your creativity will help you to make your real estate investing dreams come true. Some of the people in this book describe deals that they did with little or no money down. Even if a particular deal was completed using a chunk of the investor's money for a down payment or interim financing, don't let that discourage you if you're cash challenged. Lease options and assignment deals are possible with no money and no credit. But there are lots of other options some of which we are going to discuss in this chapter.

There are so many ways in which to finance your deals. Are there "dream-stealers" in your family or circle of friends whose negative outlook discourages you? Or they bring up your lack of cash when you talk about real estate investing? I can tell you this; they will only be allowed to steal your dreams if you let them. It's not their fault. It's a lack of knowledge; knowledge that you're getting here. Good economic times or bad, there's money out there available for the aggressive and creative investor.

Though an excellent credit score makes borrowing easier from many conventional sources, there are a number of other resources that don't even consider credit scores in their lending decisions. I love the stories we hear from happy investors who have completed deals they never thought possible. So many real estate investing dreams are never realized because of the belief that "it takes your money to make money." The lack of cash in your bank account, or a poor credit score, are no more of a barrier for the investor than any other facet of a real estate deal. Let's see just how many resources there are to provide you with capital to make your real estate dreams a reality.

Community Banks and Credit Unions

Community banks are chartered with the specific business purpose of supporting their communities and lending to business and individuals in support of local economic growth and prosperity. The local ownership and management means greater flexibility in decision-making and "relationship banking" is a common phrase describing how these banks conduct business. If you're one of their customers, you may have access to money that has been earmarked specifically for the rehabilitation of neighborhoods or distressed properties. After all, blocks of unoccupied homes, foreclosures, or other distressed properties are not good for the local economy. A community bank would have an interest in helping restore these homes and place responsible homeowners in them who will pay mortgage payments on time.

In comparing local community banks with large regional or national mega banks, the ICBA (Independent Community Bankers of America) makes some points that should get you excited about your ability to get the funds you need:

- Many community banks are willing to consider character, family history, and discretionary spending in making loans.
- Community banks offer nimble decision-making on business loans, because decisions are made locally. Mega banks must often convene loan approval committees in another state.

The Community Reinvestment Act (CRA) is a federal law that encourages commercial banks and savings associations to work with all types of borrowers in all areas of their local communities. Some banks may even have to provide a certain number of loans in an overall area, rather than just loaning funds in selected cities. Check into all the smaller banks in your areas to see if they offer any type of incentive funding rates for certain parts of the area you may have an interest in.

Don't overlook credit unions as a funding resource either. These member-owned financial institutions are formed to serve select groups with a common characteristic, such as their employment. There are large corporation employee credit unions, government worker and teacher organizations, and even credit unions serving the residents of a community. One need only be a local resident to join.

Check your area for credit unions you may be eligible to join. You just may be surprised how many there are. The larger ones with a strong member base will likely be flush with cash to lend. With deposits as low as $25 to join, why not open an account and take a look at their lending policies?

Friends and Family for Loans

A popular admonition, "don't ever borrow from friends or family," has killed more dreams that you can imagine. In fact, I've had students tell me stories of hurt feelings in their family or circle of friends when they mentioned a successful deal. In telling of how they took out a short term loan at a high interest rate, but flipped the property to pay it off with a profit, they actually learned something; their friends and family would have loved that rate of return on a short term loan.

Think about it logically. You have studied hard and are proving your expertise by getting in the game and doing profitable real estate deals. Your friends and family are right there, seeing it all as it happens. Sure, in the beginning they may think you are a bit crazy. That's normal when anyone does something different. But that will change, I promise you that. You have to change your mindset, you aren't coming to them begging with hat in hand for a loan. Instead, you are bringing them an opportunity. Suppose you have a hard money loan resource at 14% interest in the short term. A family member or friend has the money you need in savings, and its earning 3% or less. What a win-win situation if you can get your money from them at 9%. They triple their return and you save money. Not only are you saving on interest, but also you likely will not be paying them the up-front fees the hard moneylender charges.

Approach your friends and family with an investment opportunity instead of requests for loans. The goal is the same: a loan for your latest deal. But perception is reality here. If they see it as an opportunity to make more money than they're earning from other savings accounts, you'll get your loan. Your uncle may own his home free and clear. If he can take out a HELOC (Home Equity Line of Credit) at today's low rates, you can use that money and pay him a nice profitable interest rate for that short term use.

Make a list of everyone you know that would love a great opportunity to have their money working hard for them and making them money instead of them just working hard for their money. Or someone you know that would love to be a part of a great investment and earn much more than a stagnant bank account. You see how I phrased that? You are not making a list of simply people you know with money that you are going ask to borrow from. No way. You are giving people an amazing opportunity and you need to make sure you feel that way. Have confidence when approaching them and truly feel you are doing them a disservice if you do not get them to invest with you. If Chad, a 24 your old kid, can get older investors to give him over one million dollars to invest, don't you think you can? If you think you don't know anyone with money, I would bet you are wrong. And if you absolutely do not, then let me assure you that if you find an amazing deal, and market it properly, money will find you. Just ask so many of the students at **www.deangraziosi.com**.

Government Funding and Grants

Think about a room full of highly paid executives whose only goal is to stimulate the housing market and encourage investors and buyers by offering incentives and backing loans. Now, think about this room being the size of a city, with hundreds of thousands of people in it. That's just a hint at the size of the government offices and programs that are involved in the housing lending markets.

- FHA at fha.com
- Fannie Mae
- Freddie Mac
- HUD at hud.gov
- Veterans Administration
- Grants.gov
- GovLoans.gov
- GovernmentGrantList.com
- GrantsForHomes.com
- Loan programs sponsored by the individual states as well

With this many people involved in the process and markets, it's a safe bet that there are new programs and changes on a regular basis. Your time will be well-spent in researching federal, state, and local programs designed to provide funds for real estate financing in your area.

USDA Loans – More at their site at http://www.rurdev.usda.gov/
Since a U.S. Department of Agriculture loan made it possible for Jan Malek to finance a home for his family, it's worth a more detailed explanation here. Remember from Jan's story that he lost his job and home, and started investing recently with his partner Jeremy, who he met on my Web site. Jan discovered this loan program, and found a home to purchase using it, ending up putting no money into the deal at all. Here's how it works:

- In the areas covered, mostly rural areas, a home can be financed up to about 103% of appraised value.
- The borrower can even get back their earnest money and certain closing costs they put out before closing.
- There are high end income limitations you'll need to check at the time
- You can negotiate to have the seller pay part of the closing costs to get the financed amount within 103%, so you don't bring money to closing.

This is a great program to help a buyer with a home. But, there's more. Go to their site to see other programs they offer and what's going on right now. In early 2009, funds made available to finance rural rental properties. This could be a wonderful resource for your deals.

Using Your Retirement Account
This is one of the most overlooked funding sources. This one section of the book could be worth all of the money you've invested in learning about real estate ten times over. If you have an IRA, Individual Retirement Account, or you want to start one or transfer another account into a new one, this funding method could be your money resource of choice.

How It Works
There are a couple of reasons you may find this type of funding exciting. First, if you have a chunk of money sitting in a low return IRA, you can greatly increase the yield on your account. Second, all profits are tax deferred in the retirement account. As you're working inside a tax-deferred account already, you can't deduct some of the expenses, such as property taxes. Your accountant can contrast the tax impact of no deductions versus tax-deferred income.

If you already have an IRA, check with your custodian to see if you can do real estate investing under their account. Most of the traditional banks and brokerages will not allow it, forcing you to invest in the type of products they handle, such as stocks, bonds, annuities and certificates of deposit. If that's the case, you'll just need to transfer your IRA to a custodian that allows this type of "self-directed" investing. I found a number of results from a Google search of *"list of custodians for ira real estate investing."* Carefully interview them, and get a firm grip on their fee structure, as some can be quite expensive.

With the self-directed IRA approach to real estate investing, all expenses and income from the real estate sale or rental must go through the account. Title to the real estate is held in the account as well. Using the strategies and techniques I teach to my students, you'll be making profitable investments; so having the profits roll into a tax-deferred account could be a sound financial move. Fee structures may dictate the type of deals you do out of this account. If the major cost is in the purchase and sale, with lower ongoing fees for paying expenses and taking in deposits, you may find that long-term rental deals work best. Just do your homework and know what your costs will be.

There are various companies that can be used to guide you through this process. You want to ensure you follow all the necessary guidelines so a company that has experience with this can really be a benefit to you team. Several of my students have used the following companies to assist them with this type of transaction:

The Entrust Group - http://www.theentrustgroup.com/
Equity Trust Company - http://www.trustetc.com/

It is important understand how the process works so be sure to ask questions and perform your due diligence with whichever company you might select.

Purchasing the Property

What types of property can you buy? Generally, your custodian will allow raw or vacant land purchases, residential property, and commercial buildings. If you're leveraging the purchase, using IRA funds but not buying with cash outright, you'll need to see if your custodian allows this approach. There's a lot of property out there for sale, so selecting a deal best suited for this funding method is a good idea.

As we saw in the Weules' story and their deal recipes, you can also use your IRA funds to invest in larger deals as part of a group. Their land development investment in Tennessee was one of their most profitable deals, and the turnaround in time was only a few months. Don't overlook the possibility of partnering with others to do larger deals than you could fund out of your IRA alone.

You can't lease space from yourself in a property purchased in this way. And you can't live in a home purchased this way. Don't risk extra taxes and penalties trying to get around this. Consult your accountant to be sure you're operating within the tax rules or pay the consequences. You also cannot place a property you already own into your IRA. You can't buy the property from your spouse or siblings either.

What are the mechanics of a purchase? It's not difficult, but follow the rules. The property must be purchased by the custodian, and reflect that in all documents. If you put up personal earnest money, be sure that this is made known to the title company, as they'll need to reimburse you at closing. All funds must come out of the IRA.

Operating a Rental Property in an IRA

If you always remember to think of the property as owned by your IRA and not you, you'll probably stay out of trouble in this area. All property expenses, including repairs, insurance and taxes must be paid out of the IRA. Also, all income from rents must come into the IRA. If there are to be expenses up front in excess of what early income can pay, be sure to leave enough in the IRA after the purchase to pay for them. Not having the funds to pay expenses out of the IRA can force you into withdrawing the property from the account and paying penalties, so don't shortchange yourself on the front end, and make sure that income will pay expenses in the future.

Of course, you are still able to make cash contributions into your IRA according to the rules currently in effect. Since they change, check on this with your accountant. So, a small shortfall in expense money can be handled with a normal contribution if it meets the rules. As a last resort, seeing a problem coming could allow you time to sell the property out of the IRA before it must be withdrawn.

To avoid problems, get clear instructions from your custodian as to how rent checks should be made out, and how expenses will be paid. Following the rules will allow you to accumulate real estate investment profits over time, deferring the taxes until retirement. Let's talk about that. It is called "distribution."

Distributing Your Property

If you own a home in your IRA, you can withdraw it at your legal retirement age and use it as a personal residence. At the time you withdraw
the home, you may owe taxes on its current value. This will depend on
current tax law and the type of IRA you had. There are three, and you
can use any one of them for real estate investment. They are a traditional
IRA, a Roth IRA, or a SEP-IRA. Consult an accountant about which is best
for you.

Being a prudent investor, know that laws, especially tax laws, change all
the time, and so don't take anything you read here or anywhere other
than the IRS Web site or written material as accurate when you read it.
But, if you're sitting on cash in an IRA, check this funding method out.

Investors for Your Funding

I'm not just talking about real estate investors here. There are a great many
people and companies out there with money to invest. They can get better returns than bank interest by lending to new businesses, just like your
real estate investing business. Some will want a percentage of your profits
rather than a stated interest rate, but it's all about getting a profitable
deal done. If you have to share those profits to make it happen, then it's a
viable financing opportunity. For an education in how investors and those
needing funds meet and negotiate online, visit http://go4funding.com.

Other Real Estate Investors - With so many different types of properties
and real estate investment strategies, it's certain that there are other investors out there with goals that complement yours. They don't compete,
instead offering a chance to partner in deals or a market for your flip
properties. When you locate a deal and it's clear to you that there is profit
opportunity, it's just as clear to other investors. It's very possible that your
lack of all of the necessary funding is a problem others face, and combining your resources can get the deal done.

Remember Chad Merrihew's story. He never invests his own money in
deals. Instead, he locates profitable opportunities, takes the numbers
to investors, and they put up the money. From his father, his aunt,
and third party investors, Chad has put together more than 20 deals.
One of his best, in one of the worst areas, Riverside, CA, resulted in
a long-term relationship with the investor and seven more deals.

I can't be more enthusiastic about the opportunity for profits in flipping to the long-term investor. If your favorite strategy is to buy, renovate and flip, there are so many customers out there other than the retail buyer. You just have to develop your buyer base. These are long-term rental property buyers who don't want to be involved in repairs and renovation. They just want a ready-to-rent property without the other hassles. By cultivating a base of this type of buyer, you can frequently involve them early, getting interim financing that will be paid off in the sale after renovation and repairs. Your profits come from locating the deep discount buys, renovating on a budget, and re-selling profitably at a price that gives the long term investor a positive cash flow.

Like we mentioned earlier, real estate investment clubs can provide funding when you need it. These like-minded investors are there to locate real estate investment opportunities, and your strategies may overlap theirs. At the very least, you can bounce your deal ideas off of others with similar goals. In the process, you cultivate relationships that can bring you financing in the future.

Hard Money Loans

Don't be confused by the term "hard money loan." This loan type is similar to a normal mortgage in that the lender or funding source usually takes a first lien position to protect their investment. The differences in a hard money loan include:

- A lower "quick sale value" is used to determine the loan-to-value calculation. This investor isn't looking to hold a property if you don't come through with repayment. Their quick sale value is one that they believe will allow them to move the property in very short order if there is a problem. Call it a flip in a way.
- Typically, the loan-to-value ratio for this type of financing is 55% to 70% of the quick sale value. So, if the lender believes they can quickly sell the property for $100,000, they'll loan you $55,000 to $70,000 with a first lien to cover their interests.
- Interest rates on hard money loans are significantly higher than normal mortgage interest rates. But, when other resources aren't available, a hard money loan can get a deal done.
- Hard money lenders are usually smaller companies or individuals. However, there are larger regional and national lenders out there with hard money to loan as well. Here are some links to online resources you can check out:

- 1st Quick Funding nationally at http://www.1stquickfunding.com/
- Blazevic Funding Group nationally at http://www.blazevicfunding.com/
- Brookview Financial, Inc in multiple states nationally at http://reiclub.com/hml

Hard money loans are generally the most costly funding source, but you should develop these sources for use when the right deal is about to slip away for lack of short term money.

Remember even though hard money loans are more expensive due to higher interest rates it can still be a great tool in your "financing" tool box. If you use our techniques and find a great deal that you can buy at 50% off of today's fair Market value, know you can clean it up and renovate in 15 to 30 days, still sell it at a huge discount and be out of the property in 30 to 90 days. Then who cares if you are paying 14% interest instead of 5%. If you have to pay a few hundred even a few thousand extra for the money but you can realize a $10,000 to $50,000 profit from a quick flip, then who cares?

With hard money, the lender knows you don't have good credit, or money to put down. Their entire safety net is the property you are buying, so they do their due diligence to make sure the deal is as good as you say. They can reassure you that you have found an amazing deal and if they don't give you the money because they found a reason it is not worth what you say then maybe they saved you some hassle and you can move on to the next deal.

In fact, hard money lending can be such an important tool that I am going to give you another free bonus at **www.deangraziosi.com/yourtown/hardmoney**. I had my team take a clip from our live event where one of our coaches from my Success Academy spoke about hard money and the benefits it brings.

Lines of Credit

No matter how much money you have in the bank today, your net worth, or how much real estate you own, the use of lines of credit can be a wonderful source of funding for you in the future. How would you feel if you could just whip out a checkbook and write a check for a home purchase or down payment? You can with a line of credit.

Of course, this is not available to everyone. But for those of you that have equity in your home or another piece of property, it can be a great leveraged tool. It has helped a lot of my students who had access to it. Since your line of credit literally turns in to basically cash for buying great deals fast.

Local banks are a great resource for this financing method. They look at your operating business(es), your other real estate owned and assets, and credit worthiness. They may take out liens against these assets. If all of this looks good, they will give you a standing line of credit for a certain amount of money. It's not a loan yet, as you haven't used it. It's just there for use when you need it. You get a checkbook, and not even a phone call is required to access your line. As you pay it back, it's freed up to use over and over again.

Lines of credit have financed entire home purchases, repairs and renovations, with the flip of the property or a refinance in to a conventional loan paying off the HELOC and making it ready to use again. Combining this funding resource with a regular bridge loan, or a hard money loan, you can frequently put together the short-term financing to make the buy, repair and renovate, then re-sell at retail or to another investor. Local banks aren't your only resource, with these national companies offering lines of credit as well:

- G.E. Capital at gecapsol.com
- KeyBank Lines of Credit at key.com
- Wells Fargo Lines of Credit at wellsfargo.com
- BusinessFinance.com

It's all about developing yet another funding source to have at-the-ready to make a deal happen. It's the creative approaches that will make your dreams come true, so have every resource you can develop at hand.

"Flash Funding"

I can't tell you how many happy past students have told us some variation of this story:

Using my recommended sources for locating properties, they find an amazing bargain in foreclosure, pre-foreclosure or as a short sale deal. It's so good that they have lined up a buyer with back-to-back closings to pull the deal off without tying up any of their own money. But, and it's a big one, the real estate mortgage problems in 2007 - 2009 have made lenders and title companies much more cautious. No longer can our investor use the funds of the second sale deal to pay off the first purchase deal, even if they're closing within hours of each other.

There's a lot of profit in these deals, so there just has to be a way to get it done! One source for short term funding we have seen students on **www.deangraziosi.com** use with success is Coastal Funding at http://coastal-funding.com (use coupon code "Dean Graziosi"). With most deals costing about 2 points, Coastal Funding provides flash funding to make these back-to-back closings happen. They do this many times without looking at loan-to-value ratios, no appraisal, up front fees or income verification. Check them out for those "hurry-up" short term funding needs. Now I have never worked with them, so make sure you do your due diligence. But basically it should be a clean cut deal. It either works or it doesn't.

Back-to-back closing is a strategy to use when you are assigning a deal to another person and the basic assignment won't work, so you have to close on the deal first before you sell it to the new buyer. You can own the property for less then an hour and make yourself a small fortune on each deal. If you can't find short term funding to use for an hour during this double close, then a company like Coastal Funding may work for you. They wire the money right to the title company to close on the first deal, once the sale or second closing happens, they get their money back with a few points of interest added to it and you get to keep the rest of the difference as your profit. Jeremy, our 19 year old student, provided the money he had to another DG family member for a double close and made a $1,000 helping someone with a great deal. As you saw with Chip and Andrea, a title company worked the deal so they did back-to-back closings without using anyone's money. They closed with the buyer before they owned it, since funds were waiting, they closed with the seller minutes later. A good relationship with a title company can let you know if this is possible for you.

I hope you are seeing that the possibilities are endless to make deals happen. Does it work? Absolutely. Is it worth it? Undoubtedly! Success after success does not lie. Here is what I know to be fact. I have had people read my last book "Profit From Real Estate Right Now!" the light bulb goes on and they say, "Holy moly there are countless ways to make money with no money down, take them and go out and apply them. The results speak for themselves!" While others read the same exact book and get done a simply say, "You need money to make money." It baffles me. Now I don't judge. It is those who doubt what I teach that inspire me the most. They drive me to write books like this. To do the deals they say can't be done and the rewards of spinning those skeptics to successful real estate investors, has become a mission of mine and some of my greatest accomplishments outside my family. So I say this: If you are stoked about the strategies you are learning and revved-up to put them in place, good for you. But if you are letting the naysayer world we live in determine your feelings and you doubt all of this, open your mind, know that this works and you are simply a product of your environment.

I got off track a bit, but I feel it is important if I am going to give you all you need to be successful. You have to realize that you can be your biggest asset or your biggest obstacle. Lubertha said it took her six months to get out of her own way of success. After a bankruptcy and a multiple of things going bad for her, she was sour. Finally she broke out of it, realized she could do anything, and that she would be the only one to change her life. The skies opened up and deals were all around her. She got off the couch and got to life on her terms. Is she a millionaire overnight? Heck no, but she is on path to success and not even her inner voices are stopping her anymore.

I'll end with this: reality is nothing more than what you say and do. If you say "you need money to make money" or "the rich get richer" or "real estate won't work for me," then that is your reality. But if you are tired of the life you are currently living, want to build security, have a burning desire to live the life you are supposed to be living, than get those naysayer voices out of your head! Read this book with a positive outlook and get to make a life for you and your family that you cab be proud of, one that leaves a legacy. You can do this once you tell yourself that you can.

It's All About Options

I have yet to meet a student who couldn't get one or more of these funding options working to make a deal happen. This chapter gives you the tools, and all you have to do is to make sure that every one of them you might want to use is in your toolbox and ready to grab when you need it. Research them all, set up the ones you like the most for your situation, and have them ready when that amazing deal jumps out at you. In this chapter we spoke of ways to get money. But remember with lease options and assignments, you don't need any of your own money. Stories to review: we explained lease options in Greg Murphy's chapter. And we covered assignment deals in Chip and Andrea's chapter.

CHAPTER 16

Understand and Profit from REOs

You may hear investors talking about OREOs or REOs. Don't confuse these with those tasty cookies! When a bank has to foreclose and take a property back from the owner, they call the properties they hold OREOs or REOs. This stands for "Other Real Estate Owned," or "Real Estate Owned". We are just going to refer them here as REOs. A bank is a business and, like any business, wants to maximize revenues and reduce expenses. When a bank takes back a property and it becomes an REO, it is viewed by the bank as a non-performing asset.

Let's take a minute and think about this. If a bank is holding the property, they are not collecting the mortgage payment, which was the original principle and interest payment. The bank is really losing money each month because they are paying or accruing expenses every month on the property while it sits on their books. Expenses can include insurance, property taxes, utilities, security, and even possibly a caretaker. The longer these REO properties sit on the bank's books, the more expenses that add up over time. Beyond that, there are certain regulatory limits to how much a bank can loan based on their performing assets. When a home moves from a good asset category to a bad one, it can lower their lending for profits in other categories.

A few years ago, if a bank got a property back through foreclosure (REO), they could list it and it would sell fast. That is not the case during this real estate cycle, so banks are eagerly and aggressively trying to get these bad assets of their books and that can mean amazing deals for you.

Your Town Tips:
- At the end of a fiscal quarter or fiscal year-end bankers, may be more motivated to move their REO properties.
- Also, banks are subject to audits through-out the year from various compliance entities and the banks may also become more motivated to move non-performing assets before an audit.
- Complete the REO tracker form we'll provide as you contact each bank.

Banks do not want these properties on their books. Especially at smaller local community banks, these REOs can really begin to dilute profits and cause other problems when they must cut lending because of asset ratios and regulations. If a smaller bank with only a few locations has too many of these types of properties on their books, it can cause a significant strain on their operating profits. The smaller the bank, the larger the problem. This is important to know, as you can often make a lower offer to a smaller bank with a greater motivation to get rid of an REO property. They really want to liquidate that non-performing asset.

One opportunity in your local area may be contacting local small banks and inquiring about their REOs. How do you go about doing this? It's really easy. All you need is the plan we'll give you. You need to create an action plan for approaching these small local banks, get your question list on paper, and practice using it. Feel comfortable asking these questions in a conversational tone.

Here's a bank REO action plan that I know works. Just follow this plan, expand on it, practice, and don't be discouraged if you talk to a number of banks without results. It's like many strategies that my students successfully use every day. They had to use them, practice, and never stop until they found the right way to make it work in their towns.

Finding the local banks

You want to do some research to locate your local small community banks. Depending on the area, the number can fluctuate. A smaller community bank may have less than 5 branches, however there are still privately owned local banks that may even have as many as 50 branches. A little research can go a long way. If you discover that a bank was founded in a certain area, chances are they could still be privately owned. If you look at the bank's Web site, they usually have a background story about the bank and the founder. This is a wealth of information to determine its size. You now say, "I'm ready to find these banks but, Dean, I don't know how to do it or even where I should start!" That's OK, as I'm here to help! Let's go find the small local banks in your area.

There are a number of resources you can use. The good old telephone book or yellow pages are a great beginning. For the latest and the greatest updated information, you may want to access the Internet. You can just as easily go online and find the information in minutes. Here are some Web sites that I've used to locate local banks quickly:

www.yellowbook.com
www.anywho.com
www.yellowpages.com
www.switchboard.com

Whatever method you use to find them, you're looking for the smaller banks first. (Not that you can't make money with larger banks, but for now we are going to talk about the benefits of smaller, more personal banks) An example, using anywho.com, is to enter just the word "bank" in the "business name" block, as almost all have "bank" in their name. Then enter the town or zip code to narrow down the results. Of course, you're going to begin to locate great ones with words like "community," and "savings and loan" in their names. You could jump right on the phone with your question list, but you really don't have enough information to do this yet.

If you're locating them with a Web search, you should find their Web site link in the search results. If you can't find them in a business directory search, enter their name into a Google or Bing search, along with the city and state. You should get a fast top-result link right to their site. There will be a lot of information about the bank at their site, including the history, number and location of branches, and whether they do a significant amount of business in mortgages.

OK, you've built a list of small banks in your area, and you've made some notes about their size, branches and mortgage business. It's time to call them up, but what do you say? How do you get to the right person with your questions, and actually begin to build a relationship that will bring REO property purchase opportunities to your door? First, get organized so you make the conversation as productive as possible. Our first "tool of the trade" is a notebook with your call log, as Joe Jurek likes to call it, "My Call Log." Make a summary sheet for each day you make calls. The summary sheet should include the following information:

1. Date
2. Name of the Bank
3. Bank Phone Number
4. Bank first point of contact – who answered the call
5. Other Contact (Name) – maybe the bank operator transfer you to the Administrative Assistant of the Vice President of Risk Management
6. REO Asset Manager's Name
7. REO Asset Manager's direct phone line or extension

8. REO Asset Manager's e-mail address
9. Notes about anything special you discuss
10. Date of next follow-up call or e-mail

This information is written in columns across your notepaper, then going down, list each of the banks that you located. Let's get started!

Step # 1
List all of the banks you located on the Internet, with the information about each in a row under each column. The banks you located are American Savings, First Savings & Loan, and CBR Community Bank.

Date	Name	Bank Phone #	First Contact
12-15-09	American Savings	(555) 555-1000	
12-15-09	1st Savings & Loan	(555) 555-2300	
12-15-09	CBR Community Bank	(555) 555-3400	

Step # 2
Practice your approach and questions out loud before you call. Just remember to sound friendly, polite and confident with every person you speak to. Make sure the person on the other end of the phone can almost see the smile in your voice. Have your "My Calls" notepad ready for each call. Always write down as much information as possible.

Step # 3

The First Call!
Take a deep breath and relax, you're going to be great! Most of your first calls will follow a predictable path. The person answering will almost never be the REO asset manager, so you'll need to get to them. Treat every person you speak to as if they're the bank president, as it helps you to get to the person you need faster, and with fewer roadblocks.

Tip:
When the person answering tells you they're going to route your call to the asset manager, ask them to please give you their direct number and their full name in case you're disconnected. Now you have that direct number for all calls in the future.

Jot down the names of people you're routed through until you reach the right one. Knowing these names later can help when people change jobs. Let's pretend that our asset manager at American Savings is a Mrs. Bailey. When she answers the phone, introduce yourself with something like:
Dean: "Hi, my name I'm Dean Graziosi. I am a real estate investor, and I'm inquiring about your bank's REO properties. Have I reached the right person?

Once you know you have the right person, it's all about building your credibility as an investor, and getting into their good graces in order to gain access to these REO opportunities. It doesn't really hurt to mention that you're part of a group of investors, as this could get you a little more attention. Don't forget that their goal is to sell these properties, and you're a potential customer. I wouldn't limit your opportunities at this point by specifying property types, like residences or vacant land. You never know what opportunity you might locate, even for a property type you haven't considered before. The longer this conversation lasts, the better you're doing and the more you'll learn.

You have a phone number, but getting an e-mail address is an important next step. There will probably be several properties, or even a long list. You'll want as much information as possible, and offering your e-mail address for them to send the info is a good approach. Ask for their e-mail so you can send your contact information. Once you have it, and the conversation is over, it's time for the next step.

Before that next step, make sure that you've updated your notes with all of the information you got on the phone, as well as that important phone number and e-mail address info. One of the amazing things about the community that's developed on my Web site is the helpful nature of the people there. Below is a shot of a form you can use for tracking our REO contacts. Here's a screen shot, and the form is available at ***www. deangraziosi.com/yourtown/forms.***

Date	Name of Bank	Bank Phone Number	Bank First Point of Contact	Other Contact Name	REO Asset Manager's Name	REO Asset Mgr. Direct Phone Line	REO Asset Mgr. Email Address	Notes	Date of Follow-up

Very quickly, we want to demonstrate our efficiency and interest by sending that e-mail we promised. Plus, we can't get our REO details until we do. Send the e-mail to Mrs. Bailey, and it may look something like this:

> Good Afternoon Mrs. Bailey,
>
> It was a pleasure speaking with you this afternoon regarding American Savings REO properties. I look forward to receiving your e-mail of those you have available. My other contact information is below. Thank you for your time and assistance.
>
> Have a nice day. – Dean

Now in some cases, banks will outsource all their REOs to one real estate brokerage firm. If that is the case, still create the same relationship, just tweak the e-mail to fit the information you learned when you were on the phone.

You've begun this relationship by doing precisely what you stated you would do, and you sent the e-mail right away. This is a great start in gaining Mrs. Bailey's trust and making her an ally in your business. Even if she has no current inventory that interests you, it's to your benefit to keep your name at the top of her mind when new inventory comes in. If she says she has no properties on the phone, ask her if you can make contact again in a month to check on the situation. You can then e-mail or call her, or both.

Then on your call log note that you need to follow-up with Mrs. Bailey through an e-mail or a phone call next month. You might want to send an e-mail something like:

> Good Afternoon Mrs. Bailey,
>
> I hope all is well and you're enjoying the nice weather (or staying warm during winter months). We spoke last month about your REO properties and you indicated that you did not have any available. You kindly agreed to let me check with you this month in the event you received a few. Thus, could you please let me know if you have any REO properties available? Thank you for your time and assistance.
>
> Have a nice day.
> – Dean"

Once you have a list of properties, do what due diligence you can to determine which you want to visit. Use all the techniques we shared in this book from getting comparables, to using www.totalviewrealestate.com and other sources to see which properties from a quick glance look like they could be good deals. Do a drive-by, checking the neighborhoods out, and pull out any of those files we talked about before. This is another chance to use that work you've done on your drives in the past. The more opportunities you have in front of you, the more important this initial investigation and information becomes. You can zoom in on the ones that seem to have the greatest potential and see them first. Don't doubt that the bank is showing them to every person they can.

Call the bank and set up property visits with their representative or the real estate agent they're using. Don't let an agent set too tight a schedule, as you're going to want to take a careful look at these properties. This first visit is critical in setting a baseline estimate to use in your value calculations. Don't give away any information or appear over-interested in a property, even if it's screaming "super deal" to you. This is a business, and you need to take a business-like look at every property, not yielding any opinions until you're ready to make an offer.

Tip:
The Power of an E-mail!
The best way to present an offer is to submit an e-mail expressing your interest in the property. The e-mail usually works well because you can say everything that you want to say without having to worry about the banker hanging the phone up on you. It also gives the banker time to think about the offer or forward the offer to the final decision-maker. It buys you time to clearly explain your offer and to be creative in providing solutions that will work for the bank.

Here are a few examples of e-mails that you could send to the bank on their REOs:

Example # 1 – E-mail to REO Asset Manager

Good Afternoon Mrs. Bailey,

It was a pleasure speaking to you regarding the home located at 123 Washington Street. This home has 1057 square feet, and some nice features. However, I believe this REO has become a greater liability for your bank considering utilities, security, upkeep, insurance and property taxes ($4,026.40 annually). Thus, I would estimate the annual expenses are probably closer to $7,000.

Similar homes on the market in the local area are listed as follows:

- 152 Second Street (1,044 sq ft home) listed at $48,000
- 1112 Park Place (1,164 sq ft home) listed at $52,900
- 2356 Main Street (1,080 sq ft home) listed at $57,500

As you are obviously aware, the real estate market has become very slow and a great many buyers are waiting in the wings. There are several issues that would need to be addressed with the 123 Washington Street property; these include the flooring, interior doors on closets, code items, such as windows in bathrooms and the hot water heater. A kitchen update is required, as well as general finish work, etc. The exterior may require painting, cleanup and eventually a new roof. Thus, the home at 123 Washington Street would probably be listed in today's market at $59,900 or less.

I would be open to negotiate a deal that would work for both of us. I could offer a higher purchase price (near asking price) with great financing terms or a lower purchase price with workable terms. Please advise with your preference as to price or terms. I want to purchase this home if I can work out a deal that makes sense and would result in positive cash flow. I look forward to working with you and your bank to create more affordable housing to make a difference in our local community. Thank you for your time and consideration.

Have a nice day.
– Dean

Let's assume that Mrs. Bailey responded with an offer to sell as discussed in the next e-mail. This would be one way to go back to her and to move the negotiation along.

Example # 2 – Follow-up E-mail to REO Asset Manager

Good Afternoon Mrs. Bailey,

Thank you for the call this afternoon regarding the 123 Washington Street Property. You indicated the bank was looking at selling the property at $79,500 and offering a 30-year mortgage with an adjustable rate. The first 5 years would be at the interest rate of 7.5 percent.

As I previously discussed, I can balance the offer based on the relationship of the price to the interest rate. The 7.5% adjustable rate (non-owner occupied interest rate) is high based on other local bank's current interest rates and www.bankrate.com.

Also, the real estate market is still on the decline. Currently, in the local market there are much larger homes on more desirable blocks in the $65k to $89k range. If the home was listed on 123 Washington Street by a real estate agent they would probably recommend the home in its current condition be listed at $59,900 or less.

Thus, I would like to propose an offer of $59,900 with the 30-year mortgage and an adjustable rate. The first 5 years would be at the rate of 6.25%.

Or

I could go as high as $79,900 with an interest rate tied to the current prime rate (3.25%) for five years, and amortized over 30 years.

Other terms and conditions:
• No penalty for early mortgage pay-off.
• All unpaid property taxes to be pro-rated and credited to me (the buyer) through day of closing
• Seller to satisfy all other liens and bills accrued to date against property prior to closing, including, but not limited to, the water and other utility bills
• Buyer to receive title insurance reflecting clear and equitable title for the property.

- Buyer to receive $5,000 cash at closing for paint and carpet allowance
- Seller to pay for all closing costs
- Seller to pay for buyer's pest and home inspections
- Seller to provide current and updated survey
- Please advise if either of these options may be acceptable to the bank. I would desire to structure a win-win transaction for both parties. In the event we do not reach an agreement on this transaction, I would appreciate it if you could contact me in the future if you acquire any other REOs.

Thank you for your time and consideration.
– Dean

Now let me tell you a few things. First, these e-mails may look familiar. They should since they are a version or variation of Joe Jurek's e-mails that he has used to close great deals. I ethically robbed these from Joe Jurek because he is out there using these exact e-mails, these exact strategies to buy REOs and is killing it (for lack of a better word). So why wouldn't I share with you what is working right now out in the field? Don't dare be shy, scared or embarrassed to ask. If you don't ask you don't receive!

Let me confess something. I would never suggest being so aggressive if this was the beginning of 2006. The only response you may have received from an e-mail like this would be a rude e-mail back or a dismissive laugh. But times have changed; banks are hurting and ready to negotiate on price, on terms, on loans and everything in between. If you are not asking you are not receiving. This is the same type of e-mail that got Joe one of his recent properties with no money down, reduced price, great loan terms and he walked away from closing with over $5,000. Yes, it works.

Your Town Tips:
- The following other terms and condition points in the purchase offer can become bargaining points with the Bank Asset Manager.
- Always remember that information and your contacts are your keys to achieving your goals. The more information and contacts you discover, the more opportunities that may come your way.
- The REO Asset Manager holds the key to the treasure chest of REO gems! So be sure to cultivate these relationships, and the key will be yours.

Another way to locate REO properties

If you are interested in finding REOs, and want to do a little more research, go to your county courthouse or look to see if the information is available online. In some states they may charge a nominal fee to access the information online, but this could be money well spent, especially if it saves you time and effort in driving and time at the courthouse.

You want to look in the county assessor records for your local area and see if you can sort the files by property owner. Then start doing searches with the word "bank" or "credit union" in the owner title. You'll have to weed out the buildings actually owned b the banks for their own use, as well as properties in trusts with banks. However, you can usually quickly find a list of REO properties in the area.

You can also check the county treasurer tax records. The tax records may contain additional information. Check with your county to see what information may be available and how you can go about gathering it. As you gather the information on a potential REO, you may be in a better position to negotiate with the bank. You can then determine when they took back the REO, verify the current property taxes, and estimate the other current expenses paid by the bank to hold the REO.

Bankers love numbers and the more expense numbers you discover, the more ability you may have to negotiate a lower price for the REO. For example, if the costs to carry and maintain the REOs are accounted for in the "other operating costs" of the bank, the bank senior management or Board of Directors may not be paying close attention to these mounting additional costs. As you remind them of the costs, they may become more motivated to sell these non-performing assets.

There is another reason why a bank may take less than what is owed on a property. If you've ever looked at an amortization schedule for the payments on a typical 30-year mortgage, you'll see that the amount going to interest is at its highest at the beginning of the loan. That's because the interest charged each month is at the stated rate applied to the unpaid balance of the loan. As the loan balance is at its highest in the first years of the mortgage, the interest is greatest then as well.

This means that the return on investment to the bank for the mortgage money loaned is highest at the beginning of the loan, gradually decreasing as the balance is paid down. In the first few years, all but a small portion of the payment is going straight to interest, the bank's profit on the loan. If the bank is a number of years into the loan on the REO you're negotiating, they've reaped a nice profit so far, and the actual loss they take in a below-market and short sale situation isn't as bad as it looks. That's why knowing how long the mortgage was being paid, and when the property was foreclosed is valuable information. Your offer can be reduced with this type of knowledge.

Other REO Goldmines

Corporations

Many of us think of only banks as having REOs. But there are also various other entities that have REOs or similar types of property owned. These other entities can include credit unions, private lenders, corporations, etc. In some cases, a company may relocate an employee to another area of the country. As an incentive, they are willing to purchase the employee's home to get them to move to the new job. These corporations now own the home, and to the corporation it could be just another problem or issue to deal with.

This is an especially annoying issue if you're the employee at the company who has to deal with liquidating the homes that were purchased. The quicker you can get these homes off the company's books the better. It could become an out-of-control situation, with normal monthly expenses, insurance liability to the company, and the threat of having the property vandalized. For all of these reasons, these companies are highly motivated to sell the property.

Credit Unions

As with locating local community banks in your area, the same is true for credit unions. Use resources such as these Internet sites to locate the local credit unions:
www.yellowbook.com
www.anywho.com
www.yellowpages.com
www.switchboard.com

You may have to call more credit unions to find one that has an REO, but when you do, they can be even more motivated that a bank to sell the property. A key here is to network with as many people as you can. You all know someone that may belong to a credit union or work for a large organization that does relocating of staff. Network with these people and see what information they may have to help you.

Your Town Tips:

- Everyone knows someone or something that can help you with real estate investing. EVERYONE! Whether it is a professional contact, a contractor, or a buyer or seller. The challenge here is will they share their contact with you?
- Some people are reluctant to give up their contacts for one reason or another. So, make sure they know who and what you're looking for, and hopefully people will share their contacts with you. Then watch your network grow!

Auctions

Large banks, corporations or others may decide to sell their REO homes through auction companies. You can go to www.google.com and enter "home auctions" and see a number of auction companies. Some of them may be local, in your town. The following Web sites are worth looking into:

- Auction zip (www.auctionzip.com)
- Hudson and Marshall (www.hudsonandmarshall.com)
- Realty Bid (www.realtybid.com)
- Real Estate Disposition Corporation (www.ushomeauction.com)
- Williams and Williams (www.williamsauction.com)
- Bid 4 Assets (www.bid4assets.com)
- To find auctions (www.Auctionzip.com) or (www.auctionzip.com/real-estate)

Other Auctions

- Buying HUD homes: http://www.hud.gov/offices/hsg/sfh/reo/reobuy-faq.cfm
- HUD information by state: http://portal.hud.gov/portal/page/portal/HUD/states
- US Department of Veteran Affairs: http://www.homeloans.va.gov/pm.htm
- FDIC Real Estate for sale http://www2.fdic.gov/drrore/

- IRS Property http://www.treas.gov/auctions/irs/cat_Real7.htm
- Customs – Auctions http://www.treas.gov/auctions/treasury/rp/
- US Marshals http://www.pueblo.gsa.gov/cic_text/fed_prog/selerlst/selerlst.htm
- Home Overstock Auctions http://homes.overstock.com/real_estate

Your Town Tips:

- Here is a very creative technique when it comes to real estate auctions. Normally the large real estate auction companies will advertise a few months in advance of when the auctions are coming to your local area. These large auction companies will then host several "open house" weekend dates to view the properties prior to the large auction event. Some banks will be motivated and entertain a low offer prior to the real estate auction.
- You may want to track the properties in your local area that are bank owned and have been on the market for several months. If you believe they may be ready to go to auction, make a low offer a few weeks prior to an open house. This way you can get a property for a great price without having to get into a bidding war at the auction!

The Short Sale – A Demanding Niche

Before a property becomes an REO, there is a period of time when it can be a candidate for a short sale. A short sale is simply a sale to a buyer at a price less than the mortgage(s) owed on the property. Of course, since a bank holds the first mortgage, they're going to have to approve of any sale that takes money out of their pockets. It's not cash money, as the loan was made long ago, but its profit. And, there's the fact that the home was on their asset books at a certain value, with a certain cash flow associated with the mortgage payments.

Because banks have certain percentage requirements for backing their loaned funds with enough assets to cover problems, it's never good when they have to remove an asset and move it to the liability column. They now have no income from the property, plus there are costs involved in holding it. Factor in the fact that various studies have stated that it costs an average of somewhere between $36,000 and $50,000 for a bank to foreclose on a home, and you would think that any reasonable offer to get it off their books while it's still an asset would be welcome. Well, it just isn't so!

We're looking at a homeowner behind a couple of payments or more. Depending on the time line, there could be a default notice from the bank, or even a threatened courthouse steps sale date in a letter on their kitchen table. Along comes an investor who sees an opportunity. The balance owed on the loan is such that an offer reasonably lower would result in a good purchase for rental or a flip. Let's look at an example home:

- The homeowner is behind two payments and knows there is going to be another late one soon. There's no hope of selling, and they just want out without a foreclosure.
- The loan amount owed is $172,000 on a home worth about $195,000.
- You're an investor who sees opportunity, but only if you can get it for $150k.
- You approach the homeowner who is happy for you to try and do a short sale negotiation with the bank, if it helps them get out before foreclosure.

All this looks good, as you know that an offer $22k below the loan amount is still going to be better for the bank than spending $36k to foreclose, keep the property in decent condition, and market it for sale. So, you make the offer and they accept! NOT. One study says that nationally, only one out of five short sale offers ever gets to closing. Some say that's optimistic because most aren't generally known about, dying before significant paperwork is done.

Why is this the case? Nobody really has come up with one good answer. The fact is that banks are geared to lend money, not own homes or give up money willingly. They're also big bureaucracies, rivaled only by the government in their ability to stymie creative solutions to problems. Staffed up for the lending side, they don't have enough people on the problem side to handle the influx of short sale offers that have cropped up in the last few years. Then there's the lack of expertise on the part of the property owners, real estate agents and investors in how to work with a bank to make it a little more sure of a deal in a short sale.

With all of this on the negative side, why even bother with short sales anyway? The fact that they can be wildly profitable. But, as an investor, you'll need to be prepared to do a lot of work on a lot of deals to get to closing on a few. And, even if you educate yourself, learn all the tricks, and submit flawless short sale packages to lenders, you'll still get ignored and turned down a lot. It's the way of life in the mortgage foreclosure business.

But, if you want to take a stab at short sales, there is great potential for acquiring nice homes before they're damaged in foreclosure, and at prices that lock in excellent instant equity. There are investors out there who only do short sales, and do very well. It's all about getting the procedure down, and replicating your process for an efficient negotiation. And that's what it is; a negotiation with a banker's asset manager, and maybe even a loan committee making a groupthink decision. Just get ready for some frustration before you rake in those profits. Here are the basic process steps once you've located a willing owner ready to try a short sale:

1. Have them gather all relevant documents, mortgages, loan balances, default notices, and letters to and from the lenders..
2. Get home owner to sign form giving you permission to talk to the bank on their behalf.
3. Prepare a cover letter stating the desire to sell the property at a price below the loan amount.
4. Prepare a contract of sale for the stated amount.
5. Then we do what's frequently called the "hardship letter." This is both a letter and a kind of financial calamity statement. We need to:
    - Show all of the liabilities of the owner, including late mortgages
    - Show all debts, credit cards, even loans owed to family and friends
    - Total up the monthly liabilities of the owner and show that they've become more than the owner can pay
    - In effect, we're stating to the lender that foreclosure is imminent
    - Provide a value estimate for the home, showing comparable recent sales, as well as current listings that would compete if the bank tries to sell the home
    - We're showing the lender that it's going to be very difficult to sell the home, and it's likely that they still will not get their loan balance after costs of sale anyway

This set of documents is called the "short sale package." We hopefully have made substantive contact with a real person in the lender's asset liquidation or other department tasked with this type of deal. We submit our package and keep checking in regularly to try and stimulate movement in a process that can become stalled on almost a daily basis. Many failures of short sales come from buyers who get tired of waiting and withdraw their offers.

Now it's all about waiting, reminders, and patience. You can't hurry a banker, and one who's about to give up some profits is never in a hurry. But, if you can muster the patience and do all the detailed work, you stand to make a friend of a homeowner in trouble while putting a nice profit in your pocket.

Or . . . Do What Greg Does!

Remember Greg Murphy's amazing deal recipes? He finds the same owner we just talked about, a few payments behind, and wanting to sell. They're staring foreclosure in the face. Instead of trying to deal with the bank in a short sale situation, Greg goes to his buyer list and matches a tenant buyer with this home. It's students like Greg using creative solutions who can help these homeowners to sell, put a tenant buyer into the home, and build a great business in doing it.

CHAPTER 17

Success with The FSBO

The For Sale By Owner (FSBO) seller is a different seller than those who list with real estate agents and bankers who handle REOs. So, we need to learn how to market to reach them, and understand how they're different. It's all about how to negotiate effectively with FBSOs, creating win-win situations all the way through closing. Thinking about the FSBO, their real estate knowledge and experience is how we set the tone of all our marketing, negotiating and transaction processes. Generally, they will not have the level of experience of the real estate investor, so working with them to create win-win deals is the key. The FSBO may be a little more emotional about their home, so be sure to choose your comments and critiques wisely. It is often a good idea to get to know the seller on a more personal level and be a good listener. People want to do business with people they like and trust. I wrote in detail in one of my first books about people's "magic buttons;" the things that make the deal happen. You can learn those "magic buttons" by listening to your client talk. So I'll say it again, be a good listener.

FSBO Marketing in Both Directions

First, let's look at how we might meet a FSBO seller, either through their marketing or ours. After all, they are trying to sell their home, so there is some marketing on their end. And, at the same time, you're trying to locate FSBO properties before the competition sees them, so you're marketing as well. So, it's a bit like two sales people, each with their own agenda, but both open to a mutually beneficial relationship.

Why are there FSBO listings in the first place? Though there are not "set" commissions charged by real estate brokers, a number used a lot in the media is a 6% commission to sell a home. Customarily, it's split 50/50 between the listing broker and the agent who brings in a successful buyer. So, the vast majority of FSBO sellers are doing it to avoid the commissions. On a $100,000 home, that's $6,000, enough money to encourage frugal sellers to try it on their own. They may be behind in their mortgage or owe more than it's worth, so that there isn't room for a commission. Some FSBO sellers are looking at the very real possibility that they'll have to pay money at closing to get the home sold.

Of course, there are other motivations. Some people just don't trust any-one else, real estate agents as an example, and want to take the situation in hand and get it done on their own. Some are just natural "do-it-your-selfers." Others just enjoy the process. The Internet has made it a lot easier for a FSBO seller to market their home themselves. Now they can get exposure on FSBO Web sites, as well as national real estate portal sites like Trulia.com and Zillow.com. With digital cameras, online photo editing, and easy uploads to these sites, more people are encouraged to take the FSBO approach. The "why" of the FSBO listing can be important, as our ultimate purchase price is going to relate to their motivation and urgency. I'm going to share a questions list with you in this chapter. You'll see that we try to get to the root of their decision, as well as determine how motivated they are.

What the FSBO is Doing

Just a Sign - The sophistication of marketing done by FSBO sellers is all over the board. Those just not in the marketing mindset may just stick a hardware store "For Sale By Owner" sign in the yard with a hand printed phone number on it. Actually, these should be high on your target list. They are less likely to be found by buyers and investors if that's all they're doing. I shared Joe Jurek's "driving around your market" tips with you, and that's when you'll come across these potential deals. A simple sign with no other marketing makes this the only way to locate them. It makes saying "you're in the driver's seat" that much more meaningful.

When there is only a sign, your first approach can be a phone call or a knock on the door. If you're in front of the home, you can use your cell phone to start a conversation. A phone call can save you some valuable time if you find out they have placed a ridiculously high price on the home. Your polite side won't let you just walk out if you knocked and found this out while they're showing you the home. We'll get into the first conversation later in the chap-ter. Right now let's stick to marketing methods.

Don't just glance at the yard for signs. Some areas, particularly homeowner associations, restrict signage to a window, prohibiting yard signs. So, as you drive around, look at the windows as well. The smaller and harder the sign is to find, the more likely you're going to have first shot at the home. Others are not finding these homes. Less competition leads to lower offers and higher profits. I've literally seen signs smaller than a car license plate in a window! Keep a sharp eye out, as it could bring you a great deal.

Sign and Ads – The sign is almost always there, so the next phase of so-phistication in FSBO marketing is their placement of classified ads, ads in thrift papers, and possibly ads on eBay and Craigslist. In Jan and Jeremy's story we learned that Jeremy is a big fan of Craigslist for locating FSBO sellers. Of course, you still want to monitor the newspaper classifieds and thrift publications as well. There are still people out there who don't use the Internet, really! What you'll find could be anything from "Home for Sale by Owner, call xxx-xxxx" to ads with some home description infor-mation, and maybe even an email address for contact. A few may even have a photo.

Think of these newspaper and Craigslist ads as a gold mine. The gold is in nugget form, and scattered all through the mine. There are specks, and there are large nuggets. The key is to sift through enough of the dirt (or ads) to turn up the biggest value. You can't read them all, so your goal is to try and identify the best deal candidates, and spend your time in researching those. Watch for keywords that might indicate the best op-portunities, like "desperate," "must sell fast," "price reduced," "owner financing," or "need to sell now."

One of the reasons Jeremy likes Craigslist is that searching for these key phrases is much easier than scanning the newspaper classifieds. Just go to your local Craigslist site and you'll find that a search on just "must sell" will turn up a number of listings. Jan and Jeremy's strategy works best with owner financing, so that key phrase is a great one for Jeremy's searches. Once you get the hang of using Craigslist, you'll return daily to check for those big nuggets.

Some of the yard signs will also have an information tube with flyers. I suggest you always take one, even if the price is high, and your interest isn't immediate, the phone call and file copy are important. The more in-formation you have, the better. You may come back to this property later, after price reductions. Or you may use this property's info in determining the value of another one in the area.

FSBO Web sites and the Internet

A great many FSBO sellers also place their homes on the national real estate portal sites and on some of the many FSBO-dedicated Web sites. Some of these sites sell those signs, lockboxes, and brochure services as well. Visiting these sites and doing regular searches can bring some really great properties to your attention. You'll generally get more extensive descriptions and more photos on these sites as well. So if you see a sign or an ad elsewhere, you may want to search a few of these sites before you make the phone call. If it's also listed on the Web, you can print the listing and use it for notes on your call. It gives you more information that prompts you for questions when you have the seller on the phone. If the seller is using a sign provided by one of these sites, it will tell you just where to look on the Web for more info on the home.

Ads In Strangest Places

Always be alert for FSBO ads. Supermarket bulletin boards have been great resources for some of my students. And it's not just the for sale ads. The "for rent" ads on these bulletin boards give you a prospect for a sale, or an investor for your buyer list. There are also subdivision newsletters, local community papers, homeowner association newsletters, and church bulletins as examples. You never know where a FSBO will place an ad, so be alert and grab that free local newsletter for a look.

What You're Doing

Now we know that the FSBO is marketing their home so that you'll call them. But that's just one side of this great market for your real estate investing. The other side is what you're doing to get them to call you. This is the exciting part! Getting that call or e-mail could mean they haven't even put their home on the market yet. This puts you in front of any competition in making a deal happen. You're continually marketing yourself as a real estate investor in your area with the goal of getting that advanced call. But, if the call comes after the home has been on the market for a while, it could be an even better opportunity.

A discouraged FSBO may have been trying for a few months, showing their home to strangers, getting negative feedback, or maybe getting little or no activity at all. Now they're at a decision point. Should they list with a real estate agent, or is there another way? They see one of your bandit signs, an ad, or a flier, and think that it's at least worth a try to see if you can help. If they're in trouble with their mortgage, this wasted marketing time is in your favor. They're more motivated than when they first went FSBO.

So, early or late, there could be a nugget of a deal that comes right to your door from your marketing. Let's talk about some of the ways that you can market for FSBO sellers, get their attention, and get that phone call when they're highly motivated to sell their home.

Bandit Signs – You've seen these "I buy houses" signs and others like them on street corners, in yards, and anywhere where there is traffic. The point is that from nice printed up signs to a cheap white signs from Wal-mart that you write on with a sharpie, these signs work. They're inexpensive, and you never know when that FSBO has been driving past one of your signs for weeks, then finally gives up on selling on their own, and gives you a call.

Classified Ads and Craigslist – Most of the places we talked about for FSBOs to place their ads are great places for investors to advertise as well. Think about the number of FSBO sellers that are in those ads every day checking to make sure that their ad is running. There's yours, and one day the call will come. As far as Craigslist, the keyword searching that is so great for the investor is also a useful tool for the FSBO seller. I did a search on a town's Craigslist site with the phrase "buy homes" and pulled up a list of investor and lender ads. You know that some sellers are doing the same search. Those key phrases that work in the newspaper are even more valuable to you in Craigslist advertising.

Jeremy told us he used Craigslist to advertise their investing business as much as he did to locate FSBO sellers. His ads about buying homes, avoiding foreclosure, and helping homeowners in trouble do bring them business. It's free, so why not take advantage of a very popular and growing marketing tool on the Web?

Business Cards and Flyers – We're leaving flyers all around town, posting them on bulletin boards, and handing out business cards at every opportunity. A simple flyer that shows how you help homeowners in trouble to avoid foreclosure and save their credit is a powerful business building tool, especially when it's on a bulletin board among FSBO home ads. They may even need to move it over a bit to make room for theirs, creating an opportunity to read it. Don't forget the business cards for divorce attorneys, trust administrators, asset managers, and others who come into contact with homeowners every day. There have been deals done because of a referral. If one of these professionals weren't able to help a homeowner, he or she lets them know that you might be able to do something for them.

Remember examples of bandit signs, flyers, business cards and more go to *www.deangraziosi.com/yourtown/ads.*

Word of Mouth – The Weules first deals came to them through friends. All they did was let everyone in their circle of family and friends know that they were real estate investors. My students get really excited when they make the decision to move forward with real estate investing. Excitement is infectious, and your friends and family will be exposed. They have their own circles of influence, at work and in their hobbies, churches and activities. This expanding circle will bring you FSBO referrals as they hear these sellers talking about their homes. Get excited, tell others, and they'll get excited right along with you!

This could be the most valuable resource of all. To find out about a FSBO through word of mouth could be some of the best deals you discover. Often the word of mouth FSBO is very motivated because they may not yet want to put that sign in their front lawn. Their motivation to sell could be driven by a divorce, financial situation or possible probate property. The cast of characters that are competing to purchase the home is a lot smaller at this point, which gives you the early advantage to negotiate a deal. So remember to network with as many people as you can in your community and follow-up with any and all leads. You never know when the next great deal may be headed your way!

Making the FSBO Call

Joe Jurek has kindly provided his FSBO question list for us. Is Joe great or what? And, he's emphatic that you should be calling just about every FSBO you uncover. He says, *"It's not just to see if their home is a deal for you. I've found FSBO sellers to be very helpful. Whether we decide to move forward and talk more about their home, some of them are happy to tell me about other homes in the area, or about their neighbors who have expressed an interest in selling."* Just carry on a conversation, you'll be amazed by how much you can learn about a neighborhood. You may even hear something about planned development that isn't yet common knowledge.

Now we're ready to make that phone call, and we have our flyer, Web printout, and any notes right in front of us. Pen or pencil in hand, we get the seller on the phone. Right now you're not an investor, just an interested person. We're going to be friendly and speaking with a smile on our face that translates into a smile at the other end. Here are the things we're asking about and why, and the conversation can change the order around. Also you may only get through a few questions and realize the deal is not for you, just be polite and find a nice way to end the call. Here we go:

What are the basics: bedrooms, baths, garage, square footage, one or two story, etc. – This one's basic, and the seller expects you to ask these questions early on. We'll gradually work our way into more detailed information and motivation, but keeping it light and expected at first.

Get some exterior information: lot size, fencing, exterior structures, storage buildings, paved driveway, trees, landscaping, etc. – Another basic set of questions, we want to try and get the owner to give us a descriptive picture of the yard, even though we've probably seen it in a drive-by. Also, we my not be able to see the backyard.

Ask about appliances and major equipment: heating, air conditioning, included free-standing appliances – Even with standardized listing agreements and contracts, real estate agents will tell you that disputes are frequent when a buyer assumes a refrigerator or microwave is included, while the seller never intended to leave it. We need to have notes, so we can properly word our offer later to include these items.

Condition of these major items – Since we're talking about heating, air conditioning and appliances, now is when we can ask about their age and condition.

Ask about floor plan, basement: general layout and basement info – If there is a basement now is the time to ask about any problems with water. By asking about layout, we may hear something that the homeowner loves about their home, or something they wish was better.

General condition information: roof condition, recent upgrades, window/door condition, etc. – Great detail isn't necessary here, but you're looking for more major issues or renovations.

Updates and improvements to the interior – Ask about all recent upgrades to carpet, flooring, counter tops, bathrooms, and kitchens. You're trying to get an idea of how they take care of the home and how it might compare to others of the same age in the neighborhood.

Other big ticket updates like plumbing and electrical – Recent major upgrades to these items are a big positive, and may make this home stand out when compared to others for sale in the area.

What do you like best about your home? – Let them brag a little, and you may get some new information, such as the sunset views from the back yard, or the short walk to a great park for the kids.

The Why and Motivation Question – This is the perfect time to ask, as they've just told you all about how they've improved their home, so say something like, *"It sounds like you've really taken great care of your home, and it's a nice place to live. Could I ask why you're selling?"* Listen carefully, as this is when you find out how motivated they are.

What is your asking price for your home? – I shouldn't have to tell you why we're asking, but listen to how they put it. "Well, we'd like to get $ xxx,xxx," may give you a clue that they're not sure if it's worth that amount.

This is a good place to show you a portion of Joe's Property Features form. He has it in front of him during the call, and it's a simple matter to check off the features as they are discussed. And, there's room for notes. **As with all of these forms, you can get them on my Web site www. deangraziosi.com/yourtown/forms.**

Property features to consider

Property Address:		Date:		
(Place X in box and write number where appropriate)		YES	NO	Number
1.	Fenced Yard ?			
2.	Central Air Conditioning?			
3.	Patio?			
4.	Balcony?			
5.	Deck?			
6.	Garage (if so number of cars)			

Before we go on to other questions, you may be able to make a decision right now as to how much deeper you want to go in your questioning. If the price is way out of range, you may want to thank them and let them know that you're going to think it over, or not, up to you. But, if the price is in the ballpark, and you think that it may be worth some more consideration now, or if the price drops in the future, then we can move to these questions:

Property taxes and insurance costs – They'll usually be happy to share this with you. The insurance can vary based on desired coverage limits, but it's good to ask, as any issues with coverage may come up here.

Special exemptions to property tax? – States and counties often have a list of special exemptions for everything from age to veteran status. You need to know if their tax amount is low because of exemptions you won't get.

The negotiation question – Now that you've gone into dollar amount specifics, they may be getting a bit excited, as you're asking questions that others haven't. So now would be the time to ask if they're flexible on the asking price. Listen carefully to how they phrase the answer. Remember, if they are not flexible right now it does not mean they won't be in 30 or 60 days. So that is why is it good to not only have all this information but to keep it in an easy to find place.

Flexibility in financing – You may get a hint in the previous answer. You want to know if they would consider other than conventional financing, especially if it would allow a higher offer. You may find out here about mortgages on the home, as mortgages would limit their ability to accept owner or other creative financing.

Once you have all of these answers in your notes, you can do the valuation analysis to see if this property might fit your investment strategy. And, we have a chapter to help you with valuation too!

What makes this book so wonderful to me is that I am sharing techniques shared by my students who in most cases never thought about real estate prior to getting my book, never less making money with it! Yet now these student become our teachers, sharing the exact techniques that work now, in the real world. I love sharing this priceless information with you. And it is just not me looking like some bigheaded guru telling you what to do. I am stepping aside and letting my students do most of the teaching. I love it.

CHAPTER 18

Building Your Real Estate Investment Team

We talked about building a team briefly in Angie's chapter because it was such an important part of her success. A good team can allow you to leverage resources and be able to accomplish more in less time. There are many professionals who are available, ready, willing and able to assist you with your investing efforts. Though you may be able to do it all these things yourself, it's just not going to allow you enough time to leverage your knowledge and create profits through multiple deals.

So, let's go through the selection of your real estate investment team members, whether you're investing in your town or another city or state. You won't use all of them on every deal, and some of them will be used only now and then. But, waiting until you need a team player is too late. Interviewing and selection of the right people will not only make your job easier, it will make your deals more profitable. It's a little extra work up front but worth its weight in gold. Think of your real estate team in all facets of what a great team should be all about. You want team members that are professional and can get the job done. A team is sometimes only as good as their bench strength, so always try to have a deep bench of professionals that can step up quickly as their name is called!

In Chad Merrihew's section, he mentioned a potential financial partner's belief that more money could be made if all repairs and other functions were done on their own, without hiring others. This investor and Chad didn't end up doing business because Chad realized that he could do more profitable deals if he stuck to his plan, leaving things better done by others to the experts. Paying a contractor to replace the heating unit was far more efficient than doing it himself. The time saved allowed him to do another deal, making far more money than the small amount spent on the heating contractor. That's not even taking into account the fact that he didn't finish the day with sheet metal cuts and fiberglass in his jeans.

So let's look at our selection of team members starting with real estate agents, and moving through all of the others who will be helping you to build and operate your successful real estate investment business.

Selecting and Working With a Real Estate Professional

- A real estate agent can be a valuable addition to your real estate invest-ment team. Because your agent will be an important and frequently used team member, working with the right one is critical. Not only do you need to be able to get along personally, but a common understand-ing of your needs and goals is quite important. Just in case you haven't been exposed to the structure of real estate representation and who's an agent, broker or Realtor®, let's go over it quickly now.
- A broker, sponsoring broker, or qualifying broker is one who operates a real estate brokerage office and has agents or other brokers working in that office.
- An associate broker is one who has a broker's license, but doesn't choose to operate her own office, instead working under the umbrella of another broker.
- An agent is licensed only to work under a sponsoring broker, and that broker is generally responsible for the activities of the agent.
- A Realtor is one who is a member of the National Association of Real-tors, and subscribes to their code of ethics and rules structure.

In general, someone with a broker's license has had to pass a more exten-sive examination, and may have been required to operate as an agent for a period of time to gain experience. So if you are trying to make a deci-sion from among several good candidates, you could give more weight to those who are brokers instead of agents. But that shouldn't be high on your list of criteria. Many agents have years of experience and simply never wanted to move to broker level. They could be much better quali-fied than a "broker" from an experience perspective.

Here are some questions for you to ask a candidate and get a feel for whether they'll be a good real estate professional for your team:

- Time in the business
- Willing to work with new investors
- Worked with investors in the past
- An example of the best deal they ever made, how they took their exper-tise and allowed a client to have a smoother/easier deal
- Worked with banks on foreclosure/short sales
- Ever successfully handled an assignment of contract
- Invest themselves? (not always a conflict of interest)
- Willing to make low offers
- Willing to send property info regularly that matches your criteria

Those are the main considerations but, going a little deeper, you may ask:

- What days of the week are they normally available to meet or view properties?
- What business hours are they normally available?
- What is their technology comfort level? Do they feel comfortable e-mailing comps or new listings? Can they e-mail information to you?
- Does the real estate agent feel comfortable scanning and using e-mail or faxing documents to you for your signature? Some real estate agents do not want to utilize automation and always want to meet in person to complete paperwork. Due to time constraints this may not be the best fit for you, especially if you make offers on multiple properties. Now there are even special online software solutions for digital signatures. An entire signing can happen with mouse clicks, and a high quality legally signed copy sent over the Web. A high tech agent can also be high touch, but the high tech adds efficiency.
- On the high tech topic again, are they able to use their MLS system to set you up with automated e-mails of new listings that match your search criteria? Almost every MLS now has this capability, but not all agents know how to use it. You'll get all new listings that meet your search requirements, as well as alerts when prices change on those listings. No real estate professional can catch them all, so this automated alert system is really important.
- What are the best contact numbers to reach them? Always request their cell phone to reach them quickly as needed.

Over time, a real estate professional's actions will speak louder than words. As you work with them, it will quickly become apparent how they're serving your needs and how fast they respond to requests. Does the agent do everything they say they will do and in the time frame they commit to do it? When submitting offers on real estate, time is of the essence, so you want an agent that will get your offer in as soon as possible, and not dally when counter offers come back your way.

You don't have to come to a single selection right off the bat. If you can narrow it down to 2 to 5 agents, just start working with them to see how it goes. Let them compete for your business. Here's where you may trade off a little experience for an aggressive attitude and a "jump when you call" approach. Also, some agents specialize, just like attorneys and doctors. More than ever before, there are a lot of agents out there who practice "buyer representation" only. They do not list property. You may want one of them, and another agent who lists only, giving you the best of both worlds. For the listing agent side of your team, you may want to drive around and count signs. Another tactic: look at the MLS listings online and sort them by zip code of interest by, for example, single-family homes. Then do a quick count to see the real estate agents in your area that have the most listings. The most aggressive agents and the best marketers will have more signs out there with their name on them. If you also see a cell number, they are showing that they're responsive, no matter where they may be.

This business is one of timeliness. Not just in contract requirements, but also in acting on opportunities. You really need a real estate professional that's responsive and not just 9 to 5 Monday through Friday. Another tip in dealing with real estate agents to see how quickly they get back to you on a property or how quickly they find the answers to your questions. In some areas of the country, a more seasoned real estate agent may even have other associates that assist them with calls and inquires. Sometimes this team approach can work to your advantage and can help distinguish the real players in the current market.

Don't wait on this selection to do deals. If you're driving through a neighborhood and see an agent placing a sign in a yard, stop and ask about the property. Even if it's not for you, the conversation can lead to other properties, or even a referral to a FSBO that just will not work with the agent. You never know, and only networking with agents will yield these surprise opportunities. Sometimes the early bird can get the worm. If you spot a great deal before it gets listed in the MLS, you might have a deal locked up before others have a chance to even know it is on the market.

The right real estate agent, broker or Realtor can be one of your biggest assets, so finding the right one to fit your goals is a must. But if it doesn't happen immediately, don't panic. Many of my successful students went through several before finding the perfect fit. They still made money prior to that perfect fit, but it was better once they found the right person.

FREE BONUS
If you would like to see a clip from an Empowering Conversations interview I had with a gentleman that I consider the "perfect" real estate agent in today's market, go to *www.deangraziosi.com/yourtown/moneymaker*.

Repair and Remodel Contractors

Though low prices should be a consideration in the mix, this shouldn't be your primary criterion for this selection. There are other things that you should consider when working with a contractor such as quality of work, timeframe from completing a project and the clean up and care of your property after the contractor is complete with the project. In some cases, the terms of payment may be even more critical than the final price you negotiate. The more time the contractor allows you for payment could be a very important factor to measure when making a decision. Because many real estate investment strategies involve multiple offers without resulting deals, you'll need the input of your contractors and repair people on a regular basis, and many times a job and payment won't happen. So building a relationship of trust and passing profitable work to them when you can is important. You'll need estimates at times on short notice and you'll need to be able to rely on them to be reasonably accurate. Cost overruns do not make for profitable real estate deals.

Check out all contractor references, ask to see some of their work, and visit a project or two. In this industry, you want to ensure that contractors will not over promise and under deliver. One of the best referrals for a contractor is networking and speaking to other investors in the area. As you discuss certain needs, names of contractors may come up regularly. Word of mouth can be the best form of advertisement and some of the best contractors may do limited advertising. If they're primarily repair people, ask to see customer comments they've received. Even if you can't be sure that what they're saying is the absolute truth, ask how many of their jobs come in at the original bid, and how many end up going over for any reason. Tell them your intent is to make offers that will not always result in work, but may require repair estimates. You want them to be conservative and accurate, but speed will be usually be needed as well. In exchange, you'll be giving them all of your work.

For major equipment replacement, like furnaces, water heaters and air conditioning systems, a good contractor can give you advanced estimates by size of system or unit. Factoring in a little for possible error, his estimates by BTU size or A/C tonnage can be in your file, ready for you to add into your estimates before you decide on whether to offer on a property or not. Having as much information at your fingertips on the front end will make your offers more realistic.

Your Town Tips:

- Once you acquire the property, try to get at least 3 estimates for any type of major work that you are going to complete. You may be surprised at how much the estimates can vary for the same job.
- Always get every estimate for work in writing and make sure the contractor includes all costs for materials, labor, permits, etc.
- Include payment and terms when you sign a contract.
- Never pre-pay 100% of the price to any contractor. Try to negotiate a payment as completion progresses. For most jobs, I may offer a small payment at the time of contract signing, another payment at the start and the final payment upon completion of the project.
- Try to get as specific as possible with work to be completed. You want to avoid cost overruns by the contractor.
- If time is of the essence and you have a larger project for the contractor, make sure you put in the deadline requirements and possible penalty for not completing within the allotted timeframe.

In today's market, contractors can be just as motivated as sellers and may be flexible on price or terms if you just ask. There is nothing worse for a company to have employees on a payroll and have no pending jobs to complete. Therefore, some companies may work with you to be able to get the job and keep their staff working.

Accountant
Just as there was a difference in a real estate agent, Realtor and a broker, there is just as much difference in an accountant and a certified public accountant. It is important to note that all accountants are not certified public accountants. CPAs have more requirements required for their certification and are held to a higher level of ethics, integrity and a broader base of accounting knowledge. Your accounting professional will be helping with your taxes, but they're also a valuable resource in making deal decisions. Tax consequences of real estate purchases, sales and rentals can make a big difference in your ultimate profitability. You should also have an exit plan, or multiple plans, in place before you get into a deal. How long do you plan on holding a property? What's your planned method of getting it sold when you're ready? When are rental property rehab projects a good idea tax-wise? Can you offer financing in a sale that will postpone capital gains? Or if you take cash out, is it a better way to go than leaving it in and realizing interest income? How does the 1031 exchange work, and how can you use it?

There is more, but the idea is that you need a good tax professional on your team. Sit down and talk to a few of them. Develop not only a good feeling for their knowledge and expertise, but also how you think you'll get along in the future. Similar to your relationship with an attorney, your accountant is going to be involved in a large part of your life through your business finances. Choose well at first, as changes can be expensive later.

Attorney

Some of the same considerations apply to your attorney selection as they do in accountant choice. Law is a broad field, and no attorney can be proficient in all areas. You wouldn't want to be an innocent defendant in a murder trial with a tax attorney at your side. It's the same with real estate. Check on attorneys who specialize in real estate. It's not just about getting a contract drafted to your advantage. There are also situations that can develop related to environmental issues, zoning and building codes. Having the right attorney help you navigate these issues is a necessity.

Many attorneys will do a 30-minute free consultation. Find a few from referrals, friends or the Internet and set an appointment. Tell them exactly what you are planning on doing, get prices, and see if there is a set fee for a closing or only by the hour. Also, if you are going to use no money down "assignment" deals, it's good to have an attorney with experience in this area or at least is comfortable with helping you through a deal like this.

Property Management

Every bit as important as your attorney and accountant, your property manager or company is a major player on your team. If you're planning on growing your net worth and cash flow with rental properties, the person or company you choose to manage them will be with you for the long haul. And if you are planning on investing remotely like many of my students do, finding a rock star in this field is a must. One or two properties may justify the do-it-yourself approach, but any more and you should probably hire someone. The cost is minimal in comparison to the time you could be letting them do what they do best while you are out finding and closing on new deals. Remember; opportunity cost can be expensive.

If your plan is to grow your rental property holdings, make sure that part of your selection process involves a careful look at the current staffing of your candidates, as well as their plans to expand or shrink in the future. They may not have a plan for growth, but you can usually tell if they're motivated to build their business, and have the ability to expand, both in terms of personnel and finances. It isn't fun to outgrow your management team and be forced to start over with a new one, or split your properties between two.

In chapter 20 we will go more in depth on questions you need to ask and how to know you have the prefect property manager.

Mortgage Brokers and Lenders

Don't assume that the selection of mortgage companies and lenders is all about you getting funding for your deals. Many a deal has resulted in a higher profit in a retail resale because the investor was able to help the buyer with financing. This is especially true if you're working with buyers who have credit problems. A creative and aggressive mortgage broker can make the difference in the deal. And the buyer, appreciative in getting a loan they didn't expect, will pay top dollar for the home.

Remember Greg Murphy's use of mortgage brokers to help his tenant buyers improve their credit scores and buy the property through a lease purchase agreement. All along they paid market rent, taking good care of the home that some day would be theirs. Your profits in selling properties can be improved just by having the right team members on the mortgage side.

Just like real estate agents, many lenders and mortgage are specialized by type of loan. This could be just their preference, or it could be about success, or lack of it, in getting certain loans approved and through the process. Another reason a broker may not want to do a certain type of loan, or work with certain lenders, has to do with their income. If you aren't getting the financing you need for yourself or your buyers then make sure that it's only after the mortgage broker has tried several lenders and underwriters. If they only try one or two and tell you it can't be done, you may have a broker who isn't taking you to the best sources because they don't pay high enough fees.

When choosing a mortgage broker, be transparent with everything when it comes to loans you want to obtain. Make sure you let them know that you could be potentially bringing them the buyers of the homes you will be selling, assigning or finally closing on a lease option. Ask them if they assist future clients with credit repair **(If you need credit repair help, go to *www.deangraziosi.com/yourtown/creditrepair*.)**

Other things to consider when working with a mortgage broker:
- Make sure they have banks that are friendly to investors and that they have banks that do not require seasoning on homes before a refinance or new loan.
- Make sure you understand their fee structure.
- Make sure the broker can quickly get you information on approvals or options that are available.
- The broker is aware of all special incentives and programs that buyers may qualify for.

Escrow Companies

Another member of your team could be an escrow agent or escrow officer. If you are considering doing lease purchase options like Greg Murphy does, an escrow company will be a very important member of your team. The independent third party escrow agent collects and processes rental payments, mortgage payments and provide you with a monthly payment, net of a small fee. This independent third party also becomes a credible resource when a mortgage broker needs to verify timeliness and consistency of payments made by a tenant buyer to a landlord.

Title Company Selection

Depending on the state where you live and the way contracts are negotiated, you may not have a choice as to which title company to use. However, if you're doing a lot of creative and owner financing, you will probably be in control of the title company. There's a lot of similarity in services offered by title companies, but that doesn't mean that there's little difference in how they deliver those services. Selection is important.

Similar to your consideration of real estate agents and mortgage brokers, you want a responsive title company. They may do a great job of processing documents and researching title, but if you can't keep track of the process, how do you know they're on track? You want a title company that takes your phone calls, returns your messages, and lets you know early about any problems in the process.

If the company will be insuring titles for properties you plan on owning for a while, ask them which underwriters they use and how many. Underwriters are rated like other insurers on their financial stability. If you think this is incidental, know that a major title insurer was declared insolvent because they had too much invested in real estate securities during the mortgage crisis. Hundreds of thousands of paid-for policies became worthless instantly.

Various Miscellaneous Role Players on your Team

There are other miscellaneous individuals that may become part of your team. These other members could be Jim from the local Home Depot that really knows a lot about the store and materials. Another member could be your team of bird-dogs that find potential deals and inform you about them. You could have other members such as the person at the local newspaper that you contact and they take that extra time with you to craft the maximum size classified ad you can run for the price.

Your Team is Part of Your Success

Building your real estate investment team is a win-win approach. As you are more successful in real estate your team will be able to profit and become more successful as well as they assist you with your deals. I'll help you with other investors as funding members of your team in the "Funding Your Real Estate Deals" chapter. The other members here all have an important contribution to make to your success. Develop long term relationships of mutual respect and the attitude that all of the team members need to win in your deals. You may use some of them some of the time, or all of them a little of the time, but every one will come into play at some point. You want them there when you need them. Building the right team can be a continuous work in process. So as you move forward treat people better than you want to be treated and people will be there when you may need them the most.

It all comes down to your network of professionals and the "sphere of influence" around them. The more we can come out of our comfort zone and meet new people and expand our sphere of influence the more opportunities that can come your way. I have found that every new person that I meet has at least one person they may know that can assist me with my goals in real estate. Some people know great bankers, realtors, handyman, attorneys, contractors or even buyers or sellers. Thus, each day work on expanding that sphere of influence and who knows how large it may grow!

CHAPTER 19

Evaluating Repair and Renovation

Why valuation, repair and renovation all together? In so many of our deals, we're buying a property in need of repairs, and possibly renovation. So, we must have a pretty firm grip on our costs to get the property ready for sale if we're planning repairs. As far as renovation, we may recognize an opportunity in a home that's still pretty much like it was built in the 1980's while others around it have been remodeled with features today's buyers want. If we can buy it right, and do the renovations at the right cost, we can sell it for a tidy profit. But that means we better know how to come up with those renovation costs. Whether we learn to do it ourselves, call on contractors for estimates and bids, or some of both, it's important to know value before and after repairs and renovation. When looking at a potential deal, try to see beyond what others see. If you see the potential or the "hidden value" in a property and you can properly estimate the repair and renovation costs, you may not just have an okay deal, but you could have a "killer deal" on your hands!

Matt Larson, a student of mine, went from a machine worker living in a 300 sq. ft. apartment to a millionaire, all thanks to reading my books and participating in my Success Academy. He is not only a great guy, a great example of what you can accomplish, he has also become a friend and investing partner. Now I have refrained from talking about many of my deals, I did that in my previous books. But I can talk about this quick since Matt and I are partners. Together, we have bought around 30 homes together in the area he was living in Illinois. We used all the same techniques you are being taught. We bought really low by using a great real estate agent to help us make multiple low offers. The houses we're buying averaged about $50,000. We would pay cash for them, rehab them, rent them, then do a refinance of 70% loan to value. Since we bought them so cheaply, in most cases, we would get all of our money back plus rehab money then rent each one for positive cash flow. We have flipped a few for a nice profit, but we are holding most for cash flow and larger future gains. But let me get to why I am writing about it now. With the 30 houses we have done together, the average rehab is around $6,000. Plus, we are looking for the same type of home, same type of repairs needed and man they are all seemingly the same. I share this with you because it can truly become second nature to you, even if repairs are not your thing. Matt said he had never even painted a wall before he started investing. Now he can walk in to a home and within minutes know if it is another $6,000 repair home. But until you are that confident, get advice, estimates and help from someone more informed.

Whether you're flipping for resale, or holding for rental, it's critical you know how to determine value in the current market. You might think that this is all about numbers with indisputable results. That's not the case, as there are subjective factors, as well as relative value based on who's doing the buying and for what reasons. There are also different people with different goals that may be helping you to determine value, or even deciding value as an appraiser. The appraiser's role has a lot of influence, as they are working with lenders, and your financing is dependent on their valuation, over which you have no control.

The Appraiser

Before the upheaval in lending in 2006 through 2009, appraisers were generally selected off of a list by the lender, with a great deal of discretion on the lender's side. They could choose the appraiser who was more likely to give them the valuation they wanted, and the goal was to get that loan approved and collect those fees. We all know how that turned out. Now it's a bit different. There are still fights going on in legal circles and Congress to adopt more stringent rules, but the lenders definitely don't have the discretion in choices they had before.

Most lenders now are either using appraisers off of a rotating list, with whichever one is next getting the assignment. Or they're taking bids from their list, and using the lower cost appraisers. There's a lot of infighting to have these rules changed, but we're really just bystanders as investors. It just helps to know, whether we think it's right or not, that there are certain "facts of life" when it comes to appraisals:

- There is no incentive for an appraiser to over-value a property if there's a purchase price and contract. They will have to answer to the lender, their employer, if the borrower later defaults and the lender finds that the appraisal of value $20,000 over the contract price won't hold up in the market. That's why the vast majority of appraisals come in at or very little above the contract price. In today's market, some appraisers are being overly conservative and valuing properties below the negotiated purchase price. Appraisers use to use comps of similar properties that have sold within one year, however in some markets the appraisers re now using comps from sales within the past 3 months. Therefore, it is key to know what is happening in your market today.

- Pretty much the same situation exists in refinances. There's still an amount stated that the borrower needs for cash out, so a number to shoot for.
- It's not so clear-cut when there isn't a purchase contract, as in an appraisal for an estate, or a seller who just wants to know. Comparing appraisals in these situations can yield bigger differences, as there isn't a number out there that's required. With plenty of comparable properties to use in their appraisal, different homes might be chosen in this situation than in one with a purchase price or refinance amount.

So, what do we as investors need to do to help? There's little we can do, except make our properties as presentable as possible and wait for the results. However, we could offer information on the property and surrounding market. The appraiser likes to know any and all repairs that have been made. I request to meet the appraiser at each property "so I can ensure he can get in and have access to the entire property." I usually provide a packet of information based on the normal questions the appraiser may ask and the information he needs to gather for his report. I often provide an extensive list of any and all repairs and renovations made right down to the new light fixtures or doorknobs. I also like to provide a floor plan drawing with closets, exits, room measurements and any other special features. The more information I can provide, the easier it may be for the appraiser to remember when they are crafting their report. The area of town is also important. If I am on the favorable side of a busy street near a school, this could be of greater value then being on the other side of town. The other side of town could be in the same zip code, but not have the same appeal to potential buyers. The more information that I can provide to make the appraiser's job a little easier, the better professional relationship I can cultivate with additional real estate professionals.

Without a lot of detail, the very basic goals of the appraiser are:

- Understand the market, and the influences on price in various neighborhoods
- Select the very best comparable properties that have sold
- As similar as possible to the subject property in size, bedrooms, etc.
- As close as possible to the property in the neighborhood
- Sales as recent as possible
- Make adjustments to value based on differences between the comparable properties and the subject of the appraisal

In cases where there are a number of very similar properties close-by, and they were sold within the last six months, this is not too difficult or variable of a process. If there aren't enough comps close-by, then the circle is widened, but the result may not be as reliable using properties farther away, or homes sold more than six months ago. If you have access to similar homes that have sold in the area, I would just provide copies of this information as a point of reference for the appraiser.

The Real Estate Agent's CMA (Comparative Market Analysis)

If the appraiser is trying to make sure that the lender isn't taking on unnecessary risk, the real estate agent has very different objectives in mind when doing a CMA for a seller. They are trying, at least the seller hopes so, to give a seller a realistic number at which they can expect to sell their home in the current market. The word "current" is important, as the market is changing, sometimes daily. New listings come on the market, some are taken off, and others are sold. A good real estate professional will make follow-up reports to advise the seller if they need to adjust their list price.

You may end up with a real estate professional who will work up CMAs for you, using recent sales from the MLS. The MLS Association usually carefully protects this information, so only their members allowed to access sold data. So while you can't get to it to do an analysis on your own, you can learn the process and make it easier on your agent. Once you can do it yourself, they only need to send you sold reports, and you can take it from there.

The process is similar to that of the appraiser. The real estate agent locates the best comps among recently sold properties in the area. The same criteria apply, as the sell date needs to be as current as possible, and the property's location should be as close to the subject home as we can get. The agent also tries to select homes similar in style, size, bedrooms, baths, etc. Then adjustments are made to the sold homes selling prices to add or subtract for differences. It looks like this:

- You have a home you want to sell, with 3 BR, 2.5 BA, 1 car garage, ¼ acre lot, the home totaling 2450 square feet.
- One of the comparable sold properties has 3 BR, 2 BA, and 2-car garage on the same size lot. This home sold for $200,000 three months ago.

- The appraiser or real estate agent will adjust the sold price of the home in two areas in this case:
- Add the value of a half bath, as your house has an extra half bath
- Subtract the value of one garage space, as your home has a one car garage compared to the comp's two.
- So, we're raising the comp's sold price to make it more like your home for the bath, but subtracting for the smaller garage in your home.

There can be a number of these adjustments, and there are variables for distance apart, different streets, maybe a cul-de-sac, and how long ago it sold. But you get the idea. We're bringing the sold prices of our comparable properties into line with our home based on features and other variables. Over time, you can become an expert at this, needing only the sold prices and what you know about the homes from the Internet to do your own valuations. When you are able to do your own valuations, it truly gives you the advantage to make better offers and to be able to create better profit margins or a wider array of exit strategies.

Breaking news as this book goes to press comes from www.redfin. com, a brokerage that has branches in multiple large cities around the country. They just announced that their Web site will display sold prices and detailed data about homes within hours of the closing. You can access the sold homes by maps from their home page. It is expected that this will become more common soon, as the National Association of Realtors' settlement of a recent action by the Department of Justice allows online brokers to display the same data that a broker can share in person with a client.

Are Tax Valuations Useful?

Usually not. However, if a taxing jurisdiction is computerized, their valuation formula is known, and they use the latest sold price for the home, you can get a pretty good idea by working the math from the valuation back to the sold price. But, in general the other methods are better, as too many taxing authorities are behind in assessments, yielding old and inaccurate values. It's not worthless information though, as comparing the tax valuations of similar homes in different neighborhoods can help you to figure out the value of the land under the homes.

An advantage of accessed values is in understanding how the tax authority calculates these amounts. In an area that has seen properties values decline in value there could be a process to appeal a higher tax bill. If you see this in an area it could be an opportunity. For example, if a property has lowered its asking price because the property taxes are high and a buyer likes the property but does not like the annual taxes, it could be an opportunity. If you understand the tax valuation and appeal process what if you could acquire the property at a great price and appeal the tax to get them lowered. Not only will you probably already have a tax credit the seller has to provide, but also get the tax bill reduced, thus putting more cash from the tax credit in your pocket!

Another approach is to understand what is happening in the local markets. One of my students informed me two layers of tax credits will take effect in their communities in the next two years. Some property owners will have their property taxes reduced by more than 50%. Can you imagine how many sellers may not realize this and may sell their properties today because of the tax bill strain that will go away in a few years? This could be another tremendous opportunity.

Estimating Repair and Renovation Costs and Value

When we're cooking up a deal, underestimating one ingredient can lead to an unappetizing dish. It's far better to pass on a deal than to risk a loss. A little creativity in ingredient measurements is usually not a problem in our deal recipes, but using 8 ounces of the basic ingredient when 16 ounces is called for is usually a recipe for disaster.

You can invest in real estate without dealing with repairs and renovation. But a great deal of profit is waiting out there for those who can look past the things wrong with a home to the ultimate value if those things were corrected. Sometimes it is just cosmetics, like painting and landscaping. Or it could be structural and systems repairs to roofing, plumbing, heating or other major items. We could even be adding rooms, tearing out walls, modernizing, or remodeling kitchens and baths.

In the valuation information, I gave you resources for getting to the true value of the home. When extensive repair or renovation is necessary, the value at which you buy should be much less than the ultimate value once the work is completed. That's your profit once the cost of the work is paid. It's easy to see that you can lose some or all of this profit, or even have a loss, if you underestimate the cost of repairs or renovation. You'll want to use a combination of resources and methods to come to realistic estimates for repairs and renovation, including:

Contractor quotes - Some of the same considerations should be used here as with using real estate agents. Overuse without something in it for them could cut off your source. Try to find reasonable contractors who do good work and stick to their quotes. You should then use them for the work whenever possible. This will make them happy to give you quotes on a regular basis, even if a lot of them don't result in you doing the deal. They understand your need for accurate quotes for assessing the deal, so keep them in the loop for work when you can.

Your Town Tips:

- Try to do a more basic rehab first that only needs paint and carpet.
- As you become a more seasoned investor slowly take on larger projects if you desire.
- For example, start with a small one level home to do rehab and renovation and note what you learn regarding time and costs. You do not want a very large major rehab to be your first deal. The information and knowledge that you gain along the way will be priceless and increase your profit margin. It is true to assume, the more experience you gain, the higher the profit margin you will generate per deal.

Develop your team, including plumbers, electricians, heating and air conditioning contractors, roofers, carpenters and general handymen. Explain how you do business, the type of deals you look for, how you rely on their estimates and completion time frames, and that you value their services. Not only will their future work bring you profits, they may also become a resource for deals. They see homes in all conditions and areas, some in the course of working for banks or others involved in foreclosures or pre-listing repairs. Good relationships work both ways.

Books and Online Resources - Over time, if your interests run to construction and repairs, you'll begin to develop your own estimation abilities. You'll find that you can wait to contact your team, because you know pretty closely what it's going to cost to get a home to where you want it. You can make offers based on your own knowledge, allowing for some error and wait to see if there is a deal in the making. If it looks like it, then you may call in some expert advice and price estimation. You can get help in this from a number of books and online resources:

- "National Repair and Remodeling Estimator" - This book is published annually by Craftsman Book Company, and you can purchase it online from several book outlets.
- BDEG - "Building Damage Estimators Guide" - This handy guide contains suggested labor times for most residential repair procedures and pre-calculated tables that provide the amount of material required. Find it at http://www.npccrs.com/estguide.php.
- Online building cost calculator at http://www.building-cost.net/

The more you know, the less you'll risk in relying on others. If repair and renovation are part of your investing strategies, develop your own abilities, even if it's just to be able to verify the estimates and work of others. At **www.deangraziosi.com/yourtown/forms** we have great spreadsheets to help. Here's partial screen shot:

Items in need of rehab or repairs

Property Address:		Date:		
(Place X in box and write number where appropriate)		YES	NO	Number
1.	Roof (number of layers?)			
2.	Windows (need to be replaced)			
3.	Doors (need to be replaced)			
4.	Painting (exterior of home)			
5.	Treat/Paint Deck or fence?			
6.	Paint Garage ? (other issues)			

That's Cost – What's a Remodel Worth?

Every year, *Remodeling Magazine* issues a Web site report of the value of major repairs, remodels and room additions in relation to the cost. You'll find it at this link: http://www.remodeling.hw.net/2008/costvs-value/national.aspx. It's a great resource of relatively unbiased data. It's also broken out by regions, so you can zero in a little better on the data for your town.

Keep in mind that their costs are supposed to be retail, what the homeowner would pay for the job. If you're working with contractors regularly, and negotiating below-retail work, then you can adjust these percentages for a better result. Because they give the numbers for all types of room additions, bedrooms, baths, garages, and kitchen remodels, you can use these numbers in your market analysis adjustments we talked about before.

They're All Related

Whenever repairs or renovation are involved in a deal, valuation is dependent on the cost as well as the resulting added value, if any, of the work that's being done. Your ability to accurately determine after-repair value of a home can cause you to do a deal that others have shied away from. Learn as much of this as you want, and rely on trusted experts for the rest.

CHAPTER 20

Cash Flow and Property Management

Throughout the student stories and deal recipes in this book, you've seen the words "cash flow" a lot. Cash flow is extremely important to any and all businesses. It is vital to the health of any business, including your real estate business. You may even consider the cash flow as the "blood of the business". The business needs cash flow to be healthy, vibrant and in sound fiscal shape! Often, as you consider deals to pursue, you also need to consider cash flow from the deal. No matter if you are going to assign the deal, flip the deal, or buy and hold the deal as a rental property you need to forecast your cash flow while you have money tied up into the property.

How much cash will be needed to see the deal from the purchase contract acceptance to completion? If you assign a deal or use the Greg Murphy style lease option strategy, the amount of cash out of pocket in many cases could be nothing at all except maybe for some research. If you plan on a traditional flip, you will probably buy the property, make repairs and then resell. Thus the amount of cash flow needed just went up significantly. You need cash to acquire the property, cash to pay the insurance, and cash for the material and labor for the improvements.

If you sell the property on your own, rather than use a realtor that can put the property in the MLS, you will need to invest in advertising. Whether you put up small bandit style signs in the neighborhood, a large for sale sign in the front yard, or and run an ad in the local newspaper.

Typically when you hear the term cash flow in the real estate world, it is the money you have left over from the rent, less any and all of your expenses. If you have money left over each month, this is referred to as positive cash flow. If you are short each month and have more bills then the amount of rent you took in, this is negative cash flow.

Normally a mortgage payment will have a portion that goes to reduce the principal amount you borrowed and a portion that goes to pay the bank back interest for the mortgage loan.

If you have any annual expenses that may not be included in your monthly mortgage payment such as property insurance and property taxes, then you should take the annual amount and divide it by 12 to figure how much you will need each month. This provides a true and accurate picture of the cash flow from each property.

It isn't an accident that a great many of these deals are focused on buying and holding a property for long term rental with more rent coming in than expenses going out. My students shared a number of deal recipes that resulted in positive cash flows after mortgage payments, taxes, insurance, and other expenses involved in holding the property. Let's think about this type of buy and hold strategy as just another investment play.

• They could have just flipped houses, taking nice profits out in a hurry.
• Then, they could have invested those profits in a Certificate of Deposit at 3%.
• Or they could have put those profits into the stock market or bonds.

Of course, the stock and bond markets have given investors a really rough ride the last few years, with few actually retiring on cash flow from their investments. A CD at 3% isn't even going to keep up with inflation over time. What's an investor to do? Just what these students did.

• Buy and rehab homes for long term rental.
• Buy at deep discounts to value.
• Use creative funding, but always with a positive cash flow outcome.
• Collect that cash every month for as long as they hold the property.
• Take advantage of the tax advantages of owning rental property.
• Realize returns on their investments of more like 12% to 20% or more.
• Watch their value and net worth go up as the market hopefully rebounds in years to come.

These are the things you need to remember when you set out to plan your long-term property management activities. Recalling all of those great investment results will help you have a smile on your face when you're self-managing and get that late night call about a water leak in the bathroom. It's common to self-manage early in your investing, when you have just a few properties. But once you begin to see the compounding of income from multiple rental properties, you may want more of them. As you accumulate properties, you'll want to bring in others to handle the day-to-day management tasks.

I'm going to give you a lot of help in this chapter in how to market and manage your properties. Even if your plan is to immediately take on out-side management, you should have a thorough understanding of what's involved so that you can use that knowledge to interview property management professionals. So, first just a little on hiring a company, then a lot on how to manage, market, set rents, and improve your properties.

Hiring a Property Manager or Company

In the chapter on building your real estate investing team, we learned some of the important things you look for in selecting a property management professional or company. Most of those tips had to do with helping you to locate properties located in the right areas for rentals, as well as identifying the characteristics and features of a home that would make it stand out and stay occupied with happy tenants; not to mention command higher rents.

Additional considerations in selecting a property manager or management company would have to do with record-keeping, money handling procedures, expense control, how they market rentals, and tenant relations. How do they handle maintenance calls, both on the tenant side and in getting the right repair company out at a reasonable cost? There's no substitute for experience.

As in any business, knowing the competition is important in evaluating your place in the market. When it's about rental property, what you can charge for rent and how to keep the property occupied is all about how yours compares to other similar rentals in the area. Driving around, taking pictures of properties, and comparing the neighborhoods could be a first step. If there are promotional signs out, or ads offering free months of rent or other incentives, make sure to note them in relation to the property location and exterior appearance. You'll not be too concerned about a two months free rent offer for a property that's in disrepair and very inferior to yours. But, the same offer for a very similar property would be something to consider in competing for tenants.

During the drive, get the phone numbers and call as if you're a prospective tenant. At this point, you don't want to get in to see a unit and you can usually find out just about everything you know in a phone call if you ask the right questions. These questions include:
• Is there an application fee?
• Is there a lease required? If so what is the length of the lease term?

- Is there a security deposit required and if so how much?
- Does the property allow for pets and if so what types of pets are acceptable?
- Did the landlord inform you that an additional pet deposit or fee would be charged? If so, how much?
- What is the monthly rent for the unit?
- What is the total square footage of the unit?
- Does the unit have central air conditioning?
- How is the parking situation? Is there adequate street parking? Does the unit have a driveway in the front or rear of the property?
- Is there a garage? If so how many cars?
- Does the landlord pay any of the utilities such as water, gas or electric? If so, what is paid by the landlord and what is paid by the tenant?
- What is the average cost of utilities?
- Does the landlord allow a television satellite dish to be mounted to the property roof or building?
- Does the property have a patio, deck, or a fenced yard?
- Does the property have storage in the basement or attic?
- Are there connections for a washer and dryer? Are these appliances furnished?
- Are any other appliances furnished such as a stove, refrigerator or a dishwasher?
- Does the property have any other unique features such as a fireplace, wet bar, vaulted ceilings or skylights?
- How many bathrooms does the unit have? (More than one is often a great feature)
- Does the property have a dining room? If not how large is the kitchen?
- How many bedrooms does the property feature? Can the bedrooms fit a Californian King Bed and related furniture?
- How is the closet and storage space?
- Who does the exterior yard work, such as grass cutting, hedge trimming and snow shoveling, the tenant or the landlord?
- Does the property have any bonus rooms like an office, recreational room, sunroom, etc?
- If the unit requires repairs, who does the repairs and how fast do items get repaired?
- What school system is the property located in?
- What is the closest park to the property?
- I am new to the area and can you please explain what are some of the nice features of the property in general? Could you also advise of any nice features in the surrounding neighborhood in general?

Pricing and Your Rental Log

Now, take your individual property notes and their answers to the question list and compare your rental to the information you've collected. Look at them as objectively as possible, as if you were a renter about to make a decision. What is better about their unit, and the same for yours? Which would be more appealing and possibly get you to pay a higher rent? Is it because of a garage in a snowy climate, or free Internet access in an apartment project?

Do a thorough comparison, and end up with an adjustment to their rent, kind of like the appraisers did in our chapter on valuation. If your overall impression is better for their unit, then subtract some from their rent to determine what yours might need to be to be competitive. If yours is better, add some to their rent to adjust for that. Of course, your rental amount is your decision. But if you end up with vacancy time while you're holding out for another $75/month, it can destroy profitability.

Let's look at this situation for a moment. Let's say that your property is on the market with a rent of $1200/month. If you're holding out for that extra $100/month, and it should be set at $1100, how does that look in relation to the time it takes you to rent it? If it would have rented right away at $1100, you would lose $100 x 12 months, or $1200 for the year. That's one month of rent. If it takes you two months to get a tenant into the unit at the higher rent, you're going backwards. Your first year of ownership will have taken in 10 months of rent, or $12,000 at the higher rental amount. Had it rented right away at $1100/month, it would have been $13,200.

Vacancy loss is far more damaging to your bottom line than a slightly lower rent or some repairs. Let's look at this same situation six months or a year from now, when the lease is coming up for renewal. You may have had a clause for automatic increases for inflation, or maybe an automatic conversion to month-to-month rent at the current rate. There are a lot of ways you can write a lease. But, when it's time for a tenant to make a decision about the next year of their life, all bets are off. It's a new negotiation.

It's not just the fact that you might lose a tenant. If you do, your costs are going to go up for paint, maintenance, and unit make-ready for a new tenant. Then there's the dead time, usually a full month at a minimum, before you get a new tenant into the unit. So, continue to monitor your competition, and adjust your rents to the current market. Later I'll give you some property and feature improvement tips to help you to raise your rent or keep it up when others are having to drop theirs.

In my early years as a nieve young man, I handled all my own rental management. I didn't have anyone in my life to tell me not to do it all and there was more money to be made aquiring new properties than plumbing. But I was broke and felt I did not have an option. And this still may be a smart choice for your first few years or if you are handy. Now I have had a variety of property management firms. I have an old friend, who is very handy and business savvy, manging my properties in upstate NY.

Advertising Your Rental

This is a good time to talk about the difference between advertising and marketing. Advertising includes all the ways you tell people about your rental. Whether in print, on the Internet, or other ways we'll talk about here, it's the act of getting the word out to your target renter. Advertising involves decisions about methods, media, frequency and cost. It is about putting your best foot forward, promoting the features of your property, location, and any other amenities that would lure a tenant at the best rent.

Marketing is considered by many to be the same thing as advertising. And your advertising is a part of your marketing strategy. Marketing includes advertising, but it also includes something else. It's positioning your rental unit in the market in a way that makes it unique, or causes it to stand out from the competition. When you were driving around and calling the competition, you took extensive notes, contrasting their product with yours. Here's where marketing comes in. It's a plan for promoting what makes your rental different.

It's OK if it's price. Maybe you made such a great deal on the purchase that you can rent out a home or apartment below the competition and still do quite well with your cash flow. There's nothing wrong with price as the focus of your marketing, as long as you get the cash flow and profitability results you need. Actually, if price is your best feature, it can be a long term advantage. Tenants will be reluctant to move and pay more, unless it's a really great property with more features than yours. Keeping tenants in the property longer means lower ongoing costs related to turnover.

When you did your comparisons and pricing for your unit, you identified certain features that made your unit stand out, differentiating it from most of the competition. If it's location, maybe near a college campus, then that may be the thing you want to focus on in your marketing plan. It may be larger rooms, more square footage, common area amenities like a pool or hot tub, or a fireplace or garage. Whatever your unit's stand-out features, this is where you want to focus your marketing.

Your feature marketing focus can influence your choice of advertising. Back to the location being close to a college campus, you'll want to look at bulletin boards on campus, and maybe the campus newspaper. So, as you read through the advertising methods and options that follow, note down how each fits into your marketing plan. For a luxury apartment with high end amenities and higher rent, you probably wouldn't spend time doing flyers for the campus bulletin board.

The Power of a Great "For Rent" Yard Sign

We talked about the power of driving a community and getting a pulse or a feel of the local area. The same is true when looking at a rental property. Driving a neighborhood, I would often notice the properties for rent, as well as the properties for sale. The ironic thing was that some landlords had for rent signs that you couldn't read, even if you were standing less than 10 feet from the sign. Then there were the signs that were falling over, faded, hidden behind a bush or tree, in a window 25 yards away from the street, or had numbers so small you couldn't even read them with 20/20 vision.

Remember our math exercise in the lost rent from a vacant unit. People drive around and look for rentals every bit as much as for homes to buy. In fact, with rentals not having the listing power of the MLS, many renters believe that they won't see some of them if they don't drive around and look for signs. You want the sign easy to read, with large numbers clearly displayed. If a prospective tenant passes a property and can't read the phone number on a first drive-by, they may not turn back for a second look. If it's raining, and they can't read the sign, they may not get out of the car. When you're trying to rent a property for $800 or $1200, it's important to spend the money for an effective yard sign.

• If you're at a home improvement or hardware store, go for the metal signs. They're much more durable than plastic or vinyl, and they'll withstand wind and rain a lot better. I've even seen a good metal sign hold up as a goal post for the kids' front yard football game.

- Don't use a marker, no matter how nice your handwriting. Go to an office supply or home improvement store and buy stick-on vinyl lettering. Sometimes you can even find reflective lettering so that your phone number can be seen at night when the car lights hit it.
- For those cold areas of the country, use warm water to soften the ground for the sign legs. Otherwise, you may end up without the penetration and support you need. A sign laying on the ground isn't one that will get you a renter.
- When one property gets rented, just recycle the sign to another one.

What about flyers and a "Take One" tube? It's a small investment that can really bring results. In some areas, there is a MLS store where you can buy signs and these information tubes, even lockboxes. I know I have bought sign tubes myself in the past at Home Depot, so they are not hard to find. Keeping flyers in these tubes gives your drive-by prospects something to take home, as well as some nice pictures of the interior and a list of features. It's like a full color ad in a newspaper, but a whole lot less expensive, ending up in the hands of a real tenant prospect.

Signs or Ads on Bulletin Boards
Whether a local grocery store bulletin board, or one at the college campus, these are excellent places to advertise your rental unit. A color photo makes yours stand out among the many pinned to the board, and detachable phone numbers along the edge make it easy for people to take along a reminder when they don't have a pencil or the time to write down contact information. Remember most of today's computers come with some sort of program to easily create a flyer. And if you don't know how to use it get your teenage children, nieghbors or family member to whip it up in minutes. Do you want a template on what it should look like? Then grab a flyer that you like from a real esate tube or from a bulletin board. Take a quick picture of your unit and create something that looks professional.

Newspaper Ads
"Newspaper" can mean a number of different things here. The first that comes to mind is always the dominant daily or weekly paper. But there are also smaller community newspapers, church papers, homeowner association newsletters, the Thrifty Nickel, and other freely distributed local specialty papers. Remember our marketing discussion before? If a lower-than-market rent is your main marketing point, the Thrifty Nickel or a similar paper would be an ideal placement of your ad. If your rental unit

is near a large church, there may be members who would like to rent nearby. The church newsletter may take advertisements.

Here are some things to think about when making newspaper advertising decisions:
• The cost in relation to the areas covered and the circulation.
• Check different run lengths, as it may be less expensive to run an ad for a two week period than to place it for three weekends in a row.
• If one paper also gives you a free online listing with your ad, it could be a better choice, even at a slightly higher ad cost.
• Let the ad run a while, even if you get a tenant quickly. They may change their mind before finally signing a lease. You can also take backup names in case there's a problem. Keep these names and numbers, as you may find another property that is perfect for them.

Never think of a for rent ad as having the sole purpose of getting a tenant for a specific unit. Throughout this book, students have shown you the value of building lists of buyers and sellers. There's just as much value in doing the same for renters. Plus, they frequently move from renting to buying at some point.

Craigslist and Rental Sites
There are specialty home and apartment rental sites on the Internet. A search on Google with the phrase "home rentals" will give you plenty of sites to research. Some are free to the landlord, making their money on ads, while some charge a small fee. Other free sites make money offering products or services like yard signs and those "Take One" tubes. If it's a free listing, you have little to lose, just the time to enter your property information.

Craigslist is a really great resource. It's free, and has a section just for housing rentals. The National Association of Realtors states that more than 80% of home buyers begin their search on the Internet. Though I haven't seen a similar study for renters, it has to be a very similar situation. You can not only list your features, but also include color photos, something that would be very expensive in a newspaper. It's a busy world, and busy people love the Internet for research. People also like to do their shopping first on the Web, avoiding a phone call and possible sales pitch. If your area is covered by Craigslist, you should definitely use this resource.

Without going in to an indepth marketing lesson, I want you to think about your titles and your message. Think about it, the title on a

Craigslist ad (or any ad for that matter) is nothing more than a headline. Like the headline of a newspapaer that makes you pick it up or a headline on Yahoo.com that makes you click on it. You want to make sure you capture something appealing in your headline. So here are some quick lessons:

Make sure your headling has a strong benefit. It has to be short and powerful, one or two words. Here is a good task. Go to Craigslist and look at other apartments in you area and see what headline pops out at you. While I am writing this, I went to Craigslist and looked at apartment headlines in Ohio. I just picked randomly. It's exactly what I thought. Some of the short headlines has simply the "options"…

$575/3br–AMELIA 3BR 2BA $575 MONTH

While others stood out for me because they gave me a "benefit" with just a few words

$595 2br - Grab your keys - Leave your Money in the bank!! Free Rent till 2010.

$625 Wrong Season — Right Price. A very special home in a very special place.

Now these last two ads really stuck out for me and would be the ones I clicked on. All the pictures and explanations of the property in the body of the message mean nothing if someone does not click on your headline. The is especially true on Craigslist which is a great Free resource for you.

Now one last lesson. When you write your message about the property you want to rent, make sure your content is benefit-driven not option-driven. You can say "it is close to bus stop," that is an option. But what is the benefit of that? How about rewording: "Leave the car at home and save gas. You're a hop, skip, and a jump from public transportation!" If you are close to a major highway you could simply put the option "close to highway" or you could write "Cut down on your commute time with easy access to major highway!" Small changes, but you changed each to a benefit. Now if you are using a traditional classified ad, of course you need to be short, but with the power and flexibility of Craigslist and other online outlets to advertise, you can use more words and be more creative in your explanation. If you can, include pictures and take the time to snap good ones. If they don't look good to you, they won't look good to anyone else.

When You Get The Call

The more units you own, the more important this next tip will become. Have your own unit description sheet in a binder and ready to read when they tell you which home or apartment they are calling about. It's easy to forget to mention some feature or item that may have been the very "hot button" for that caller. To lose a tenant, and maybe a month's rent, because you forgot to mention that there's a new washer and dryer would be a shame.

Remember those questions you asked about competing rental units when you were researching your market? Well, get ready to hear many of the same questions from these potential tenants. So your sheet should have all of the answers ready for your conversation. You could have your next tenant on the line, so don't lose them because you don't have answers to their questions in front of you.

That takes care of what they're going to ask you, but what are you going to ask them? We'll go into other questions in more detail in the application process, but a few very basic questions to help you in deciding whether to proceed with this caller might include:
• Their time frame for rental. If they're calling for a unit four months out, and you only have one ready right now, put them on your follow-up list.
• Ask about pets.
• How long is their current lease, and how long was the previous one?
• What do they like most in a unit, and your unit?
• How did they find you? This is important information to track for future advertising decisions.
• Ask them if they can provide solid references

QUICK TIP:
After you have several units and if you are still doing it yourself you can get set up with a company like COA Network (www.coaphonesolution.com) and get set up with multiple extensions for voice mail. You can leave all the information about each unit on a message and then ask callers what they need. You will attract the renters you want and repel the ones that

are not a fit before you even talk to them. This allows you to cut down on talk time and speak with qualified prospects only.

If this conversation goes well, it may be the time to show the unit. Don't wait for them to ask if you're happy so far with the conversation. It's OK to ask them "When can I show you the unit?" Always assume that when they hang up, they're going to call another landlord on their list. The old saying "he who hesitates is lost" is true in this case. If you think this could be a good tenant based on this conversation, try to set up a meeting to show the unit.

Because people can be unreliable, especially when they view themselves as the customer, you may end up waiting in the unit with a no-show for a tenant. For this reason, you might want to schedule back-to-back showings, but make sure you allow enough time with each prospect. This can save you from a useless trip, but also allows these prospects to see that others are interested in the unit. A little perceived competition works in your favor.

When I was doing this, I would schedule them so they would overlap on purpose. Then I would have two people there at once. I can't tell you how many times the first person looking said, "You know what? I'll take it!" when the next person showed up. Everyone loves a little competition.

The Application and Selection Process

Not every person who wants to rent your unit will be a good tenant. Your task is to ask the right questions, do the research, and make sure that your decision will result in a tenant who pays their rent on time and doesn't damage your unit. (Remember that when you are ready most if not all management companies have strict criteria that you can ask them about before placing a person in your home) Some of this is history, with a request for past landlord contact information. You may want to pull a credit history, or there may be a local resource to check how people pay their rent. For any background or credit checks, you need written permission, so have that spelled out in your application. Just above where they sign, have a statement that authorizes you to collect this information.

There are specialty services on the Internet that provide these services to landlords, and charge a reasonable fee for doing so. It can be well worth it, and you may be able to charge an application fee to your prospect tenant to offset some or all of this cost. Check out what others are doing in the way of charging the prospect, as you don't want to send them away by being the only one in your area requiring this payment, or requiring significantly more for an application fee than the competition. Just do a Google search on "landlord application services," "tenant credit checks," or similar phrases to locate online services.

Rather than listing a bunch of information requirements here, locate a legal rental application for your state of residence, get one from an attorney, or have an attorney approve one you get online or at a business supply. You'll be getting a great deal of personal information, references, current and previous addresses and phone numbers, work history, current employment, income, and more. If there's going to be a social security number required, and there probably will be for a credit check, you'll want to be up-to-date on requirements for securing this information. Locked files and a shredder are two definite requirements.

Promises aren't taken as bank deposits. You'll be told at times that a tenant can't sign the lease "until Friday when I get paid." Or, there's some other reason they can't sign a lease today. Just keep showing the unit, and building your tenant list. Have a backup ready. If you think they're sincere, then they shouldn't mind a small non-refundable deposit to hold the unit. Just remember that it's not leased until the lease is signed and rent collected.

They're In! Managing Your Unit

There's another name for tenants: "customers." The best way to reduce your long term costs from turnover is to provide a servicable and nice unit and good service to your tenants. Property management is about collecting rents, doing repairs, renewing leases, and sometimes even evicting tenants. But, for the most part, it's about keeping tenants happy so they'll renew their lease, and even at higher rents as time goes forward.

Be nice, but rules are rules. Your lease should spell out the rules of occupancy, pets allowed, tenant responsibilities and yours. If it's detailed and clear, and you go over it with them at move-in, most problems are avoided. But, if there is a situation developing, you should be able to enforce the rules and lease terms. You can do this nicely, but you need to do it. Letting one tenant skirt a rule will only result in problems, as other tenants will find out.

It's their home, so treat it that way. You own it, but it's your tenants' home. Always remember that, and treat their home with respect. No matter what the state law says you must do, request entry when you need it, keep major equipment like heating and air conditioning in good order, and make repairs promptly when needed. Have an efficient problem reporting process in place, and make sure the tenants know what it is. They need to know who to call and when to call with problems or questions.

Your reward is the rent. Don't forget why you bought the property, and it's role in your financial future. Payment of rent isn't an option, and you need to make it clear in the lease when it's due, penalties when it's late, and what happens when it's late enough to kick in legal action. You'll definitely be operating with state laws for your rules, so keep up with the latest, and consult an attorney if you're not sure about a situation.

Tips for Cost Control and Unit Improvements

Costs of Turnover

Tenants leave, and this will always be the case no matter how great our unit or service. People move for jobs, families grow, and tenants become owners. You're going to have move-outs, and this creates costs in getting the unit move-in ready for the next tenant. This is true even if they were careful and there is no real damage. Just the normal wear and tear of living in a structure creates things we need to fix for the next tenant.

When you have multiple rental units, standardizing paint colors, materials, window types and heating and cooling units will save you time and money in the long run. Using the same basic colors in multiple units will allow you to buy in bulk, and also speed up the readying process for the next tenant. Standardizing heating, cooling, appliances, and lighting will create the same savings by allowing you to keep spare parts in stock. It speeds repair calls as well, as your repair service knows what to expect when they're called out.

Use a detailed condition checklist for a walk-through with the tenant at the beginning of the lease, and again at move-out. When you're holding a deposit for damage with rules as to what can be charged for, you need to have a signature from the tenant showing the condition at move-in and acknowledging the problems at move-out. This keeps your costs pegged to your original budget, not variable for things you shouldn't pay for.

Improvements for Rent Increases and Value

We'll talk more about exit strategies in the last chapter of the book. But you've heard some of my students explaining their exit strategies that were part of every deal from the beginning. Knowing how you're going to dispose of a property should be something you plan before you buy it. It's no different for rental units, houses, condos or apartments. At some point, you'll be selling this property. What you sell it for, and the appreciation during your holding period, can be enhanced by improvements over time.

The trick with a rental property is to balance the end game with the game as it's ongoing. You may not be able to raise rents for some improvements that will increase value at resale. Or you may be able to make some great improvements that will allow you to get more in rent, but they aren't necessarily going to be that valuable at resale. Remember the chapter on value and renovation. I gave you links to sites that provided the pay-back for certain remodels and room additions. Even if a kitchen remodel isn't going to get you back but 50% of cost at resale, it may allow you to raise the rent enough to recoup that cost many times over in the time you own the property.

From the "first impression" at drive-up, to the amenities in your unit that tenants really want, there are so many ways to improve a rental property. And the costs can be anywhere from almost nothing to major capital improvements. Here are some of the ways in which you can make your property better in the eyes of your tenants, possibly increase rents, and in some cases, increase resale value later:

• Simple landscaping to make the outdoor areas look nicer.
• Keeping exterior doors and window screens free of damage.
• Some apartment projects are getting higher rents for an affordable service that carries trash bags placed in front of doors to the central trash bins. It's a small service, but one that busy people love when they are hurrying off to work.
• Just about any scratch, dent or chip in floors, walls or counter tops is worth repairing. It's an overall impression of your unit that contributes to what the renter is willing to pay to live there.
• If floors are carpeted, replace it once worn. You can select lower nap carpet for easier cleaning, something people value.
• Tile or wood floors should be refinished or treated between tenants for a better look.
• Watch what the new home builders are advertising, as they keep up with the in-demand features. If you can renovate the kitchen or put in a skylight, it can make thousands of dollars in rent over the years.

• Garages, carports, or attic/basement conversions can bring increased rents and higher resale value.

NOW you can hire a property manager!

Now that you know what's involved in effective property management, you can determine its value. For a few properties, you can use what you've learned here to self-manage and put more money in your pocket. But as your holdings grow, at some point you'll be considering a property management solution. This sounds great, right? So here are some of the questions you may want to ask a property manager when you interview them:

1. On average how long does it take you to rent a vacant unit?
2. Based on the location, size and condition of my unit what is the rent that I can expect? - *(Ask questions to see their knowledge of the local market)*
3. Do you have a handyman on staff and what is their hourly rate?
4. Is the handyman licensed and bonded?
5. Do you have a certificate of insurance for liability for any and all contractors that may perform work at my property?
6. How and where do you advertise vacant units? Is this cost absorbed by the company or charged to the client?
7. What is their fee structure, of course? Do they offer a better rate in they would manage multiple units for you?
8. Do you handle all issues or unforeseen problems that may arise with a tenant?
9. How long have you been in business?
10. When repairs are made is the charge for the amount of the repair or do you add a service fee?
11. Will I receive a monthly statement of activity, does that include copies of any receipts for items that I was charged an additional fee?
12. When I check your references, what would the worst thing that someone could tell me about you or your company?

CHAPTER 21

Cashing In On the Exit

We have discussed a smorgasbord variety of exit strategies and some may have been more "tasty" or appealing to you than others. There is no right answer for what the best exit strategy may be for you or your local area when it comes to real estate investing. Each student may take a different exit strategy or approach and fill their plate based on their own aspirations or the current market cycle they are in. The good thing about exit strategies is the more options you have for a property, the better the deal could turn out to be.

Often we could explore one strategy but if that strategy should happen to fall through, what is our "Plan B?" Over time, your exit strategies may continue to change and develop into additional strategies. As you gather information, you will develop strategies for your local market and be able to create your own recipe for success. I have met a number of investors that started with bad credit and no available cash. After they did a few deals, like assignments for instance, they were able to expand the types of deals they were able to do. The ability to have some additional cash from completed deals may enable you to buy and hold a property as a "buy and hold for rental" for your future. Plus, while they were making money, they were also paying off old bills and improving their credit, opening up a new avenue for them. Please remember: real estate investing is an evolution and the longer you are in, the more you will define your game and expand your options.

Do you like to hike in the woods? If I'm hiking in unfamiliar territory, I really want to be sure that I can find the car again when the hike is over. Going into the woods, I might use a compass, a GPS with the car location set, or just notice where the sun is so that I can put it on the opposite side on the way back. Maybe it's just going along a stream, with the simple plan of following it back. But I always have some way to make sure that I don't get lost...my woods hike exit strategy. Yes, I got lost once in the Adirondack Mountains in Upstate NY about 15 years ago and lets just say I'll never do that again.

Investing in real estate involves buying AND selling. It may be buying options or tax certificates, not property itself. Then there are strategies that involve flips and resale in the short term, or holding a property long term for rental income. One thing that's common to all of these deals is that they aren't forever, so we need an exit strategy. Joe Jurek tells us very clearly that he never enters a deal without a written exit strategy. Greg Murphy showed us his buy side lease purchase, with the exit strategy of a sell side lease purchase as well. Chad Merrihew told us that his first deals in college were entered into without any exit strategy and he ended up with more tied up in them for longer than he wanted. Chip and Andrea plan a 30-day or less exit strategy when they are locking up a deal. Angie is keeping all her properties to raise her monthly cash flow. In 6 to 10 years she can retire on that flow of cash or sell out when the market hits a peak.

Sometimes things will not go as planned. It's a common theme across all of my students' deal recipes. They have some type of plan for the eventual disposition of the property. The exit strategy can play out in the very short term with a flip, or many years from now with the sale of a rental property. It's not what your exit strategy is that's most important. It's that you have one or more BEFORE you enter the deal. It is better to have a plan in hand and one in your back pocket rather than lose a good deal with no back-up plan!

Buy, Assign or Bird-Dog

When you can locate a great deal through your marketing, one that no other investors have discovered, you may be able to execute a very fast-developing exit strategy. Say you have your buyer list, and your marketing generates a call from a homeowner who is behind in payments, and has given up being able to sell their home. Their situation is really bad, and you can buy the home and resell it to an investor for a profit extremely fast. You have seen those examples from students right within this book. They used cash, a HELOC, even family or investor money.

Now if you have little or no money, you can take that same deal, get it under contract with an assignment clause and go to your buyer's list and assign that great deal to someone who can buy it fast. You never own the property, never personally pay for the property; you are just locking it up and handing the deal off to someone else. You may make a bit less, but you risking nothing.

Lastly, you may want to make a real quick buck and be a bird dog. You are not buying the property, you are not locking it up on contract, and you are simply finding a great deal and forwarding that deal to a buyer who would love it. Letting the seller and your buyer work directly together and asking for a "bird dog fee" for making the connection. Some people have been paid as little as a few hundred dollars for this type of deal, I know Chip and Andrea did this on their first deal and made $4,400. Some people have made 10 times that for larger deals.

The Buy and Rehab to Sell

In this scenario, you're just holding on to the home a little longer while you do repairs and rehab work to increase the value for sale at retail or to another investor. The retail buyer approach requires more marketing, and your exit strategy should take into account that you may be holding it longer than you planned. As for selling to another investor, you can take the same approach as the as-is flip, just stretching the time frame a bit for the work you have to do on the property. You still have decided on the exit strategy going in, and you may even have the buyer on board before you buy and start work.

The Buy and Hold for Rental

There is an exit strategy for each type of deal you have in mind. You may want to acquire a property that will have a positive cash flow each month, appreciate in value over time, and hold it as a rental. The most important thing to you may be the accrued equity build-up you get each year as you pay down the mortgage and acquire more equity in the property with each payment. In the future you can decide your strategy, based on your need and the current market cycle.

When and how do you plan on selling the property? You could go into this deal knowing that you can do a sale to a tenant buyer, like Greg Murphy does. You'll set them up with a lease, and they'll pay toward an agreed purchase in the future. There are set times and deadlines, and you should have sold the house by that time if all goes according to plan. If you loses your tenant buyer, you have the same exit strategy, but you just need to go out and find another tenant buyer.

If you're going to take the landlord route, you'll be holding the property long term, possibly for years. You might do some interim funding, like a refinance to get a better interest rate or to free up cash for other deals.

But you're continuing to rent it out until it's time to sell. Generally, when the appreciation has been such that there's a nice profit to take out or to roll into another property with a 1031 exchange transaction, it is time. This "rolling up" is both an exit and an entry strategy, as you end up with a more valuable property with the taxes deferred.

Your exit strategy over a longer period can change, as lives change and tax situations can be different over time. So it isn't a problem if your exit plan changes, but it is a problem if you go into a long-term rental deal without some plan for your eventual exit. It forces you to think about the tax and later life issues that everyone has to plan for. Plus, it is fun to think about the appreciation and if you get x number of properties how much you could cash out with, or how much cash flow you need to quit your job or even retire. My buddy, Matt Larson, was able to quit his job two years to the day he bought my book because he had enough rental monthly cash flow coming in that it replaced his paycheck.

Selling Your Investment Properties

All of these exit strategies short of dying and leaving the property, or donating it to charity, will involve a resale eventually. We've looked at the importance of making a smart and well-researched purchase, as that sets the basis for our future profits. Now it's time to take care of the other end of the deal, the sale of the property. Here we hope that we've enjoyed some appreciation over the holding period. And if we bought at a discount to value, or bought in a down market like when I am writing this book, we locked in some equity at the beginning and hopefully all that can do is go up.

Condition and Curb Appeal

In a fast flip, especially when our buyer is another investor, we may be doing little or no rehab work or repairs. If you've had the property a while, or if you're getting it ready for a retail sale, you'll want to present it in the best light possible to generate the highest selling price.

This doesn't necessarily mean spending a lot of money in beautification, in many cases, the little things bring big results. Landscaping, exterior paint and trim work, or just cleaning the place up can generate "curb appeal." Realtors will tell you that buyers are quick to say "let's not even go in" if they are turned off when they first drive up.

It may seem silly, but agents will also tell you that the way they arrive, meaning the directions you give them, can make a difference as well. If there are two or more sets of directions you can give to the home, use the one that takes the prospect through the best looking neighborhoods and streets. It's true that they will eventually drive by the homes with the peeling paint and tall grass in the other direction, but it would be better if that happens after they've seen the home, liked it, and are investigating further. If they see them on the first trip in, they may just opt to not go in at all.

If you are attached to the property, you may not see things that stick out to others. Get advice. I'm talking free and cheap advice. Ask your realtor to stop by and look at the outside and ask if they see anything that bothers them. Ask a neighbor or friend the same question. So many people get used to a dirty door where the dog scratches to come in or an old dead tree in the side yard. You need to look at your property through fresh eyes; how you looked at it for the first time.

List With A Real Estate Agent Or Not

Generally, the local MLS, Multiple Listing Service, is where a great many buyers end up being exposed to the home they eventually buy. This is because Realtors are showing them around, and the MLS has all of the listings for all member Realtors. So, for exposure in a focused marketing venue with a great many brokers seeing your home, listing in the MLS is very effective.

Of course, then you have both sides of the commission to pay. That's the half that goes to the listing broker, and the half that goes to the buyer broker that ends up bringing the successful purchaser. Most of the For Sale By Owner (FSBO), listings out there are in that status in an attempt to avoid all or half of this commission. If they offer a commission to a buyer agent, they'll avoid just the listing half, but many sellers hope to make it happen and put that money into their own pockets at closing.

One approach that can work for you, particularly in good markets, is to try it on your own for a while, listing with a Realtor if you don't get a buyer in the first month or so. Another thing to consider is if you've been working closely with one or more agents in your property purchases and valuation activities. You may find that they will be less helpful in the future if they never get a listing from you. And, never forget that commissions are negotiable. This is truer of small or single practitioner brokerages than the larger multi-agent firms. You might want to work with a broker who is the sole broker in his/her firm, or the owner. They'll be better able to be creative in commission structures.

There may be another reason for going on your own. If we've built a great book of buyers, perhaps we'll just contact them all and make the sale without any marketing. But, if we're more interested in the higher price we may get in the retail market, we're going to want to present our property in as many effective marketing channels as we can. The Internet has radically changed the world of real estate marketing, and this is great for you. You can get worldwide exposure for your property at little or no cost on the Web.

If you do decide to list with a real estate agent, work with them at the very beginning to come up with reliable and accurate comparable sale numbers for the CMA. Even in fast markets, overpricing can kill your showings, and in slow markets, it's almost a sure trip to the bottom of the list for showings and a long, long time on the market. So get the price right from the beginning. And have your agent do follow-up CMAs if it's been on the market a couple of months or more. Things change, and your home won't sell if you're chasing the market.

Now a quick note. If you are going to market the home yourself, use the same marketing lessons I shared with you on renting your own property. Be benefit-driven in your marketing and advertising. Take the time to find other great ads and model them. Take flattering pictures and present your home in a manner in which it would have attracted you to it when you were buying not selling. This may take an extra hour, but could return you thousands and thousands of additional revenue.

For Sale By Owner Web Sites

There are a great many for sale by owner Web sites, as you'll see if you do a search on "FSBO" or "sell your home by owner", or similar terms. These three are some of the largest:
www.Owners.com
www.ForSaleByOwner.com
www.HomesByOwner.com

Most of these sites offer a free listing, with photos and descriptive information. They may also offer you lockboxes, yard signs and other items that the "for sale by owner" seller needs. Some will also "syndicate" your listing to other sites like Google Base, Oodle, Trulia and others. This syndication multiplies your exposure, while all you had to do is enter the listing once at the FSBO site.

The National Association of Realtors has annual survey responses showing that 84% of home buyers used the Internet in their home shopping process, so you can see that good exposure there can make all the difference. Some of these FSBO sites also offer access to MLS listings at flat rates, some as low as around $300. This is one way to avoid the listing side of the commission, but you'll need to offer the buyer side to the agent members of the MLS, or you'll get no showings. Then there's Craigslist, which you are probably sick of me writing about, so I won't. I'll simply say it could be a great option to sell your own homes if you use the right marketing techniques. Refer back to the advice I gave about renting and apply it here to selling.

From Entry to Exit – Your New Life Starts Now!

Now we come to my exit strategy in writing this book. It ties in with my larger goal of helping more people to realize their dreams and become successful and financially independent through real estate. Remember my Seven Levels exercise in Chapter 2? When I did it, what was my seventh level answer?

"Because I want to be in control of my life so that I can help everyone I love around me to evolve to the next level."

That's my exit strategy for writing this book, to help you to evolve to the next level. Now, my "deal recipe" to get that done was to prove through real people with real deals in real towns, that you can do this. My recipe:

The Ingredients
- Real stories of students in all types of financial situations
- Some students with seemingly insurmountable life and financial problems
- Examples of a great number of real deals with different strategies
- Alternate methods when the one used in the recipe isn't available to you
- Real and valuable resources to help you to learn your town's real estate market, locate deals, negotiate them, fund them, and play them out to your profitable exit strategy
- And most of all not only give you the "What" and "Why" but most importantly the "How"

Preparation

This part was simple in the planning, but long in the doing. I needed to assemble these students, get their stories, assemble the detail of their deals, show you how they did it, and give you other tools and resources to do it, even if their strategies, techniques or funding options aren't available to you.

Book Garnish and Presentation

This is where you have to help me to realize my book exit strategy and my Seventh Level dream. Read what you have to in the book again. Find the student or students you can identify most with. Read their story again. Understand that they're no different from you, and that you can do this if they did.

Then, read the deal recipes again. Find the ones that seem like they can work for you in your town with your resources. If you're challenged in one funding resource, read the "Funding Your Real Estate Deals" chapter again or Greg Murphy or Chip and Andrea's chapter again until one strategy works for you. Then go to ***www.deangraziosi.com*** for inspiration and wisdom from these students and many others that aren't in the book, but are out there doing successful deals every day.

If would like to do what many of the students in this book and countless other successful students have done around the country and be a part of my real estate Success Academy then call to see if it is a fit at **877-219-1473**.

All I know is that the only way these strategies work is if you are going to take action with them. Know that you will make mistakes, get confused and even fail. But that is when you brush yourself off, remember your big "why" and get back in the game so I can put you in a future book.

My exit strategy for this book is your real estate investing success!

Don't let me be frustrated in my Seventh Level, please. It's your town, your dream, and your next step!
As you get to know your area, the type of properties, the pricing, etc. you will begin to formulate a strategy of what your niche may be. There are usually several factors that will help you determine your niche:

• The local area, types of property and pricing
• Your financial situation and your available resources. There are opportunities whether you are staring with no money and bad credit or you have some available cash and have good credit.
• Your niche will also be determined by what you enjoy doing. Some people may enjoy buying and holding properties for future streams of income; while others enjoys finding and assigning deals to make cash quickly

Whatever you preference, there is something for everyone. You may have to try a few things to determine what may be your niche are. Once you determine this, learn everything you can about the subject. You almost want to become the local expert. As you gain the knowledge and experience your ability to assess deals will become faster and faster. Once you master one area, you can then expand your niche or begin to learn another area. If you find deals outside of your niche area, those are okay too, you just have to try to stay focused and the deals will begin to materialize.

When thinking about finding your niche, consider each of the techniques you may be able to use. You will discover the techniques you feel most comfortable with and the ones that you may benefit most by employing them in your local area. You can use some of the techniques we already discussed, make some modification to the techniques, and even create new techniques along the way.

Congratulations! You now have the information you need to take action in real estate investing. I know you will be a success and be taking immediate action. Others have blazed the trail before you, so the path is there for you to explore and discover!

I want to say one final thing before I sign off. As silly as this sounds, I'm proud of you. You overcame busyness, naysayers, doubt, fear, skepticism and probably many other obstacles to get to the point of finishing this book. I commend you. Don't let your knowledge go to waste. Continue on this journey and make it a reality for you and your family. I'll be here to help all I can through our Web sites, weekly video blogs, monthly teleconference call and our real estate Success Academy. I'll do my part, you do yours. Thanks! ;-)

INDEX

Acknowledgments

I want to thank the wonderful students who participated in this book. They were not paid to do so, they did it out of pure willingness to help others succeed. They let me into their homes, some flew to Arizona so I could interview them in person and others allowed many phone calls back and forth to get all the details right. They took time out of their busy schedule to unselfishly share all they could.

When we set out to fly all over the country to meet these students in small towns and big cities, I figured they would all be good. But quite honestly, I figured maybe we would get 50% of them to really share the "nuts and bolts" of how they did it. I mean they worked hard to figure this out, right? Well, all I can say is I am so sorry for underestimating my students. Each one could not do enough to share what they could to help YOU reach the goals you desire. Thanks to each of you for being so self-less. You are all making the world a better place and you have touched my heart.

A sincere thank you to Gary and Jill, Angie, Lubertha and Bernadette, Jan and Jeremy, Eric, Joe and Stacey, Greg, Chip and Andrea and Chad. Each of you are amazing investors who overcame challenges, obstacles, naysayers, bad credit, no money and so many other of the things that could of stopped you. But you didn't allow it to and now the results you are receiving are not only awesome, they are well deserved.

I have to give a very special thank you to Joe Jurek. Joe was instrumental in helping me make this book all it can be. He went over and above anything expected of him, willing to help in any and every area he could, and the benefits are in black and white on the pages within this book. Joe and Stacey – a sincere thank you.

To my entire staff for all you do and to Jim Kimmons for helping me turn my sloppy grammar in to proper English, a big thank you as well.

And most importantly I am the luckiest man in the world to have a loving, caring family who supports me to follow my passions. I thank you always and forever.

Our Real Estate Success Academy has the mentors that can help guide you to success!

No other advanced training program on the planet has the unique qualities our program has. We have combined the right amount of wisdom, direction, confidence, capabilities and inspiration to get you out there doing deals and making money in record time.

Sherry Carlson
Coaching Experience: 2 years
Investor Experience: 20 years

Gregg Howell
Coaching Experience: 8 years
Investor Experience: 12 years

Dianne Dowd
Coaching Experience: 11 years
Investor Experience: 30 years

Casey Poppinga
Coaching Experience: 3 years
Investor Experience: 3 years

Dawn Erling
Coaching Experience: 7 years
Real Estate Experience: 15 years

Bill O'Connor
Coaching Experience: 4 years
Real Estate Experience: 29 years

Jeff Jensen
Coaching Experience: 6 years
Investor Experience: 6 years

Tom Flood
Coaching Experience: 5 year
Investor Experience: 25 years

Nathan Street
Coaching Experience: 6 years
Real Estate Experience: 12 years

Craig Mitchell
Coaching Experience: 2 years
Real Estate Experience: 8 years

Eric Wolff
Coaching Experience: 1 year
Real Estate Experience: 11 years

Patt Jacobs
Coaching Experience: 6 years
Real Estate Experience: 11 years

Our entire coaching staff has a combined 234 years of real estate experience!

Call today and see if "Dean's Real Estate Success Academy" and his amazing coaches are the perfect fit to help you reach your goals, just like it has been for many successful students before you.

Call us today at 1-877-219-1473